CW00537348

Snubbing
GOD

Snubbing
GOD

The High Cost of Rejecting God's Created Order

VICTOR KULIGIN

Foreword by David J. Ayers

LEXHAM PRESS

Snubbing God: The High Cost of Rejecting God's Created Order
© 2017 by Victor Kuligin

Lexham Press, 1313 Commercial St., Bellingham, WA 98225
LexhamPress.com

First edition by Weaver Book Company.

All rights reserved. You may use brief quotations from this resource in presentations, articles, and books. For all other uses, please write Lexham Press for permission. Email us at permissions@lexhampress.com.

Sources used throughout this book have their bibliographic information either in the footnotes (if they were only used for illustrative purposes) or in the bibliography (if they make a substantive contribution).

All Scripture quotations, unless otherwise indicated, are from the Holy Bible, New International Version®, NIV®. Copyright © 1973, 1978, 1984, 2011 by Biblica, Inc.™ Used by permission of Zondervan. All rights reserved worldwide. www.zondervan.com.

Scripture quotations marked ESV are from The Holy Bible, English Standard Version® (ESV®), copyright © 2001 by Crossway, a publishing ministry of Good News Publishers. Used by permission. All rights reserved.

Scripture quotations marked NKJV are from the New King James Version®. Copyright © 1982 by Thomas Nelson, Inc. Used by permission. All rights reserved.

Scripture quotations marked KJV are from the King James Version.

Charts and illustrations are used with permission of copyright holders.

Print ISBN 9781683591405
Digital ISBN 9781683591412

Cover: Caines Design
Interior Design: Nicholas Richardson
Copyediting and Proofreading: Line for Line Publishing Services

I dedicate this book to my father,
the hardest-working man I know,
for teaching me the value of a solid work ethic.

CONTENTS

MORE THAN TWENTY-FIVE YEARS ago, J. I. Packer seconded an observation that American Protestantism was "3,000 miles wide and half an inch deep."[1] Things have changed since then. It is now closer to an eighth of an inch.

We are in the grip of cultural, social, and political challenges that promise to transform the deepest, most foundational areas of existence in ways that will make us unrecognizable not only to our ancestors, but also to ourselves. Modern people are fundamentally altering what it means to be human, trying to control our own evolution, to be our own gods, while erasing the one true God. No one seems to know how to hit the brakes.

In the midst of this we have the professing church, called to be salt, light, a prophetic voice, a city on a hill. Yet in terms of their knowledge of reality and the Bible, average evangelical Christians (and often the intellectuals and academics as well) don't know the basic facts, logical categories, applicable Scripture texts, or doctrines needed to think about and respond to these many challenges. Even where that isn't true, they often seem more anxious to endlessly accommodate the ancient faith to modern sensibilities and political correctness than to stand for it. At times they seem embarrassed by orthodox faith. Sadly, many are selling their orthodoxy cheap, like Esau exchanging his birthright for lentil soup. And many who refuse to exchange orthodoxy for the latest fashions are still woefully reluctant to take public, costly stands for it. Across the board, we are reminded of the late Francis Schaeffer's famous observation that the modern church has become addicted to personal peace and prosperity.

Thankfully, there are many notable exceptions to this grim prognosis, and I thank God for every one of them. Among these is Victor Kuligin, and among their contributions is this excellent, bracing, challenging book. Dr.

---

[1] Quoted in Leland Ryken, *Worldly Saints: The Puritans as They Really Were* (Grand Rapids: Zondervan, 1986), x.

Kuligin is a fine scholar with a fascinating resume that includes education and experience in engineering, business, and theology. His service of training pastors and leaders in South Africa for more than twenty years has given him an outsider's point of view, even as he has remained in touch with developments in the evangelical church in Europe and North America. His message and tone is conciliatory, compassionate, but uncompromising. As an old friend has often reminded me, faithful Christians should be motivated by love of God and their fellow man to maintain a stranglehold on the Word of God. And that is what this book encourages us to do.

Dr. Kuligin's analysis is that we have been too quick to compromise a clear understanding of and fidelity to the Bible in order to accommodate science as a new arbiter of truth. This includes an uncritical adoption of evolutionary theory, often "baptized" or "corrected" by theistic add-ons and assumptions. We end up with a God markedly less than the God of the Bible. This God has allowed "design flaws" in creation because he didn't really design it, at least not totally. We have a second Adam but not a real first, historical Adam who was created by God's own hand. With this, much of what we rely on for the gospel in the New Testament has to be jerry-rigged rather than trusted. Can the genealogy of Jesus be traced to Shem, Noah, and Adam? No. Did God really author marriage and make a distinct man and woman from one flesh and then, through marriage, one flesh again? No. Did we all sin in Adam? No, maybe, kind of.

In this book we are reminded that it is naturalistic science, not historic Christianity, which makes the great leaps of faith—something from nothing, life from inanimate matter, complex thinking organisms capable of art, physics, engineering, and compassion from a long process of impersonal chance variations. When and how did so many Christians come to believe that this story makes more sense than David looking across the Milky Way on a clear night, in awe, and seeing the glory of an incredible God who designed every particle of it, and who also fearfully and wonderfully made him? Naturalism has led in our day to homosexual marriage, abortion on Holocaust levels, "mercy" killing, and sex change operations, among numerous innovations that threaten to erase human dignity and personhood. More "progress" we can barely imagine awaits us in the near future. Should I trust the people and worldview that has given us things like that, while rejecting truths that gave us what is now the fleeting glory of Christian civilization? Dr. Kuligin is calling us back to rationality in the best sense, not asking us to substitute reason with some sort of blind leap in the dark. This book will help us do that.

Snubbing God is strong medicine. The reader will find it challenging at points—morally and intellectually. Few will agree with everything in it. Yet Dr. Kuligin has no desire to only preach to the choir, though certainly encouraging the saints is part of his aim. He is trying to get us to pull up short, to think, to reconsider the marvelous truths, and righteous demands, of the Bible and of its Author.

The tides of change are getting rougher, the swells higher and closer together, the currents more treacherous. As we try to walk through this surf into the future, bringing our loved ones with us, how will we stay on our feet? How will we stand? By reading books like this that challenge us and point us back to the One we have been snubbing.

—David J. Ayers, Assistant Dean,
Alva J. Calderwood School of Arts and Letters;
Chair, Department of Sociology; Professor of Sociology,
Grove City College (PA)

Downloaded from

As CHRISTIANS, WE LIVE in a wonderful time in history. In my lifetime of a half century, I have seen an increasing animosity toward the gospel and its proclamation of salvation in Jesus Christ alone. Along with this declaration has come a growing assault on Christian morality. Make no mistake, the two go hand in hand. Deny the supremacy of our Savior Jesus Christ and you will undoubtedly deny his lordship and the subsequent morality he expects. We are moving from a society where being a believer was easy, to one where proclaiming your faith is increasingly dangerous.

Let me be clear. I am not happy that our society is abandoning the ethical underpinning that has, in large part, made America great. As that Christian foundation erodes, so will our country. However, I must take Jesus at his word. When he tells his disciples, "Blessed are those who are persecuted because of righteousness" (Matt. 5:10), I believe him. To be persecuted for our faith in Jesus is a high blessing and honor.

Persecution has a wonderful way of weeding out the pretenders and shoring up the faithful. Now is the time for believers—genuine Jesus followers—to stand up and be counted. We might find the numbers are not as high as they once were, but this is not a moment for despair. Often, after a time of bitter persecution, God has used his Spirit to work in incredible ways through a society. Any student of the early centuries of the Christian faith can attest to this. The persecution recounted in Acts 7 and 8 produced the missionary journeys recorded in Luke's account of the early church. Wave after wave of Roman maltreatment for several centuries worked to strengthen the faith, not destroy it. As the second-century apologist Tertullian attested: "The blood of the martyrs is the seed of the church."

We need to recapture that hopefulness again. This is not the time for doomsday predictions prevalent in Western Christianity, such as, "The U.S. Supreme Court's legalization of gay marriage is the end of American society as we know it." I've heard numerous Christians say things like this. It may, indeed, be the end of society "as we know it," but we must not discount how God uses persecution to strengthen his church, not weaken it. In an atmosphere where Christianity is under attack, this is the perfect time for us to be Christ in the world.

Let's be honest. The number of "Christians" in our country has been grossly inflated because of the ease and comfort that has come with being an American believer. I have a hunch that if some of these self-professed American Christians were dropped into Iran or North Korea, their claim of faith would happily cease. When it is comfortable to be a Christian, the ranks will swell. Throw in a little oppression, though, and we might find our numbers voluntarily dwindling.

I can imagine starkly different responses to the following two scenarios:

Scenario 1: "Are you a follower of Jesus? Great! Here's a new leather-bound Bible. Come join our small group."

Scenario 2: "Are you a follower of Jesus? Here, take this blindfold and stand up against that wall while we put a bullet in your head. Oh, you aren't a follower of Jesus? Sorry for the confusion."

However, it usually is not all that neat. It is like the man who says he would sacrifice his life for his wife if a train were coming and he had to push her out of the way. But ask him to love his wife in the little things each and every day, and he might have major difficulty.

"I would take a bullet for Christ," we boldly proclaim, sounding like Peter just before Jesus' arrest. But when a servant girl questions our views on homosexuality or gay marriage and yells "bigot" and "homophobe" for all to hear, we might flinch more than we expected. When a slap in the face from our immoral society causes me to back down from my faith, I certainly won't take a bullet for Jesus.

Some estimates are as high as 100,000 believers in the world each year who lose their lives for their faith in Jesus, but we are not at that point yet in America.[1] However, I may be sued for refusing to use my farm for a gay marriage, or I might be falsely accused of misogyny because I

---

[1] See line 28 from Gordon Conwell Theological Seminary's Center for the Study of Global Christianity report: www.gordonconwell.edu/resources/documents/StatusOf GlobalMission.pdf, accessed May 12, 2016.

believe the Bible places men in the position of authority in the home and church.[2]

With this book I intend to address some "hot potatoes" in our world, such as gay marriage, abortion, and animal rights, and how a biblical understanding is opposed by a secular view that has at its heart an outright disregard for God's design for his creation. I expect to anger just about everyone with something I say. That's okay. Sometimes the best way to tackle a contentious issue is to allow the blood to boil. Adrenaline is a wonderful teacher. Debate often gets a bad rap.

I have a simple goal: put the issues before fellow believers, create awareness of how deeply these matters run in our society, and provide some guidance about the best way forward. I do not claim any grand schemes. Christian discipleship in the twenty-first century largely looks like Christian discipleship in any century.

Jesus calls us to follow him in an antagonistic world. "If the world hates you, keep in mind that it hated me first . . . A servant is not greater than his master. If they persecuted me, they will persecute you also" (John 15:18, 20). Let's embrace this calling as we ought, but let's not go down without a fight.

Victor Kuligin
Cape Town, South Africa
November 2016

---

[2] This comprehensive study by the Pew Research Center claims that Christianity is the most persecuted religion in the world: "Religious Hostilities Reach Six-Year High," www.pewforum.org/2014/01/14/religious-hostilities-reach-six-year-high/, accessed January 12, 2016.

ACKNOWLEDGMENTS

THANK YOU TO MY wife, Rachel, and our children, who gave me the time and space to complete this project, even when it meant taking time away from them.

Thank you to David Ayers for writing his insightful foreword to this book and for his encouragement through the years.

I had several friends read all or portions of the book. Of special note is Wayne Harbuziuk, my friend for nearly thirty years, who read the whole manuscript and offered helpful improvements, as he has done with my previous books. Robert Zins, Johan Kruger, and Steve Aaron read through the chapters on science and evolution, providing valuable insights. Good friend Bob Martin gave me great material to consider on environmental ethics, and another friend who wanted to remain anonymous nonetheless needs special recognition for reading through the whole book with a keen eye for detail, giving me substantial improvements.

Thank you to the editor, Maria DenBoer, for her helpful corrections. I'd also like to thank Sarah Summers, who helped improve the quality of the graphics in this book for publication.

Lastly, as I wrote this book over a span of about fifteen months, when it seemed that virtually every day something was happening in the world that was relevant to the main thesis of the book, Jim Weaver showed considerable patience as he awaited the manuscript. Thank you, Jim, for your willingness to publish this project and for believing along with me that it is important.

Defining the Conditions of the Debate

Wecannotuseelectriclightsandradiosand,intheeventofillness,availourselves ofmodernmedicalandclinicalmeansandatthesametimebelieveinthespiritand wonder world of the New Testament.

—RUDOLF BULTMANN[1]

THE RELEVANCE FOR OUR generation of the first three chapters of Genesis is truly amazing. Even as an evangelical Christian, I am flabbergasted how an ancient book written three and a half millennia ago can be so applicable to the twenty-first century. In eighty verses, hot topics like gay marriage, evolutionary theory, gender equality, and human sexuality are affected. Much of what I write in this book comes from the ancient truths penned by Moses 1,500 years before Jesus.

I am equally amazed at how ignorant some Christians are of this crucial book from the Old Testament. To be sure, the accounts of Cain and Abel, Noah, Abraham, and Joseph are well known by most believers, but few practical lessons are gleaned from them these days. Noah has become little more than a cute children's story that produces colorful books and vibrant toys. I am all for making the biblical accounts familiar to our youngsters, but when they are consigned to the children's section of the bookstore, things have gone astray.

On the other hand, many people dismiss Scripture. After all, what can

---

[1] Rudolf Bultmann, *New Testament and Mythology* (Minneapolis: Fortress Press, 1984), 3–4.

we possibly learn from a worldview so primitive and backward? However, I believe the Bible to be the very words of God.

Moses records events that happened much earlier than his lifetime. Perhaps he consulted writings and oral traditions from primeval human accounts, but there are some things he could not possibly have received from previous human histories. "In the beginning God" is where Moses starts, but when God created, no one else was there to observe it. As such, the only commentary on the history of creation of any value must come from God himself.

Skeptics will say Moses reworked ancient legends when he constructed his own creation account. They are free to believe such things. We all have our presuppositions, those ideas we assume are true and on which we build our arguments. Mine is that the biblical authors were inspired by God when they wrote down his infallible and flawless words. I believe Scripture has consistently proved this over the centuries.

This means that even an ancient book written about incidents happening thousands of years ago not only could be relevant today, but must be. If this is God telling us what happened "in the beginning," then we need to take note. The Bible is not just true, it is God's truth. This is where it all began, and where I begin.[2]

Assuming the veracity and relevancy of the book of Genesis, I repeat myself: I am amazed how germane it is to the twenty-first century. It is here that we find God laying out the foundations of the earth, shaping the world to his specifications, and placing humans in it.

It is no accident that Genesis is placed where it is in God's Word. Someone who does not understand Genesis will not adequately grasp the rest of the Bible. Its first chapter lays the foundation for everything else.

Culture Wars

I read a lot about the so-called culture wars in America. While at times these wars are sensationalized, the fact is Christian ideals are under attack. No doubt gray areas abound, but I see concerted efforts in Western societies to push Christian principles to the fringe or even to criminalize them.

---

[2] The Bible is also relevant because, despite cultural and technological changes through history, human nature remains the same.

When Christianity first came to Europe, it found a world steeped in paganism. It took centuries for the faith to build a thoroughly Christian society, even if pockets of paganism still existed. I am speaking in broad strokes and do not mean to paint a rosy picture, but Christian ideals ruled the day in most segments of European society. This was similarly true for the early decades of American history.

Today, the West is moving toward a neo-pagan worldview that is decidedly hostile to Christianity. Atheism is on the rise, coupled with scientists who are aggressive evolutionists. The "onward Christian soldier" is met with a militant homosexuality that redefines family and marriage in its own image. The battle is on and in many respects Christianity is losing.

The godless worldview of the atheist will inevitably lead to a godless society that embraces godless values and principles. However, while I argue against the atheist's position, it is not the focus of my book. The atheist will never alter his view until he experiences a radical change of heart through the Holy Spirit.

My concern is with Christians who buy into secular ideals for science, gender roles, human sexuality, and so on. They say that homosexuality is quite okay, or they incorporate evolutionary theory into their theology because they have been taught it is good science.

My purpose is not to "name and shame" these Christians. First, I do not have exhaustive knowledge of their viewpoint; they may have subsequently changed their perspective.

Second, there is a certain "guilt by association" that takes place. Good Christians are wrong on this or that point, but it does not negate everything they say. Unfortunately, the creation account is occasionally used as a litmus test for genuine faith, and if some believers do not subscribe to a young earth or a literal seven-day creation, they are written off as heretics. There is good, honest debate about these important matters among genuine brothers and sisters of the faith.

Third, even though I have strong opinions about these issues, I have no intention of belittling fellow believers who disagree. While it might be true that some Christians simply kowtow to the latest scientific or cultural fad, I surmise that the vast majority of evangelicals who believe in theistic evolution, for example, are doing so in good faith and from an honest (albeit inconsistent) reading of Scripture. As a Christian I must give them the benefit of the doubt. Are they wrong? Most certainly. Could I be wrong? That is always possible. If these debates do not come with a healthy dose of humility, they can only result in discord.

I will frequently refer to "science" in this book, but I do not view the scientific enterprise as monolithic. There is good science and bad science. The former is done with God in mind and the latter is not. This does not mean that an atheist cannot invent or discover something of great importance to humanity, but science driven by the atheist's godless materialism will eventually result in drastic consequences. If I refer in a derogatory way to "science," it is this type of atheistic science that I have in mind.[3] Science whose pursuit is "chasing after the thoughts of God" is always a noble undertaking.[4]

Lastly, I reject the supposition that the Bible is open to interpretation, while science is unquestioned fact. Whenever a paleontologist digs up a fossil, that finding is open to interpretation just as much as a verse from Genesis. Both involve presuppositions and subjective analysis.

The Created Order Defined

My book's title, *Snubbing God: The High Cost of Rejecting God's Created Order*, assumes that we understand what the "created order" is. It is the recognition that God made things in a precise way, and ignoring that design is to work against God's purposes for his creation. Not only must God be recognized as the Creator, but we must also affirm how and for what purpose he made the heavens and the earth.

In chapter 5 I will talk about God's fine-tuned creation specifically designed for humans. When we reject this principle, we do so to our own detriment. It is like digging a ditch with a golf club. You could get a little ways, but eventually the club will break under the stress. Similarly, God's creation has been ordered a certain way, and ignoring this order will bring damage and potential ruin.

This has profound ramifications for how we live our lives. Male and female roles, the beauty and complementary design of the genders, and

---

[3] Some call this "scientism," an exaggerated trust in natural science as a tool for understanding all truth regardless of the discipline.

[4] Or in the words of astronomer Johannes Kepler (1571-1630), "Thinking God's thoughts after him."

humanity's relationship to the environment—all contentious twenty-first-century issues—are addressed in the created order.

This order of creation is frequently noted throughout Scripture. For example, Paul invokes God's design when he speaks about marriage and the function of the church (Eph. 5:31–32). Throughout the Bible, we see the sovereignty of God powerfully displayed through creation. Often we envision God as Savior and forget that God as Creator has equally important implications for our lives.

Some Christians say that Paul's first-century commands on the role of women in church or on sexual immorality are irrelevant. Subsequently, these same people find truths written 1,600 years before Paul to be equally inconsequential. However, if we do not endeavor to return to God's design, we can expect the continued unraveling of his creation.[5]

Is Genesis a Real Historical Account?

Recently an evangelical friend told me that her pastor noted from the pulpit that the early chapters of Genesis are not actual historical accounts. He was caught up with the scholarship that suggests there is no historical Adam; Genesis is historical fiction. "We know snakes can't talk," he emphatically stated, which for him sealed the argument. My friend was less than pleased with this disillusioning statement since she has been a member of the church for thirty years. Her mind raced through the possibilities: "Does my pastor really believe Balaam's donkey spoke? What about Jonah and the whale? And what does this say about Jesus' resurrection?" Her foundations were shaken that morning.[6]

This is nothing new. Christianity has experienced several centuries of questioning the historical veracity of the Gospel account of Jesus. If we are going to question whether or not the biblical account of Jesus is accurate, we might as well question the minor players too. Much liberal scholarship today sees Abraham as nothing more than a literary fabrication by the

---

[5] Jesus refers to the writings of Moses as historical fact and relevant for his disciples, so when some Christians imply that Genesis is not applicable for our time, they tread on dangerous ground.

[6] My friend's fears are well founded. A well-known evangelical scientist believes the stories of Adam and Eve, Job, and Jonah "do not carry that same historical ring" (Collins, *The Language of God*, 209). Yet, he provides no grammatical evidence for this.

redactor of Genesis. Talking snakes are swept away, deemed on par with parting seas and men who walk on water.

Forget the atheists. These miraculous stories are distrusted by self-professed Christians, people who believe in God's existence. While it makes little sense to me to say you believe in God but do not believe he can do miraculous things, nonetheless many liberal Christians are anti-supernatural in their approach to Scripture, all the while proclaiming they believe in a supernatural God.

However, more and more *evangelical* Christians are beginning to state such things, like my friend's pastor. This is highly troubling. If you do not believe in the historical first Adam, I see little reason to believe in an historical last Adam (Jesus).[7] The two are intimately linked in Paul's arguments in both Romans 5 and 1 Corinthians 15.

The reason why some evangelicals are jettisoning a traditional reading of the first Adam is because they believe science (especially evolutionary science) contradicts it. To be consistent, these evangelicals should reject all miracles on the same "anti-scientific" grounds. The biblical worldview of creation, meaning, and purpose has always been antithetical to the reigning secular or pagan context.

I have no doubt that a serpent spoke to Eve in Eden. Nor do I doubt that Jonah was swallowed by a great fish, or that God made a "cosmic bet" with Satan about the fate of Job, or that Jesus, the God-man, literally died and literally rose from the dead.[8] As these events are related, it is difficult for me to believe that someone who doubts, say, a talking serpent, would proclaim a resurrected man. Such discernment, though, is left to God who perfectly knows each person's heart.

It is important for my readers to understand why I believe in the historicity of these accounts, and it is not simply because I believe God can do

---

[7] Whereas liberal Christians question the miraculous Jesus of the Bible because of their anti-supernaturalism, evangelicals who question an historical Adam normally do so based on evolutionary assumptions that point to the "first man" evolving from lower primates.

[8] Kevin DeYoung notes, "In the Gospels we see Jesus reference Abel, Noah, Abraham, Sodom and Gomorrah, Isaac and Jacob, manna in the wilderness, the serpent in the wilderness, Moses as the lawgiver, David and Solomon, the Queen of Sheba, Elijah and Elisha, the widow of Zarephath, Naaman, Zechariah, and even Jonah, never questioning a single event, a single miracle, or a single historical claim. Jesus clearly believed in the historicity of biblical history" (*Taking God at His Word*, 104).

anything he wants to do. It rather has to do with the pedagogical value of fiction (or lack thereof). Let me explain.

A fellow lecturer told his Bible class that it did not matter whether the biblical character Job was real or fictional. For him, the point of Job's book is to teach us about suffering, and the historicity of Job is immaterial to that lesson. I cannot disagree more strongly, and hopefully this illustration will help clarify why.

Suppose you are going through a difficult time in your life. Perhaps it is from the death of a close relative, or you struggle with a debilitating illness. Just like the psalmist who felt abandoned by God in his deepest time of need, you feel lost and adrift in your suffering, with no sense of God's care. In this state, you ask me to bring you wise counsel and comfort.

I tell you a story about a man who built a spaceship to travel to Venus. Due to a technological breakthrough, he was able to equip his vessel with heat-resistant panels, making it safe to venture close to the sun. Unfortunately, along the way the panels failed and his eyes were burned out of their sockets. With all hope seemingly lost, in his despair he called out for help and God rescued him.

What would your reaction be to my story? Would you thank me for the incredible comfort I gave you? Or would you look at me with a glare, wondering how I expect this silly story to assist you? After all, there is no man who has traveled to Venus.

Would it help if I couched my tale in biblical-sounding language? "And God said to the man, 'Cannot the Creator of all things give back your sight? Cannot he who measured the oceans in the palm of his hand return to you your eyes lost to the sun I equally created?'" This talk would avail little because you know the story about the spaceship to Venus is fabricated.

Fiction can provide little comfort for the realities of life. It is akin to telling someone struggling through financial difficulty, "Don't worry, you'll win the lottery." Or to a man who lost his legs in a car accident, "Let me read you a story about a man who drank some sugar water and his legs grew back overnight."

The real God of creation acts in the real events of human history. Our Christian faith is not rooted in esoteric platitudes or ethereal propositional truths to which we grant our mental assent. Our faith is rooted in concrete experiences, with God breaking into history in amazing ways. If you doubt a talking serpent or a worldwide deluge or a man being swallowed by a great creature of the deep, why believe a dead man came back to life three days after his demise?

Which brings me back to Genesis. Once we reject the premise that the opening chapters of Genesis are real human history, we empty it of legitimate value. Forbidden fruit is just that: a real piece of fruit hanging from a real tree. In a real garden a real serpent spoke to real human beings, from whom all of humanity descended.

Anyone who disagrees with this simple presupposition might as well stop reading at this point because the conclusions I formulate only make sense when presented as genuine historical events. Otherwise, someone could always say, "Well, you say marriage was instituted by God in the Garden of Eden, but we know there was no garden or no real 'first humans' as the Bible tells us." At which point all bets are off, and you can make Genesis mean anything you want it to mean, or worse, ignore it altogether.

The Need for a Prophetic Voice

As our society turns from its Judeo-Christian roots, many Christians have decided it is pointless to fight against it. "We won't be listened to anyway, so why bother?" However, a defeatist attitude serves as a self-fulfilling prophecy and guarantees that our fears will be realized. Is it not better to speak out against those elements in our society destroying God's plan and purpose for his creation?

Noah stood alone as the only righteous man of his generation (Gen. 6:9). How difficult it must have been for one man to live among an entire race that God declared "wicked," "corrupt," "violent," and "evil" (Gen. 6:5, 11–13). Yet, despite the incredible tide of ungodliness in his day, Noah was a "preacher of righteousness" (2 Peter 2:5).

The prophet Jeremiah was given an incredibly difficult task: to declare an oracle that was counterintuitive to Israel's presumption as the covenant people of God, antagonistic toward the false prophets who preached a contrary message, and dismissive of the monarch who saw his power being threatened. The situation in Judah was so dire that God challenged Jeremiah in this way:

> Go up and down the streets of Jerusalem, look around and con-
> sider, search through her squares. If you can find but one person
> who deals honestly and seeks the truth, I will forgive this city. (5:1)

The Israelites had embraced false religions, crafted worthless idols, and
fostered the vain hope that treaties with other pagan nations would save
them from the destruction threatened by Nebuchadnezzar's Babylonian
armies. All the while the false prophets preached peace, but God told
Jeremiah that doom was surely coming. Drought, famine, and sword were
the lot of the rebel covenant breakers; a day of disaster would soon be upon
them.

This was no easy task and Jeremiah knew it. In fact, he consistently
complained to God that this undertaking was too burdensome. Listen to
Jeremiah's lament and see if it is not similar to predicaments Christians
find themselves in today:

> I am ridiculed all day long; everyone mocks me. Whenever I speak,
> I cry out proclaiming violence and destruction. So the word of the
> LORD has brought me insult and reproach all day long. (20:7b–8)

American Christians are in a similarly perilous position. However, this is
not the time to despair. If we do not declare the word of the Lord, who will?

Jeremiah cursed the day he was born, accused God of deceiving him, and
wished he had been slain while in his mother's womb, so difficult was the
task God laid before him (20:7, 14, 17). Yet there was something in Jeremiah,
despite the opposition from without and turmoil from within, that compelled him to proclaim the Lord's will.

> But if I say, "I will not mention him or speak any more in his name,"
> his word is in my heart like a fire, a fire shut up in my bones. I am
> weary of holding it in; indeed, I cannot. (20:9)

We need a similar prophetic voice today, one that cannot help but
declare God's will for his creation. Let us immediately dispel the post-
modern myth that our opinion is intrinsically valuable. It is not if it is
wrong. The only opinion that matters is God's opinion; our opinion is
worthwhile only if it agrees with him. As such, we must declare God's

word in a world increasingly hostile to it, for it is the only hope the world has.

The Way Forward

There is a purposeful order of topics I tackle in this book. I begin discussing science and religion. Many evangelicals have had their trust in the Bible eroded by what they think are scientific facts that disprove traditional biblical teaching. In the first two chapters I argue that science and theology can co-exist when science is relegated to the position of "handmaiden" of theology.

Chapters 3 and 4 deal with the created order and its relation to evolutionary theory. I highlight several failings of evolutionary theory and why it is not an adequate scientific position for Christians to incorporate into their interpretation of biblical creation. Once the issue of science is dealt with, hopefully more evangelicals can trust the Bible again.

Chapter 5 deals with the sanctity of life and humans as made in the image of God. Chapter 6, covering animal rights and the environment, only makes sense once the special status of humanity is established.

Chapters 7 through 9 touch on gender roles and sexual morality, among the hottest ethical issues of our time. Chapter 10 covers what the created order has to say about marriage and the family. I then conclude in the epilogue with a few comments on godly wisdom. By the end of the book, I hope you are as astounded as I am at how relevant the opening chapters of Genesis are for our generation.

CHAPTER ONE

God's Created Order
and Scientific Enterprise:
Its Philosophical Underpinning

Faithisthegreatcop-out,thegreatexcusetoevadetheneedtothinkandevaluate
evidence.Faithisbeliefinspiteof,evenperhapsbecauseof,thelackofevidence.
—RICHARD DAWKINS[1]

WE LIVE IN A special time in human history. Watch a program depicting life a relatively short time into the past, where if you needed a limb amputated, the doctor gave you a swig of whiskey and told you to bite down on a stick while he lopped off the appendage. Advances in medicine are helping us live, on average, twice as long as humans did two centuries ago. Ours is a privileged place in the history of mankind, a slice of time that represents at most 5% of humanity's existence given the biblical timeline.

Much of the wonder of our day comes from the technological advances that have swept over us at breakneck speed. When my wife's parents first went to the mission field in the late 1950s, they took a ship that spent three months getting to their destination. Fast forward to today, where a friend flew from the United States to South Africa, spent four days speaking at a conference, and flew back home in time for his classes to resume after the university's weeklong spring break. I can type an email, hit the send button, and a friend eight thousand miles away will answer me in the next minute. This continues to amazes me.

---

[1] From an untitled lecture presented at the Edinburgh Science Festival (1992). Positive Atheism, "Richard Dawkins Quotes," www.positiveatheism.org/hist/quotes/dawkins.htm, accessed November 16, 2015. In Dawkins's 1996 acceptance speech for Humanist of the Year, he likened religion to AIDS, mad cow disease, and smallpox.

The thing is, my in-laws left for the mission field not that long ago. People are still alive, like my grandmother, who vividly remember World War II. Changes in technology that used to take generations now take months. The first computer I recall from my childhood, the Commodore 64, had as much memory as an email today with a small picture attached. We are incredibly blessed.

Nonetheless, these improvements have come with a downside—the greater our technology, the greater our hubris. The more we learn about the world around us, the less we feel the need for God.[2]

Science Has Removed Mankind from Its Rightful Place

Some readers may ask, "Hasn't science removed *God* from his rightful place, not humans?" Yes, but there's a caveat. Science done wrongly eliminates God, but good science need not. There is no inherent conflict between science and religion.

Humanity has been relegated to an increasingly insignificant position in the godless materialism that drives much of the contemporary scientific enterprise. In removing God from science, mankind is equally removed. The God-centered theology of Christianity places a higher value on humanity than does the man-centered worldview of the secular scientist. When God is exalted to his rightful place, humanity comes along for the ride. However, when mankind attempts to usurp God's position, humanity is cast downward to destruction, and usually a destruction of its own doing.

For brevity's sake, I will highlight three scientific findings from the past five hundred years that have facilitated humanity's removal from its privileged place in the cosmos.

Before the discoveries of Polish astronomer Copernicus (1473–1543), speculation existed that the earth was not the center of the solar system. However, it was difficult to ignore the empirical evidence seen every day as the sun moved across the sky. By the Middle Ages, the terra-centric model of creation was used by the Roman Catholic Church to speak of humankind's

---

[2] The Scandinavian research center Sintef claims that 90% of all the data the human race has ever produced has been generated in the past two years. This only increases our arrogance, giving us the false impression that we "know it all." BBC News, "Web Porn: Just How Much Is Out There?" www.bbc.com/news/technology-23030090, accessed October 10, 2015.

special place in God's plans, so that when Copernicus proposed a heliocentric model, opposition came from clergymen and scientists alike. In time, though, the heliocentric model won the day, and the earth was demoted to just one of many orbs orbiting the sun.

Driven by seventeenth-century Enlightenment ideals, humanity in the coming centuries reveled in its newfound freedom from the tyranny of ecclesiastical oppression. Enlightened people claimed that religious tradition stifled discovery and creativity. Science was seen as the great liberator.

Building on the nineteenth-century biology of his day, Charles Darwin (1809–1882) proposed a common ancestor that eventually evolved into all life on the planet. The grand conclusion was that humans are nothing more than advanced animals. Visit any natural history museum and you will see Darwin's "descent of man," as apelike creatures morph into modern *Homo sapiens*. So much for human beings as special creatures made in the image of God.

Sigmund Freud (1856–1939) furthered the decline of mankind with his supposition that humans are sexual beings driven by hidden urges. If Darwin said that humans are nothing more than advanced apes, Freud concluded they are sexually repressed apes driven by unconscious and largely uncontrollable forces.

So-called science has cast humans down from their privileged position by eliminating God's special imprint on them. To be clear, Copernicus's discovery was not a bad thing; it certainly did not contradict anything in God's Word. Science done properly is highly beneficial. Nevertheless, it cast the earth from the center to the outskirts.

Darwinism did the same thing in spades. Not only are we not the center of the solar system, we are not all that special here at home. Whereas the God-centered construct of the Christian worldview gives great value to mankind precisely because we are the pinnacle of God's creative activity, Darwinism casts humans back to the dirt. We are no more important than extinct mollusks, with the same fate awaiting us. It is a world where both love and hate are biological accidents, survival of the fittest rules, and the person whose genes are distributed the widest in the pool wins.

If Freud did not put the final nail in the coffin, he certainly contributed to the hammering. Stripped of our special place in the universe and relegated to the animal kingdom as hairless, upright, lingual apes, we humans have had our craniums cracked open by the science of psychology to reveal subconscious forces beyond our control that drive every decision we make. As a result, the concept of God is nothing more than wish-fulfillment by humans who have invented a coping mechanism to get through a cold, cruel world.[3] Humans no longer find their value from above. Now it comes from within, but more likely, humanity has no real value at all.[4]

Whether it is the removal of humans from the center of the cosmos (Copernicus), or humanity as an accidental by-product of random biochemical mutations (Darwin), or humans as subject to unconscious impulses beyond their control (Freud), the necessary conclusion comes into focus. As philosopher Richard Tamas notes, "[Man] was not God's noble creation with a divine destiny, but nature's experiment with an uncertain destiny."[5]

While science was supposedly liberating humanity from its enslavement to ecclesiastical authority and religious superstition, it was sadly removing humans from the very Being who made them special and unique. Instead of being free to serve God, humanity was free to serve itself, which is just another form of enslavement; humans focused solely on themselves are self-destructive.

This is best seen with the invention of the atomic bomb. Science progressed in the past century to such a "zenith" that humanity invented a relatively easy way to eliminate humanity. While I cannot imagine a world without telephones, automobiles, and computers—all very good things— surely we went too far in the invention of weapons of mass destruction.

This is what happens when science is divorced from theology. When the scientific enterprise moves from "chasing after the thoughts of God" to "making the world a better place for humans," inevitably this self-centered, anthropocentric pursuit will result in conflict. Perhaps I am naïve, but science done with God at the center would not produce inventions that destroy the very pinnacle of God's creation. Rather, it is science divorced from God that yields chaos.

The majority of the scientific disciplines were founded by Christian

---

[3] If Freud is right and humans devised God as a coping mechanism for life in a harsh world, it is curious that we invented the God of the Bible who is far more frightening than anything the world could throw at us.

[4] While Copernicus, an avowed Christian, made a right scientific observation about our world, both Darwin and Freud were decidedly anti-Christian. It is not coincidental that their scientific conclusions are damaging to the Christian faith.

[5] *The Passion of the Western Mind*, 327.

theists, but in the subsequent generations, as greater scientific discoveries were made, this theism softened to a deism that relegated a disinterested and uninvolved God to the outskirts. Deism eventually blossomed into atheism, accompanied by her ugly sister, secular humanism. The well-known adage is apt: in the eighteenth century, man killed the Bible; in the nineteenth century, man killed God; in the twentieth century, man killed man.

In the biblical account, humanity has always been a part of the creation (Mark 10:6), but with a longer, evolutionary scenario, *Homo sapiens* is an insignificant blip on the timeline of the cosmos, not the pinnacle of God's creative activity. For the biblical creationist, mankind's existence is concurrent with the cosmos, not an appendix to it.

We are told that religion has no place in the science classroom. If this wish were truly realized, there would be no end to the heinous, humanity-destroying hubris of a science driven by atheistic materialism. If the science behind the pacifist Albert Einstein's (1879–1955) theories could be used to make the atomic bomb, what will become of us once science is dominated by atheists who believe humans are nothing more than advanced animals?[6]

Science for the sake of science, and science for the sake of humanity, are not good enough. Science must be coupled with theology in order to keep science honest.

Don't Science and Religion Contradict Each Other?

A popular impression today is that science and religion are natural enemies.[7] Galileo is frequently the "proof case" for this conclusion. However, this misleading portrayal creates an unnecessary tension that impedes scientific progress.[8]

---

[6] Christian morality has eroded over the decades in lockstep with the rise of evolutionary theory.

[7] For example, see Andrew Dickson White's *History of the Warfare of Science with Theology in Christendom*.

[8] Colin Russell notes, "The conflict thesis, at least in its simple form, is now widely perceived as a wholly inadequate intellectual framework within which to construct a sensitive and realistic historiography of Western science" ("The Conflict of Science and Religion," in *Science & Religion: A Historical Introduction*, ed. Gary Ferngren [Baltimore: Johns Hopkins University Press, 2002], 7). See the chapters in this edited volume on Copernicus (chapter 7) and Galileo (chapter 8).

Often what is missed with Galileo is that science was wrong. The church-men and clergy weren't the chief enemies of the discoveries of Galileo (and Copernicus before him). It was scientists who vehemently opposed the new findings. Galileo did not make a biblical point, he made a scientific one: the well-established science of his day was mistaken.

The vast majority of today's scientists embrace evolutionary theory, and this causes angst for some Christians. But science is frequently wrong. The beauty of the scientific method is that it is open to correction. The moment people claim evolutionary theory is really fact, and there is no way to think otherwise, they have stumbled off the path of solid science and into the realm of dogmatism. Ironically, many scientists are just as "religious" with their brand of dogma as any churchgoer.

Consider gravity. We observe what happens when something falls to earth, and while the original theory of gravity by Isaac Newton (1642–1727) explained most things, it could not account for anomalies like the abnor-malities with the orbit of Mercury around the sun. However, Newton's the-ory worked well with most large objects.

In the twentieth century, Einstein's general theory of relativity showed how particles at the quantum or atomic level contradict Newton's theory. Thus Einstein's theory improved Newton's. Today there is hope for a unified quantum gravity theory that explains both the macro- and micro-worlds simultaneously. Three hundred years after Newton we are still trying to determine how gravity works, and new explanations may make the old ones obsolete.

However, if you had lived in the mid-1800s and dogmatically declared that science knew everything about gravity, you would have been wrong. "Gravity is a fact" would have been an accurate statement, but "The present theory about how gravity works is a fact" would have been incorrect.

This is often the problem with scientists who speak about evolutionary theory. Consider a couple quotations in this regard:

"The statement that organisms have descended with modifica-tions from common ancestors—the historical reality of evolu-tion—is not a theory. It is a fact, as fully as the fact of the earth's revolution about the sun. Like the heliocentric solar system, evolu-tion began as a hypothesis, and achieved 'facthood' as the evidence in its favor became so strong that no knowledgeable and unbiased person could deny its reality."[9]

"One thing all real scientists agree upon is the fact of evolution itself. It is a fact that we are cousins of gorillas, kangaroos, starfish, and bacteria. Evolution is as much a fact as the heat of the sun. It is not a theory, and for pity's sake, let's stop confusing the philosophically naïve by calling it so. Evolution is a fact."[10]

These quotations are instances of dogmatism, not science. "We are here" is a fact, but "how we got here" is subject to debate. Evolutionary theory is one potential answer to that question, as is biblical creation. It is fallacious to pretend the evolutionary answer is fact. "We descended from apelike creatures" and "we did not descend from apelike creatures" are mutually exclusive propositions, but which one best supports the observable data? One is not automatically fact and the other fiction. As with the theory of gravity, apples fall to the ground when they detach from the tree, but why? The fact is apples fall, but how we explain this phenomenon is a theory that can be disproven later as more information becomes available.

Experimental versus Historical Science

Christians who are quick to jump on the modern scientific bandwagon, making their biblical interpretation fit the findings of science, fail to recognize the distinction between different types of sciences. There is "hard," or experimental, science, the kind learned in the high school laboratory. We know that one part sodium and one part chlorine make table salt. This science involves observation, hypothesis, experimentation, theory, and conclusions. You can see it. You can touch it. You can experiment on it and test your theories. The findings are repeatable.

However, there is another kind of science called forensic, or historical, science, which is not subject to the same method. When someone digs up

---

[9] Douglas J. Futuyma, *Evolutionary Biology*, 2nd ed. (Sunderland, MA: Sinauer Associates, 1986), 15.

[10] Richard Dawkins, "The Illusion of Design," *Natural History* 114, no. 9 (December 2005): 35–37. According to Dawkins, someone is not a "real scientist" if he disagrees with evolution.

a dinosaur bone, the hard science is that the bone exists. Conversely, how it got there, what the beast looked like, and numerous other factors are up to forensic investigation. This science is vastly different from hard science. It is subject to numerous assumptions that, if wrong, can create errant conclusions.[11]

In the quotes above, atheists claim that the postulates of evolutionary science are in the category of experimental science, when in fact they are historical science. They claim fact when all they are saying is theory. Unfortunately, many Christians overlook this distinction.

Along with calling theories facts, some scientists make religion the natural opponent of progress. The article "Study: Science and Religion Really Are Enemies after All" attempts to prove that the more religious you are, the less innovative you will be.[12] "There is a significant negative relationship between religiosity and innovativeness," it concludes.

Unfortunately, the media consistently frame the conversation as if science and religion are in mortal combat, like the article "Creationists Take Down Another Top Professor."[13] Its title is needlessly provocative, making it appear that "top professors" all over the country are getting booted from their jobs because they are honest scientists being harassed by creationists. I read the article vainly waiting for proof for its title.

In fact, a Christian college changed its statement of faith and one of its professors could no longer sign it. He was not fired. There were no staged protests by fundamentalists to have him removed. The theological landscape of his college changed during his seventeen-year tenure, so he voluntarily left. I respect such a man, but I do not value an author who sensationalizes the issue.

---

[11] A publication distributed in American public schools from the National Academy of Sciences (NAS), *Science, Evolution, and Creationism* (Washington, DC: National Academies Press, 2008), makes this very mistake, portraying evolutionary theory as hard science (10–12). Download it for free here: www.nap.edu/catalog/11876.html (accessed June 22, 2016). We will look at this document in more detail in chapters 3 and 4.

[12] Chris Mooney, "Study: Science and Religions Really Are Enemies after All," Moyers & Company, http://billmoyers.com/2014/09/09/study-science-and-religion-really-are-enemies-after-all/, accessed August 21, 2015.

[13] Karl Giberson, "Creationists Take Down Another Top Professor," *The Daily Beast*, www.thedailybeast.com/articles/2015/07/19/creationists-take-down-another-top-professor.html, accessed September 19, 2015. The article comes with a picture of Darwin with an upside-down red cross in the middle of his forehead.

Science and the Bible should never contradict each other, as they both find their source in the one Creator. If we do find an incongruity between the two, then we have misunderstood one or both of them.

It is best to say that religion and the *current* scientific view are at odds. When scientists tout that science is "self-correcting," they imply that it is often wrong.[14] In fact, rather than simply knowing that science is "self-correcting," wouldn't it be better to also know how often it has been wrong, how long it has doggedly held to wrong theories, and how many times it has been wrong without yet being corrected? Do we as evangelicals want to hitch our interpretation of the Bible to a discipline that has been and will continue to be wrong? As Jonathan Sarfati aptly notes, "If we marry our theology to today's science, we may well be widowed tomorrow."[15]

For example, in 2015, a Hungarian-American team of astronomers discovered a "giant new structure" in space that measured more than five billion light years across. Calling it a "huge surprise," one astronomer on the team noted: "If we are right, this structure contradicts the current models of the universe." An article reporting the discovery said that if the measurement of the object is correct, "scientists will need to radically revise their theories on the evolution of the cosmos" because current models for how the universe formed cannot account for an object this size.[16]

Laypeople are consistently led to believe through news accounts, school textbooks, and other media that cosmologists know with certainty how the universe formed. However, as the report notes, we may need a "paradigm shift in astronomy" now that this object has been discovered.

I had a conversation in 2015 with an astrophysicist who teaches in a South African university. He said, "We know with absolute certainty that the universe is 13.8 billion years old, within a few hundred million years." I admit to extreme skepticism with such precision about an age that, by the

---

[14] John Ioannidis from the Stanford University School of Medicine argues that science is *not* always self-correcting: "Why Science Is Not Necessarily Self-Correcting," http://pps.sagepub.com/content/7/6/645.ful, accessed May 1, 2016.

[15] *The Genesis Account*, 4.

[16] Bryan Nelson, "Astronomers Discover Humungous Structure One-Ninth the Size of the Observable Universe," Mother Nature Network, www.mnn.com/earth-matters/space/stories/astronomers-discover-humongous-structure-one-ninth-size-observable-universe, accessed August 20, 2015.

way, has changed during my lifetime. In high school I was taught that the universe was 17 billion years old.

To be clear, I do not mind new discoveries that cause us to rethink old theories. That is what good science is all about. What I do mind, though, is when science is portrayed as both "self-correcting" and "infallible," when theories are portrayed as facts that cannot be questioned (while demonizing religion for doing much the same thing), and when Christians make the Bible subject to this mutable scientific enterprise.

Scientists cannot say that if Christians question their findings, they must be wrong, while also saying that the beauty of science is that it is subject to correction. These scientists want to have their cake and eat it too. When science needs to change, we are told how wonderful it is, and when scientists are just as dogmatic as any religionist, we are told that their approach to "facts" cannot be questioned. This is nothing more than hypocrisy in scientific garb.

The charge that the Christian faith kills good science is, quite honestly, laughable.[17] I maintain the exact opposite. Adopting biblical history does not kill science, it makes it fruitful. Science done with the assumption of God's non-existence and non-interference will by necessity produce false conclusions. Only science performed with the biblical God in mind is good science. Rather than religion killing science, it is godless science that kills humans.

It is no accident that the scientific enterprise took off after the Reformation, when the reformers brought back a literal interpretation of the Bible, as opposed to an allegorical one. A more objective understanding of God's Word brought back an objective understanding of God's creation, making the modern scientific enterprise possible. This is why twentieth-century American anthropologist and natural science writer Loren Eisely pointed out that it was the Christian worldview that "finally gave birth in a clear, articulate fashion to the experimental method of science itself."[18]

It is the orderliness of the creation made by an orderly God that makes the scientific method possible. It is why we expect tomorrow to be like

---

[17] Ker Than, "Intelligent Design: 'The Death of Science,'" Live Science, www.livescience.com/9361-intelligent-design-death-science.html, accessed August 19, 2015.

[18] Loren Eisely, *Darwin's Century: Evolution and the Men Who Discovered It* (Garden City, NY: Doubleday, 1958), 62. This is why cultures that held a cyclical view of time or viewed nature as a willful entity that should not be violated did not foster scientific endeavors like Christianity did.

today, why nature is not erratic but has universal laws that we can measure, and why humans have a mind suited to investigate their universe and use the laws of logic for the task. Once we remove the theological foundation, we have cut from under science the legs on which it stands.

Apologizing for the Bible

Science, when performed with God at its heart, should never contradict God's revelation found in his holy Word. Nevertheless, the Bible *does* oppose the philosophical underpinnings of atheistic materialism, which is the driving presupposition of the scientific enterprise today. Science must become the handmaiden of theology. However, when theology is held hostage by a militant, atheistic science, both pay a heavy price.

Unfortunately, the truths of Scripture and science are often played against each other by Christians, frequently portrayed as the "two books" of God.[19] The one "book" is science, which teaches us about the material realm, while the other "book" is the Bible, which covers the spiritual realm. Any apparent contradictions are usually eliminated on the premise that "the Bible . . . was not written with the intention of being a scientific textbook."[20] On the surface, this looks like a promising approach.

Yet there is a fine line between saying "the Bible is not a science textbook" and "the Bible is scientifically inaccurate, but that's okay, because it is not intended to be a science textbook." Unfortunately, when Christians say the former, usually they mean the latter. If science says A and the Bible says B, then the Bible must be wrong since it is not a scientific authority, only a religious one. This is verbalized with the catchy yet misleading idea that the Bible is about "how to go to heaven, not how the heaven goes."[21] For starters, why can't it be both?

Some Christians say what really matters is the *who* of creation, not

---

[19] Joel Hunter, "The Perils and Promise of Preaching the God of Two Books," BioLogos, http://biologos.org/blog/the-perils-and-promise-of-preaching-the-god-of-two-books, accessed August 30, 2015.

[20] Driscoll and Breshears, *Doctrine*, 80. Well-intentioned evangelicals imply that if the Bible is proved to be factually inaccurate, it does not matter because the Bible was intended for spiritual, not scientific reasons.

[21] This sentiment, supportively quoted by Driscoll and Breshears, has been traced to Galileo, who may have been quoting a Catholic clergyman (ibid., 81).

the *how*.[22] They argue that the main thrust of the Genesis account is that God is the Creator, and any conclusions beyond that—especially if they stumble into the realm of "science"—are missing the point. I cannot more strongly disagree. If the *how* is not accurate, why trust the specifics about the *who*? Besides, if God is the ultimate author of the Bible, he can get the scientific facts correct as well as the spiritual ones since he is the Father of both.

The Bible contains spiritual truths, but these truths are couched within the real, physical world. God communicates them in a concrete manner, through historic acts like the flood and the incarnation. As such, with these spiritual truths we expect some content about the physical realm and its history. We can hardly believe that the world was deluged by water in Noah's day if we do not have some idea about the properties of water. Such a book would have to affirm both spiritual as well as scientific truths.

At times, it appears that evangelicals create newfangled proposals simply to skirt their embarrassment at how wrong the Bible is, with the implication that Christians must make their biblical interpretation fit the science of the day. However, it is nonsensical for evangelicals who proclaim the Bible as the very words of God to then say that it is inaccurate about the *how* of God's creation. I expect skeptics to take this low view of Scripture, but not fellow evangelicals who believe in the rather unscientific notion that a dead man came back to life after three days.

It is becoming more popular within evangelical scholarship to say that the opening chapters of Genesis are nothing more than a poetic portrayal of the origin of the universe ("God made it"), not the details of the process he used to do it ("God made it *this way*"). With this approach, we need not be distracted by the sequence and specifics of each day of creation.

One proposal is the literary framework hypothesis (LFH). Here is how the LFH is typically portrayed when it comes to the seven days of creation:

---

[22] This comment from theistic evolutionists Karl Giberson and Francis S. Collins is a case in point: "The Genesis account does not tell us how God created—only that God did create and that human beings are a part of God's plan and not an accident" (*The Language of Science and Faith*, 206).

Literary Framework Hypothesis

Day 1 – creation of light

Day 4 – creation of light-bearing objects

Day 2 – creation of sky in separating the waters

Day 5 – creation of sky and water creatures

Day 3 – creation of land and vegetation

Day 6 – creation of land creatures and humans

Day 7 – God rested

A beautiful symmetry exists with this scheme, and in Hebrew thought, this kind of balanced portrayal is quite common, such as the use of couplets in Hebrew poetry. Proponents of the LFH avoid the apparent contradictions that exist between the Genesis account and scientific consensus, especially when dealing with the age of the earth. Because Genesis is not a precise description of the procedure used by God, it makes little difference if the "days" are twenty-four-hour periods or geological ages of hundreds of millions of years.[23]

One problem with reconciling science with biblical creation is that according to science the earth formed after the sun, whereas in Genesis God made the sun on day 4, after he made the planet. The appeal of the LFH is that these contradictions melt away since the Genesis account is not providing a precise chronology. We could change the order of the days, flipping day 2 with day 3 and day 5 with day 6, and still have poetic symmetry since the *how* of creation is not the point of the passage.

However, there is a false dichotomy in the LFH. Why can't the passage be communicating both the *who* and the *how* of creation? The reason is because this contradicts the conclusions of science. Again, the eternal Word of God is made to conform to the tentative findings of a fallible discipline. My guess is once you adapt the Bible to scientific findings, you will always do so, even as the scientific consensus shifts.

Besides, the order of the creation days may be important for reasons other than scientific. Early church father Basil (329–379) saw a significance in God waiting until the fourth day to make the sun and moon since they were heavenly bodies worshiped in Moses' day.

---

[23] The LFH also eliminates the problem with having literal, twenty-four-hour days before the creation of the sun on day 4. How do you have "evening and morning" when there is no sun to demarcate them? However, in order to have a "day," you only need to have a fixed point of light and a rotating planet.

> However, the sun and the moon did not yet exist, in order that those who live in ignorance of God may not consider the sun as the origin and the father of light, or as the Maker of all that grows out of the earth. That is why there was a fourth day, and then God said: "Let there be lights in the firmament of the heaven."[24]

Even further, things are not as neat and tidy with the LFH as its advocates claim. There is significant overlap in the events of each day, making the balanced triads not so symmetrical. For example, the "seas" are not gathered together until day 3, not day 2 (where the "waters" appear as the sky is created). To say that the creation of the fish and birds of day 5 exactly equates to day 2 is inaccurate.

Also, the LFH relies on the assumption that the Genesis account is not historical narrative but poetry, yet there is no hint in Genesis itself that the early chapters are meant to be treated any differently from the later ones. Why is there skepticism among evangelical scholars that the story of Noah and the flood is not historically accurate, but the account of Abraham beginning just three chapters later is? Genesis moves seamlessly forward over twenty generations from Adam to Jacob, even taking pains to record detailed genealogies along the way (chapters 5 and 10; see also 1 Chronicles 1–8). Christians who treat Genesis back to Abraham as history, but then treat the preceding material as myth, are being inconsistent.

The most powerful argument in favor of the historical reliability of the creation account is that Jesus and Paul refer to events of Genesis as history[25] and Jesus' genealogy (Luke 3:23–38) goes back to Adam. Implying fictitious figures in the genealogy of Jesus is tantamount to including Paul Bunyan or Huckleberry Finn in the genealogy of an American president.

Look at Hebrew poetry in Psalms and Job and compare it to the Genesis account. A straightforward reading of Genesis makes it obvious that it is

---

[24] Homily VI:2 (New Advent, www.newadvent.org/fathers/32016.htm, accessed October 12, 2015).

[25] John 8:44; Romans 5:12–21; 1 Corinthians 15:21–22. The chronicle of the faithful in Hebrews 11 gives no hint that we should understand Moses and David as historical figures while Enoch and Abel are mythical. There are other places in the Old Testament where the opening chapters of Genesis are considered history (e.g., 1 Chron. 1:1; Eccles. 3:20; see a more comprehensive listing in Barrick, Lamoureux, Walton, and Collins, *Four Views on the Historical Adam*, 217–18).

not meant to be poetic. I cannot shake the feeling that scholars who are desperate to make Genesis 1 a poetic portrayal of creation do so not for linguistic or exegetical reasons, but because if they do not, the Bible will contradict the science of the day.[26]

I find it shocking that evangelical scholars are jettisoning traditional biblical views for the shifting sands of science. In chapters 2, 3, and 4 we will consider other ways these scholars meld the Genesis account with modern scientific findings.

"All Creation Is Mine"

The opening chapter of Genesis tells us how God made the heavens and the earth, but since God is mentioned thirty-two times in thirty-one verses, we can glean much about *him* from this chapter too.

The very orderly, systematic layout of the chapter communicates that God is orderly and systematic. There is a formula that runs throughout the six days of creation: God speaks, what he says will happen happens, God declares it good, and each episode concludes with the phrase "and there was evening, and there was morning—the X day." There is purpose and direction throughout the account.

There is a simple beauty to God's creative activity. He has designed the "kinds" of creation, each with its unique traits, all in a precise balance with the other animate and inanimate components. He designed the dragonfly and the woolly mammoth, the flagellum on bacteria and the eyelashes on ostriches. God enjoys engineering precision as well as flamboyant artistry, such as the plumage on a peacock or a cuttlefish's vibrant colors.

We either believe we are "fearfully and wonderfully made" (Ps. 139:14), or every single thing we see is accidental. Consider how atheist Richard Dawkins sees the world:

> Charles Darwin showed how it is possible for blind physical forces to mimic the effects of conscious design, and, by operating as a cumulative filter of chance variations, to lead eventually to

---

[26] For a thorough critique of the LFH see *As It Is Written* by Kenneth Gentry Jr.

organized and adaptive complexity, to mosquitoes and mammoths, to humans and therefore, indirectly, to books and computers.[27]

Note that a "blind" process that is up to chance at every level is compared to the intelligence and creative genius of God the Designer. For the atheist, science takes the place of God. This is why Dawkins and his ilk speak dogmatically about scientific findings. Science is their religious object of worship. Instead of being a tool by which humans are able to chase after the thoughts of the Creator, science has become an altar at which naturalists worship.

Genesis 1 also speaks of God's power. He simply says the word and creation is born. The number of stars in the universe is around 10^{25}. If we had a super computer that could count ten billion stars per second, it would take more than thirty million years to count them all! Yet the prophet Isaiah records this about our transcendent Creator:

> "To whom will you compare me? Or who is my equal?" says the Holy One. Lift your eyes and look to the heavens: Who created all these? He who brings out the starry host one by one, and calls forth each of them by name. Because of his great power and mighty strength, not one of them is missing. (40:25–26)

While some scholars conjecture that the plural "let *us* make mankind in *our* image" (Gen. 1:26) is the language of a kingly court or God speaking to angelic beings, it is best understood as a clue to the Trinity.[28] This only makes sense once the revelation of God's Son is complete, but this early peek at the Trinity makes it clear that God has revealed more about himself in the opening chapter of Genesis than we typically realize.

God's nature is firmly established at the start of Scripture. "In the beginning God" says as much about God as it does about the beginning. He has always been here, which also communicates his eternality. In the opening chapter of the Bible, we have a course on the doctrine of God.

As we run down the attributes of God enumerated in Genesis 1, we

---

[27] Richard Dawkins, "The Necessity of Darwinism," *New Scientist* 94, no. 1301 (1982): 130.

[28] Plural pronouns for God are also used later in Genesis (e.g., 3:22; 11:7).

might miss a fundamental truth glossed over by our modern world. As the Creator, God owns everything he has made. There is not a single element of the cosmos that he does not have a right to claim as his own. He is sovereign Lord of all.[29]

We have no problem saying this when speaking about comets and nebulae, but when it comes to humans, we frequently object. The desire for human autonomy runs deep within our veins. This was at the heart of the serpent's temptation: "you will be like God."

Because God is the owner, he has the right to determine what will be done with his creation. Note I did not say *the* creation, I said *his* creation. As such, God makes the rules. No one was there to counsel him on where to peg the speed of light, or at what temperature water freezes, or where to set the acceleration of gravity's pull. God determined these, and then placed mankind in this creation.

The imagery of a potter and his clay is used in Scripture to portray the relationship between God and his creatures.[30] The apostle Paul employs it to speak pointedly to those who question God's ways (Rom. 9:20–21). It is a perspective we ought not lose, especially in those moments when we are tempted to ignore God's design for his creation. If we dwell on the portrayal of humans as lumps of clay, we may be offended by such a low depiction of creatures made in his image. But when finite humans are compared to the sovereign, eternal, omnipotent, transcendent Creator, the analogy—humans are to God as clay is to a potter—is perfectly apt.

As we move through this book, we need to keep this perspective in mind. When we elaborate on the sanctity of life, recall that God is its author. When we speak about the gift of sex, remember that God created it and knows best how it is to be used. Genesis 1 sets the tone for the rest of the Bible and the rest of human history: we are God's creatures, subject to his rule, created for his glory. Once we forget this fundamental truth, we will lose respect for life, our environment, and our responsibilities in it.

---

[29] In Genesis 3 God is also revealed as Judge and Redeemer.
[30] For example, Isaiah 29:16; 45:9; 64:8; Jeremiah 18:1–6.

CHAPTER TWO

God's Created Order
and Scientific Enterprise:
Its Practical Outworking

Because there is a law such as gravity,
the universe can and will create itself from nothing.

—STEPHEN HAWKING[1]

IN THE 1968 MOVIE *2001: A Space Odyssey*, humans find a perfectly machined monolith with proportions of 1:4:9 on the moon. This discovery leads to the inevitable conclusion that there is intelligent life somewhere in the cosmos, and in the movie's sequel, humans reach Jupiter's moons where they encounter this alien intelligence. The irony of this materialist conception is that the same people who claim that design is a sign of intelligence—in the case of the monolith—reject a Creator for the universe, which displays even more complex design.

The same incongruity is seen in the 2014 movie *Interstellar*, which has its protagonist scoffing at religion, yet deduces in the discovery of a wormhole outside Saturn that intelligent life exists elsewhere. Ultimately (spoiler alert!) humans are saved by themselves—as more advanced humans from the future. A divine savior is unnecessary when humans can do the trick, a materialist's dream.

At the heart of scientific enterprise today is atheistic materialism. God does not exist, and everything we see can be explained via purely

---

[1] Adam Gabbatt, "Stephen Hawking Says Universe Not Created by God," *The Guardian*, www.theguardian.com/science/2010/sep/02/stephen-hawking-big-bang-creator, accessed December 12, 2015.

natural means, without supernatural meddling. When we discussed "bad science" in the previous chapter, it was atheistic materialism in the crosshairs.

For centuries Christians have used powerful arguments against atheism. One is the cosmological proof for God's existence: everything in the universe is contingent on something else, with a beginning and an end. From the largest star to the smallest microbe this is observably true.

Atheists postulate that the universe has always been here, or that it popped into existence by itself. In the quote at the opening of this chapter, we see that one of the brightest minds of our generation, astrophysicist Stephen Hawking, maintains that the universe created itself.

The psalmist writes, "The fool says in his heart, 'There is no God'" (Ps. 14:1). Surely Hawking's declaration falls into this category. When atheists claim a self-creating universe, Christians should never apologize for their "unreasonable" faith. I can go into any second-grade class, hold up a computer and tell the children that it made itself, and be laughed out of the room. Forgetting for the moment that Hawking assumes the law of gravity—something that would not exist were it not for the universe's existence—this is nothing more than a circular argument.[2] It is all Hawking has left once God is removed from the equation.

It is unreasonable to conclude that a universe containing only contingent material is itself not equally contingent. Movies like *2001* kick the problem down the road, implying that life came to earth from extraterrestrials, which produces the question: where did *they* come from? As clever as *Interstellar* is with treating time and gravity as extra dimensions, the movie falls short on the fundamental question of origins. There must be something that by necessity exists—what we call a "necessary being"—in order for all contingent being to exist. Atheism is left ignoring the question, or declaring the universe as self-created.

How Old Is the Earth?

One thing has consistently vexed me as a biblical creationist and a lover of science. For the past seventy years contemporary science has affirmed that

---

[2] Circular in that the universe must have self-created because we have the law of gravity, yet the law of gravity could not exist without the universe.

the earth is 4.54 billion years old. Young earth creation (YEC) claims that by moving from Adam's creation and adding up the biblical genealogies found in Genesis 5 and 10 and elsewhere, the earth is about six thousand years old. This plain reading of Scripture appeals to me, but it butts up against science's conclusions. Is there a way to reconcile the two?

According to claims made by modern science, the earth is 750 million times older than the YEC conclusion. Christians who are inclined toward YEC, but who are put off by the wildly differing calculations, have tried to smooth over the discrepancy by noting that genealogies in the Old Testament frequently skip generations. For example, a father and a great-great-grandson might be the most noteworthy people in their clan, while the insignificant men in between were skipped in the genealogy. Therefore, some YEC proponents say the earth is between 10,000 and 20,000 years old, but this hardly eliminates the problem. We are still talking about whether you want a large Domino's pizza or a pizza the size of Texas. There is simply no way to gloss over the discrepancy between the Bible and the claims of contemporary science by elongating the genealogies.

Perhaps God wants it this way, forcing us to either trust his Word or trust the best conclusions of modern science. However, this false dichotomy encourages the wrongheaded thinking I criticized in the previous chapter, that science and theology are mortal enemies. I rather believe they can be reconciled because they both find their foundation in the one God who established them.

We could ignore science altogether and accept what many Christians over the centuries have concluded: God made the heavens and the earth in six, literal, twenty-four-hour days. He did not incorporate evolution, nor did he allow for large periods of time during this creative process. He simply did what Genesis says he did: directly fashion creation within the time period specified. This position, called fiat creationism or biblical creation, is the view I hold. Still, this does not address how science and Genesis could be so discordant. If possible, I want to find a way to reconcile the two.

Many evangelicals agree with this sentiment but have proposed theories that demote the biblical revelation to the backseat of the car, with science in the driver's seat. Here are the main attempts at building into Genesis the billions of years required by modern science for the age of the earth.

Gap Theory and Historic Creationism

The gap theory assumes a large amount of time transpiring between Genesis 1:1 and 1:2, on the premise that God's "first creation" expressed in verse 1 was subjugated to chaos (as a result of Satan's fall from heaven), and verse 2 begins God's re-creation of the earth. In this way, billions of years can be built into this "gap" between the opening two verses of the creation account. Fossils and old rocks are explained with this theory, while literal, twenty-four-hour days can also be maintained for the "second creation" that took place after the chaotic gap.

However, this view has been thoroughly debunked by evangelical scholars.[3] The simplest shortcoming is that the account does not read like this. Are we really to assume that billions of years transpired between verse 1 and verse 2? This implies two creations, when the account only speaks of one. Further, from a scientific point of view, it does little to assuage the evolutionary consensus concerning humans. While it could account for old fossils and rocks, it maintains that humans are several thousand years old. In short, it does not reconcile things.

A view similar to the gap theory is "historic creationism."[4] It makes a distinction between Genesis 1:1, which is God's creation of the cosmos, and the second verse and following that are concerned with God's preparation of the earth for its inhabitants. Again, billions of years can be built into verse 1—with the added benefit of avoiding the chaos of the gap theory—thus affirming modern scientific conclusions about the age of the universe.

Nevertheless, historic creationism suffers from most of the problems of the gap theory while adding some new ones. For starters, the distinction between verse 1 (the creation of the universe) and verse 2 and following (the forming of the earth) is not so neat and tidy. Verse 1 does not say, "In the beginning God created the heavens"; it includes the earth as well, and on day 4, the sun, moon, and stars are created, which involve the heavens. Granted, day 4 could be speaking about what appeared from the earth's perspective, as in the stars were now visible, but historic creationism still

---

[3] A helpful book is Weston Field's *Unformed and Unfilled.*

[4] See Driscoll and Breshears, *Doctrine,* 89–90, 93. The authors build their view on John Sailhamer's approach in *Genesis Unbound.*

relies on a vast distinction between verse 1 and verse 2, something the text does not reveal.

My main objection to both of these theories is that neither of them is evident from a plain, straightforward reading of the account. Would we posit these views if we did not feel the heat from modern science breathing down our necks? Both theories are created to appease scientific suppositions. Remove the necessity for billions of years, and they both melt away.

Progressive Creationism, or the "Day-Age" Theory

My tenth-grade daughter came home from high school one afternoon and told me that her teacher that morning had encouraged debate between the students about the origin of the universe. Other than herself, there was one student standing for the Christian worldview, while many were outspoken atheists.

As she unpacked the discussion, my daughter asked a substantial question: could there be millions of years *between* the creation days? On the first day God created light, and then he waited for an amount of time approaching a geologic age before he created the sky on day 2, and so on. In this way the massive time periods of modern science could fit into the biblical account.[5]

This is initially appealing. I would love to have a workable scenario where the findings of science and the teaching of the Bible correspond perfectly. Much like the gap theory, my daughter's proposal appeared to solve this conflict.

However, as we explored the biblical text, things started to fall apart. For one thing, on the third day God created the land and its vegetation. If there were hundreds of millions of years without photosynthesis until the fourth day when the sun was created, all the vegetation would have died out.

We also have a problem with the Sabbath. How an Israelite ordered his week's activities was likened to how God created. "For in six days the LORD made the heavens and the earth, the sea, and all that is in them, but he rested on the seventh day" (Exod. 20:11). The theological balance between creation week and the Jewish week is lost if in actual fact God did not create

---

[5] Some call this the "intermittent-day theory."

in a literal week but rather in days intermittently sprinkled over billions of years.

Obviously, God did not require six days to make creation. He could have done it in an instant. That being the case, perhaps God purposefully made the universe in six days and then fashioned mankind's week after it, in order to give us a permanent reminder of his creative activity. Regardless, the intermittent-day notion is not tenable.

Some Christians note that the Hebrew word for day, *yom*, can refer to literal days and to ages or periods of time. Much like my children ask me, "Dad, in your *day*, what did they do with such and such?" the Genesis account may be using *yom* to refer to a distant age. In fact, we see it used this way in Genesis 2:4.[6]

There are numerous problems with this "day-age" approach (known as progressive creationism). The first problem is that the Hebrew *yom* never means a long period of time when it has a number attached to it. There is no hint that idle time exists between the Genesis days, or that the days are akin to geologic ages. Later in Genesis when it rained forty days and forty nights during the great flood (7:12), nobody thinks this means forty thousand years. Rather, the plainest reading of the text makes the best sense. Not only does Moses number each day of creation, but he also notes "there was evening, and there was morning." How clearer can he be?

The second problem with progressive creationism is that we have the same drawback as with my daughter's theory. Even if God took his time and created over millions of years, we have an ecosystem that cannot survive until the sun arrives on the fourth day.

A third problem is similar to gap theory and historic creationism. While we have a sufficient amount of time to satisfy geological science, we have not eliminated incongruities between the biblical text and other scientific disciplines. For example, whereas cosmology says planets form after stars, Genesis has the sun and stars forming after the earth is made. Evolutionary science likewise contradicts the biblical sequence for the appearance of birds, fish, land animals, and vegetation.

---

[6] Some say that this is taught in the biblical phrase "with the Lord a day is like a thousand years, and a thousand years are like a day" (2 Peter 3:8). However, this is a poetic way to speak of God's eternality, not a mathematical formula we can use (see Ps. 90:4, where it is clear in context that the psalmist is speaking about God's everlasting nature). Time places no limitations on a Being who is eternal.

The long ages of progressive creationism also demote humanity from the pinnacle of God's creative activity to merely an appendix, as mankind emerges in the last 0.002% of creation's existence.

A final problem involves death. Death is a punishment from God because Adam and Eve sinned (Gen. 2:17). But with progressive creationism, death existed for billions of years before Adam and Eve arrived on the scene. Some argue that Genesis merely speaks of human death, but I find this unconvincing. While the plain biblical teaching is that death is a consequence of sin (Rom. 5:12–14; 1 Cor. 15:21–22), according to progressive creationism all around Adam and Eve animals were tearing each other apart. Paul says the earth was subjected to decay due to the fall (Rom. 8:20–21), necessitating a new heaven and a new earth, which further suggests that death, even in the animal kingdom, was only a reality after Adam sinned.

In the consummation of all things, death will be eliminated (Rev. 21:4), apparently in the animal kingdom as well. Isaiah envisions a messianic age where the wolf and the lamb feed together, and a lion eats straw like an ox (Isa. 11:6–7; 65:25). That our first parents were vegetarians (Gen. 2:16) also speaks against death in the animal kingdom. Only after the fall does God slaughter an animal to provide Adam and Eve with clothing (3:21). Because death and sin are intimately linked (1 Cor. 15:56), it is theologically difficult to reconcile this biblical teaching with the scientific notion that death was always part of the picture.

When compared to fiat creationism, though, progressive creationism has some benefits, one being how to account for visible light from distant stars. Another theory, though, must first be explored.

Mature Creationism

One possibility for reconciling Genesis with science is "mature creationism." It posits that God made the universe with the appearance of old age. This intriguing view accords well with Adam and Eve, who surely were created as mature humans as opposed to embryos or infants. Twenty-four hours after Adam was formed from the dust of the earth, he may have appeared to be fifteen to twenty years old, even though he was only a day old. Why couldn't God do this with the rest of creation?

When we think of God making fully formed trees or elephants, this is not problematic. The difficulty comes with light from distant stars. God could have made the light "in transit," giving the appearance of age, but this makes God appear deceptive. Light is not simply a thing, it is also information; it communicates history. When we see a star exploding, an actual historical event supposedly took place millions of years ago, but according to mature creationism, that incident never occurred. God merely created the light to make it appear to have happened.

We are told God made Adam from the dust of the earth and then made Eve from his rib. There is nothing deceptive about God telling us how he made our first parents, even though they had an appearance of age. However, there is a difference between creating Adam with the appearance of age, and creating him with the appearance of history. What if God created Adam complete with scars, implying that Adam received a childhood injury even though he was never a child? Creating scars on Adam would indeed be misleading; creating light in transit is equally deceptive.

Because progressive creationists build billions of years into their theory, the light from distant stars actually traveled that far. Young earth creationists, though, do not have that luxury. How do they address this problem?

Speeding Up the Light?

Light, which acts as both a particle and a wave, is one of the fundamental forms of energy. Einstein's well-known law $E = MC^2$ shows the relationship between energy, the mass of an object, and the speed of light. Even a tiny piece of matter has an incredible amount of energy stored in it. It is a wonder that light is among the first items catalogued in Moses' ancient creation account.

Light travels fast, but the universe is huge. A beam of light from our planet takes 2 seconds to get to the moon, 4 minutes to get to Mars, 5 hours to get to Pluto, and about 4.3 years to get to the next star in our galaxy. The nearest galaxy is 2 million light years away, the nearest cluster of galaxies 20 million light years from us. And we have merely scratched the surface.[7]

However, as fast as light is, it is not fast enough to account for starlight

---

[7] The distance from the earth to the edge of the universe is approximately forty-six billion light years. Wikipedia, "Observable Universe," https://en.wikipedia.org/wiki/Observable_universe#cite_note-21, accessed December 16, 2015.

millions of years away when, according to YEC, the whole universe is six thousand years old. Biblical creationists have proposed altering the speed of light or envisioning the distance as greatly reduced in the past, but these solutions have severe drawbacks. For many skeptics, this hindrance alone is the deal breaker when it comes to accepting a young earth, but should it be?

For starters, creationists are not the only ones who have a predicament with light travel. If the Big Bang theory is true, then our entire universe exploded from a singular point, expanding into a fireball that eventually formed everything in space. This fireball initially had uneven temperature distribution, making it possible for various types of matter to form in the universe. Today, though, we measure this temperature from every corner of the cosmos, and we find that it is incredibly uniform. This cosmic microwave background radiation is used as proof for the Big Bang.

However, this scenario has a glitch. In order for hotter regions to share their heat with cooler ones, the energy must be distributed from one end of the universe to the other. Think of a bathtub. As you add hot water at one end, the heat is transferred through the water until the bath is at equilibrium. You do not have one end of the tub that is scalding hot and the other end solid ice.

The same happened with the universe, accomplished through radiation that moves at the speed of light. But given the vastness of the universe, and the estimate of its current age, there is not enough time for this to have happened. This cosmological conundrum is known as the horizon problem. Evolutionary cosmologists have had about sixty years to figure out an explanation, but no proposal is a clear winner.

One solution is to postulate that immediately after the Big Bang, a period of rapid "inflation" occurred (literally in a split second, and faster than the speed of light) followed by, for some unknown reason, a slowdown to the rate of expansion we see today.[8] Cosmic inflation is not without its detractors, most notably one of the originators of the theory, Paul Steinhardt, who has since changed his mind. For one thing, we do not see normal explosions behave this way. It is a rather ad hoc theory with

---

[8] For more substantial material, begin with this NASA webpage, "Dark Energy, Dark Matter," http://science.nasa.gov/astrophysics/focus-areas/what-is-dark-energy/, accessed December 2, 2015.

virtually no empirical data to back it up. More work is needed beyond the thirty years since inflationary theory was suggested.[9]

Science is up to correction. This is a good thing, but do evangelicals want to marry their reading of the Bible to the latest scientific findings? As recently as the 1990s, cosmologists changed their view on the expanding universe. Previously it was assumed that gravitational forces would cause the expansion to slow down and eventually collapse upon itself, but since the Hubble Telescope began recording readings far deeper into space, it was observed that the universe's expansion is *accelerating*. Where is the energy coming from that is causing this explosion to increase in velocity?

One way to explain this phenomenon is with dark energy, that mysterious entity that along with dark matter supposedly constitutes 95% of the mass-energy of the universe. However, we know very little about this dark stuff, and scientists postulate that we need a new theory of gravity superior to Einstein's.

By the way, secular scientists have also proposed variable speed of light theories, despite the challenges changing the speed of light creates with known physics.[10] To get around the horizon problem, you either alter the speed of light or adjust the distance it travels, as inflationary theory does.[11] Perhaps a theory that combines both is closer to the truth.[12]

---

[9] A helpful illustration of the "history of the universe" according to current scientific theory can be found on Wikipedia, https://en.wikipedia.org/wiki/File:History_of_the_Universe.svg, accessed December 4, 2015.

[10] For example, Eugenie Reich, "Speed of Light May Have Changed Recently," New Scientist, www.newscientist.com/article/dn6092-speed-of-light-may-have-changed-recently/, accessed December 10, 2015; Jesse Emspak, "Speed of Light May Not Be Constant, Physicists Says," Live Science, www.livescience.com/29111-speed-of-light-not-constant.html, accessed December 10, 2015; Wikipedia, "Variable Speed of Light," https://en.wikipedia.org/wiki/Variable_speed_of_light, accessed December 10, 2015.

[11] Altering the speed of light has a double benefit. Not only does it solve the distant starlight problem, but it also affects radiometric dating, as nuclear reactions and decay are related to the speed of light.

[12] Another possibility involves manipulating time. From Einstein's relativity theories we know that, depending on one's perspective, time runs at different rates. Therefore, according to the "earth clock," God made the universe in six days. Other parts of the universe experienced different rates of time. However, while this might address the horizon problem, it does not address YEC challenges to geology and evolutionary theory.

I bring this up for an obvious reason. Before we abandon any young earth ideas because they cannot account for light from distant stars, we need to recognize that nobody else can either. Progressive creationism, gap theory, and historic creationism have time built into their theories, but since they rely on the amount of time science provides them, they too have the horizon problem.

I ask myself, "Am I willing to abandon the most natural reading of the Genesis account, and the apparent young earth that results, for theories that have critical scientific drawbacks? Do I make the Bible subordinate to science?" I must answer in the negative.

How Did We Get 4.54 Billion Years?

In the mid-seventeenth century, Bishop Ussher famously set the date of the earth's creation at October 23, 4004 BC, using calculations made from biblical genealogies and the Hebrew calendar. In the following century estimates for the earth's age began to move upward, based on little more than guesswork. No sophisticated methods for dating were yet invented.

However, given assumptions about the incremental formation of rock strata, most geologists believed that the earth could not possibly be just six thousand years old. By the late nineteenth century, and in light of Darwin's new theory that necessitated lots of time, estimates for the earth's age moved up into the tens of millions of years. Discoveries of dinosaur bones measuring the size of large living rooms allowed imaginations to run wild. Was it true that whole species of creatures came into existence and then out again in only millions of years?

The upshot is that geology and paleontology worked in lockstep as estimates for the earth's age steadily increased until the 1950s, when through radiometric analysis of uranium and lead, the age of the earth was set at 4.54 billion years, a figure largely uncontested today.

These two scientific fields continue to work together in what biblical creationists call rather circular logic: fossils are often dated by the layer of strata they are found in, and the strata have dates linked to the type of fossils discovered there. In fact, radiometric rock dates that do not agree with the presupposed age of the fossil evidence found with the rock will be presumed contaminated and thus discarded. This happens more often than laypeople are led to believe. The paradigm drives the conclusions, with data contrary to the paradigm ignored.

One assumption of geology shared with evolution has been uniformitarianism (signified by the adage "the present is the key to the past"). Present-day observed rates of erosion or sedimentation can be extrapolated backward, and because forming of rock strata or carving of a canyon takes a lot of time, the Bible's timeframe cannot be accepted. For example, the Grand Canyon is believed to expose two billion years of the earth's geological history as the Colorado River gradually cut through the layers of rock. Coupled with this is the large amount of time necessary for evolutionary changes to occur from simple to complex organisms through incremental adaptations. This is usually portrayed with the geologic column neatly divided into periods, with fossils depicted in all the right places throughout the record.

The problem with this tidy formulation is that nowhere on the planet does the entire geologic column exist, except in high school and university textbooks. It is a patchwork depiction driven by assumptions of deep time and long ages, with the basic framework largely created in the 1800s from local observations on the British Isles. It is a paradigm built on uniformitarian assumptions that need to be questioned, not blindly accepted.

Granted, there are more and more scientists who are recognizing that catastrophic occurrences must be taken into consideration, like giant meteorites pounding the earth or massive volcanic eruptions that dramatically change the landscape.[13] Still, these theories remain the minority position, with uniformitarianism still king.

Creationists have long argued that it did not take millions of years for the Colorado River to make its mark through the Grand Canyon, when the recessive stages of a worldwide flood could accomplish the task in a very short time. Assuming a steady rate of erosion over such a long stretch of time is not good science, it is mind-boggling naïveté. Biblical events like the flood are usually denied by geologists either on the grounds that the biblical record cannot be trusted, or that the flood was limited to the Mesopotamian basin. Again, it comes down to what you trust: the history of the Bible or the interpretation of modern-day geologists.

---

[13] Already a classic in the field is Derek Ager's *The New Catastrophism*.

Radiometric Dating

All of this bickering about history and distant events is moot since today we have very sophisticated machines that can date just about anything, right? There is a common misconception that a piece of mysterious material is thrown into a radiometric dating machine and out pops its age. It seems so simple, so straightforward, but the actual process is hardly that. It is not akin to sticking a thermometer into your son's mouth and immediately acquiring an accurate temperature. It is rather like using the thermometer and with the first reading, he has a raging fever of 105°F. You do it again and realize your son is suffering from hypothermia with a reading of 93°F. Several other thermometers yield answers that generally fall into this range, but not all of them. Yet the myth that radiodating is a highly accurate "geological Rolex" continues to be perpetuated in science classrooms and throughout the media.

In 2013, our family took a fascinating ninety-minute tour through Cango Caves in South Africa. The guide told us that the stalactites and stalagmites are millions of years old. When I asked how we know this, he said, "Through carbon dating and radiometric analysis."

After thanking him for his answer, I leaned over to my son and told him that carbon dating is good up to roughly 98,000 years. Few people realize that carbon dating cannot produce dates for dinosaur bones or for rocks of hundreds of millions of years. However, its accuracy is suspect even when used for items dated within its effective range.

A recent example involved dating the so-called Gospel of Jesus' Wife manuscript unveiled by Harvard University professor Karen King in 2012. Carbon dating a fragment from the papyrus initially gave the manuscript a date of 404–209 BC, hardly accurate for a document speaking about the biblical Jesus.[14] The problem with all dating methods is that there are assumptions that go into the process, and if those assumptions are wrong, the outcome will be erroneous.

Many kinds of radiometric dating methods are used today. Among

---

[14] Simon Gathercole, "5 Reasons Why the Gospel of Jesus' Wife Is a Fake," *Christianity Today*, www.christianitytoday.com/ct/2015/july-web-only/5-reasons-why-gospel-of-jesus-wife-is-fake.html?utm_source=ctweekly-html&utm_medium=Newsletter&utm_term=17786756&utm_content=369251558&utm_campaign=2013, accessed September 29, 2015.

the more well-known are uranium-lead, potassium-argon, and rubidi-um-strontium dating. The science behind radiodating is straightforward. Atoms of an unstable, radioactive element (called the parent) decay into a stable element (called the daughter), like radioactive uranium transform-ing into lead. This transformation is measured by the half-life of the radio-active element.

For example, half of the most stable isotope of uranium will decay in 4.468 billion years into the daughter element. Thankfully, we don't have to sit around and wait for half to decay. We merely observe the rate of decay over a specific period of time and extrapolate the half-life.

It sounds easy enough, but radiometric dating is based on key assump-tions, and each of these is problematic.

1. *It assumes a constant rate of decay over the entire life of the sample*. But this is not necessarily true. We already know that the half-life of other elements, such as cobalt-60 and silicon-32, is affected by the distance between the earth and the sun, which changes over the course of a year. Cosmic rays, neutrino bursts, and changes in the atmosphere or in the Van Allen radia-tion belt that encircles the earth can all affect the radioactive decay of an element. We cannot know that uranium's half-life will not be altered over 4.5 billion years, especially when we use a tiny, extrapolated measurement to determine it.[15]

2. *It assumes the original sample was 100% parent element, with no daughter element present*. But we have no way of knowing this, and even the tiniest amount of daughter element present in the original sample would radically throw off the radiometric date.

3. *It assumes a closed system that has not been contaminated*. But this is quite an assumption, especially when dating a rock that is supposedly hundreds of millions of years old. Is it safe to conjecture that no daughter element ever got into the sample subsequent to its initial formation? The same goes for the parent element. What if more of the parent was added later? The rate of decay of a radioactive element can also be affected by the presence of another radioactive element, or by high pressure, or by leaching chem-icals. We must believe that the original sample sat there, unmoved and

---

[15] Carbon dating has the same problem, where the present ratio of carbon-14 to car-bon-12 in the earth's atmosphere is assumed to be constant, projected into the past. Half of all carbon dates are discarded because of the inaccuracies of the method.

unaffected by anything outside itself, for hundreds of millions of years, in order for radiodating to be accurate.

Consider a lit candle on your dining room table. You can measure the current burn rate of the candlewick, but if you were asked how long the candle has been burning, that depends on how big the candle was initially. If you were not there to see it lit, then your answer to the question would be guesswork. Even if you were told the original length, this does not provide you with enough data. What if the candle had been lit, extinguished, and relit a week later?

It is one thing to say a certain rock is determined via radiodating to be 300 million years old; nobody is in a position to say otherwise. But what if we had samples of rock with an undisputed age that were tested by radiodating and found to be falsely dated? Fortunately, we do.

One involves the eruption of Mount St. Helens in 1980 and the resultant lava dome that was formed over subsequent years. The eruption provided a perfect opportunity to test the accuracy of radiodating methods since we knew that the rocks had recently formed.

Potassium-argon dating of Mount St. Helens rocks that had formed less than 2 decades earlier produced ages that ranged from 350,000 to 2.8 million years old.[16] Eventually geochronologists concluded that argon must have contaminated the samples, but meticulous care was taken throughout the whole process. The other possibility is that argon was in the rocks from their very formation, throwing off the calculations and contradicting a major assumption used in all radiometric dating. If excess daughter element can cause false conclusions for rocks of *known* age, why should we trust the method when it comes to rocks of unknown history and age?[17]

To add insult to injury, different dating methods yield wildly different

---

[16] For a detailed explanation, see Steven A. Austin, "Excess Argon within Mineral Concentrates from the New Dacite Lava Dome at Mount St. Helens Volcano," Creation Ministries International, http://creation.com/excess-argon-within-mineral-concentrates, accessed December 2, 2015.

[17] Interested readers should research radiodating of rocks from Mount Ngauruhoe in New Zealand or Salt Lake Crater on Oahu for other examples. This study from Harvard University found trees on the volcanic island of Rangitoto carbon-dated to about 1,000 years old, but buried under lava radiodated to 145,000 to 465,000 years old: "Excess Radiogenic Argon in Young Subaerial Basalts from the Auckland Volcanic Field, New Zealand," http://adsabs.harvard.edu/abs/1969GeCoA..33.1485M, accessed December 11, 2015.

results, and previously popular radiodating methods have given way to newer ones because the older methods were deemed inaccurate. How soon will it be before scientists give up on the newer methods for the same reason?

Scientific Evidence for a Relatively Young Earth

At this point, some readers might respond, "That's all well and good. The plainest reading of the Bible is that the creation is young, but what scientific proof exists to back up that claim?" Before answering, though, I emphasize that I do not require scientific proof when the historical witness of God found in Scripture already points to a young earth.[18] Nevertheless, it will be helpful if scientific verification exists for a young earth, especially when most scientific disciplines (e.g., cosmology, evolutionary biology, paleontology, geology) indicate otherwise.

First, a caveat. If I declare a rock of unknown origin to be ten thousand years old, instead of ten million, I am making the same mistake I criticize others for making. We cannot be dogmatic about the age of an object for which we have no historical record. However, if my straightforward reading of the Bible is correct, then nothing on this planet can be more than roughly six thousand years old. Not one single thing.

Therefore, when I argue against the long time periods of geology and evolution, this does not imply that I know an exact age. Still, I can point out the limitations of the long-age theories and if another plausible explanation exists for a younger age, I have no reason to doubt the biblical report.

For example, finely laminated sediments are assumed to have occurred gradually over millions of years, but Mount St. Helens deposited 8 meters (25 feet) of the stuff in one afternoon. Large canyons can be formed rapidly, as scientists in 2015 reported concerning the 28-kilometer-long, 100-meter-deep Jokulsargljufur Canyon in Iceland, which is now believed to have been formed by catastrophic flooding several thousand years ago.[19] More

---

[18] Some evangelicals say that Genesis is mute on the earth's age, or at least non-committal. However, Genesis is written as historical narrative, complete with genealogical tables giving us a calculable date from Adam to Abraham. The Bible is not ambivalent on the issue. The author of Genesis goes out of his way to provide his readers with precise time markers.

[19] BBC News, "Canyon Carved by Three Short, Savage Floods," www.bbc.com/news/science-environment-31356229, accessed November 30, 2015.

recently, the California Institute of Technology reported that a 2.2-kilo-meter-long, 7-meter-deep canyon through solid bedrock was carved in just 3 days of heavy flooding in Texas in 2010.[20] While this does not prove the age of other canyons like the Grand Canyon, it does call into question the assumption of gradual erosion taking tens of millions of years. Rapid formation of coal, opals, and even diamonds strongly suggests that long ages are not required for these processes.[21]

Petrification is another process that has been assumed to occur gradually over long periods of time, but studies have called this into question. One shows that petrification of wood took from seven to thirty-six years in hot springs in Japan, not the tens of thousands of years students are usually taught.[22]

Perhaps the best evidence for a young earth is soft tissue discovered in fossils supposedly millions of years old. *Smithsonian Magazine* reported paleontologist Mary Schweitzer's discovery of a thin network of blood vessels in a *Tyrannosaurus rex* bone purportedly 68 million years old.[23] Since this discovery a decade ago, similar findings have been reported elsewhere, including soft tissue in other fossils dating back to the Jurassic period, which allegedly lasted 145 to 200 million years ago, and even one marine fossil supposedly 425 million years old complete with eyes, gills, and other soft tissue intact.[24]

---

[20] ScienceDaily, www.sciencedaily.com/releases/2010/06/100620155748.htm, accessed November 29, 2015.

[21] Andrew Snelling, "Growing Opals—Australian Style," Answers in Genesis, https://answersingenesis.org/geology/rocks-and-minerals/growing-opals-australian-style/, accessed November 21, 2015. At LifeGem the ashes of your loved one can be made into genuine diamonds in about six months (www.lifegem.com/, accessed September 2, 2016).

[22] H. Akahane, T. Furuno, H. Miyajima, T. Yoshikawa, and S. Yamamoto, "Rapid Wood Silicification in Hot Spring Water: An Explanation of Silicification of Wood during the Earth's History," *Sedimentary Geology* 169 (2004): 219–228. See also John Pratt, "Petrified Wood: Days or Millions of Years?" Joseph Smith Foundation, www.josephsmithforum.org/research/papers/petrified-wood-days-or-millions-of-years/, accessed November 21, 2015.

[23] Helen Fields, "Dinosaur Shocker," *Smithsonian Magazine*, www.smithsonianmag.com/science-nature/dinosaur-shocker-115306469/?all, accessed December 16, 2015.

[24] Phys.Org, "New to Science: Find from 425 Million Years Ago with Body, Limbs, Eyes, Gills and Alimentary System Preserved," http://phys.org/news/2012-12-science-million-years-body-limbs.html, accessed June 22, 2016.

These discoveries expose the incorrect assumptions that drive evolutionary science. The first false assumption, by their own admission, is that organic tissue cannot be preserved for very long. According to one scientist quoted in the *Smithsonian* article, this assumption inhibited scientists for the past three hundred years from ever looking for soft tissue in fossils.[25] Now that soft tissue has been discovered, evolutionists are scrambling to find an explanation.

The second false assumption involves time. Instead of questioning their basic premise of millions of years, evolutionists set out to explain how soft tissue could survive this long. One possibility is that iron in the dinosaur's blood served as a sort of formaldehyde, preserving the soft tissue. Lab tests have confirmed that blood vessels soaked in iron-rich liquid could "remain recognizable after sitting at room temperature for two years."[26] This was done in a controlled laboratory by intelligent scientists overseeing the experiment, but two years is a far cry from Jurassic period dates. This time it is the difference between a large Domino's pizza and one the size of the continental United States.

An obvious solution to this conundrum is that the bones are not tens of millions of years old. Recognizing this, one California State University scientist discovered soft tissue in a triceratops skull, but when he suggested the fossil could be as young as several thousand years, he lost his job.[27] The assumption of deep time is so ingrained in evolutionary science that it is virtually impossible to question it. Incredibly, Schweitzer is worried that fossils cracked open and exposed to air will quickly degrade the soft tissue, and yet she believes some mysterious mechanism kept the tissue intact for two hundred million years.

In the following chapter we will see why evolution cannot do what its proponents claim it does, with important evidence from genetics. For now it must be noted that with each generation of a species, additional mutations

---

[25] While this is not a false assumption if the fossils are several thousand years old, it highlights the way the evolutionary worldview impedes good science.

[26] Stephanie Pappas, "Controversial T. Rex Soft Tissue Find Finally Explained," *Live Science*, www.livescience.com/41537-t-rex-soft-tissue.html, accessed November 26, 2015.

[27] CSB Los Angeles, "Lawsuit: CSUN Scientist Fired after Soft Tissue Found on Dinosaur Fossil," http://losangeles.cbslocal.com/2014/07/24/scientist-alleges-csun-fired-him-for-discovery-of-soft-tissue-on-dinosaur-fossil/, accessed December 10, 2015.

are added to its genome. Eventually these mutations accumulate to such a level (called the "genetic load") that the organism breaks down. It stands to reason that organisms could not have lasted for the tens of millions of years assumed in evolutionary theory.

Does It Really Matter?

Somebody might say, "So what? My faith is not affected by whether that star in the distant sky is ten billion years old or only a few thousand." Granted. But all these sciences are related. The deep time assumed for star formation is also the deep time required for evolution. If the assumptions used for radiometric dating of rocks here on earth can be wrong, what about the suppositions made concerning the formation of stars billions of light years away? Long ages are necessary for the current evolutionary theories to seem plausible, one of them being that we evolved from apelike creatures over millions of years. Surely this idea affects your faith, right?

When compared to an age that comes from a straightforward reading of the Genesis account, I am reluctant to grant science an automatic pass when it declares a ridiculously older age. I certainly am not going to excuse the discrepancy with, "Well, the Bible isn't a science textbook." When I see how many assumptions go into radiometric dating methods, and how the slightest error in one of them can have a dramatic effect on the final age produced, I hesitate to jump on the old earth bandwagon.

Much of modern science assumes the non-existence of God and then comes to its conclusions. Many Christians errantly believe they can take those conclusions and stick God back into the equation, without any need to alter the scientific findings.

The age of the earth has always vexed me. It still does. But should Christians uncritically accept what scientists tell us, given the shortcomings with dating methods and knowing how tentative the scientific enterprise is?

Evolutionary theory relies on long time periods, but as we will see in the following two chapters, regardless of the amount of time, evolution cannot do what atheists claim it does.

CHAPTER THREE

God's Created Order
and Evolutionary Theory:
A Theological Perspective

It is absolutely safe to say that, if you meet somebody who claims
not to believe in evolution, that person is ignorant, stupid, or insane
(or wicked, but I'd rather not consider that).

—RICHARD DAWKINS[1]

BEFORE THE BIG BANG theory was adopted about sixty years ago, the reigning scientific consensus was that the universe was infinite. There was
incredible speculation about other worlds with other lifeforms. If the universe had been around forever, life must have appeared elsewhere.[2]

Evolutionary theory was born in this age when the universe was ageless. Given an infinite amount of time, an infinite number of possibilities
existed, like the ridiculous notion that an infinite number of monkeys
typing on an infinite number of typewriters would produce Shakespeare's
Hamlet. During those decades, conservative Christians were castigated for
believing that the universe had a beginning.

Science now teaches that the universe had a beginning, and the "singularity" from which the cosmos exploded was about 13.8 billion years ago.
The problem is that 13.8 billion years, while a very long time, is nothing

---

[1] *The New York Times*, April 9, 1989, section 7, p. 34, in reviewing the book, *Blueprints*,
by Donald Johanson and Maitland Edey (New York: Penguin, 1989)].

[2] Benjamin Wiker's fascinating article, "Alien Ideas: Christianity and the Search
for Extraterrestrial Life," catalogues speculations about life on other planets (*Crisis
Magazine*, www.crisismagazine.com/2009/alien-ideas-christianity-and-the-search-for
-extraterrestrial-life, accessed September 16, 2015).

compared to infinity. This is not a small recalculation. The difference is between a finite age and an infinite one. All speculation about what could happen given an infinite amount of time should be off. Yet, evolutionists today largely work on assumptions laid down by Darwinists in the nineteenth century.

In the previous chapter, we looked at Christian views attempting to reconcile the Genesis account with modern scientific theories. None of them incorporate biological evolution, which certain Christians deem a major shortcoming. In this chapter and the following one we will investigate what some evangelicals consider the best explanation of origins, theistic evolution. But first we need to define "evolution."

What Is Evolution?

"Evolution" has evolved, such that the word means different things to different people. Any small change in the allele frequency of a species is "evolution" to some; moving from Adam and Eve to their firstborn child is a form of "evolution."[3] However, when people usually speak about evolution, they imply something much grander than a change in skin tone. They are referring to big-picture evolution, where we move from a one-cell organism to complex *Homo sapiens*.[4] For my discussion, I will use "evolution" for this big-picture portrayal. I will refer to the incremental changes within species as "variation within kinds." In seeing variation, atheists make the wrong leap to big-picture evolution.[5]

Creationists need to be clear on this distinction. Nobody in his right mind denies variation. The only way variation could not exist is if Adam and Eve produced children who were genetically identical to themselves

---

[3] The allele frequency is the measure of relative gene variants in a particular population.

[4] I've seen this light-heartedly labeled as "from fish to philosophers," or "from microbes to microbiologists," or "from slugs to scientists," or "from germs to geniuses," or "from particles to people," or "from goo through the zoo to you."

[5] Some use "microevolution" to refer to variation and "macroevolution" to refer to big-picture evolution, but "evolution" as a process has many assumptions that come with it, making "microevolution" a misleading term. "Oh, it's the same evolution, just on a smaller scale" is errant reasoning. It is difficult to not smuggle in big-picture evolution when using the term "microevolution."

in every way (clones). Any room full of people immediately proves variation.[6]

Christians who say "I don't believe in evolution" sound uninformed. "I don't believe humans evolved from apelike creatures" or "I don't believe all life on the planet descended from the same one-cell organism" are preferable statements. We ought to be careful how we phrase our disagreements.

Whenever breeders create a new breed of dog, they are performing artificial selection that results in variation within a kind. No Christian should disagree with this. Dachshunds were not in the Garden of Eden. They have existed for about three centuries. However, a canine "kind" was created in Eden and from it came the hundreds of canine breeds we have today.

Therefore, when we see statements like these, keep in mind the various ways the word "evolution" is used.

- "Evolution is as much a fact as anything we know in science."[7]
- "Evolution as a process that has always gone on in the history of the earth can be doubted only by those who are ignorant of the evidence or are resistant to evidence, owing to emotional blocks or to plain bigotry."[8]
- "There is no doubt in my mind that biological evolution is a fact. It is also clear to me that human evolution is a fact. And in light of the recent genetic evidence, it is a fact that humans did not descend from only one pair of humans."[9]

In one sense (variation) the above are true, but in another sense (big-picture evolution) they simply are not. Which do the above authors

---

[6] Evolutionists call variation "descent with modification," but this smuggles in big-picture evolution with the assumption that all life on the planet descended from one common ancestor.

[7] Brown University professor Kenneth Miller in *Finding Darwin's God: A Scientist's Search for Common Ground between God and Evolution* (New York: HarperPerennial, 2007), 57.

[8] Theodosius Dobzhansky, quoted in Laurence Moran, "Evolution Is a Fact and a Theory," Sandwalk, http://sandwalk.blogspot.com/2011/08/evolution-is-fact-and-theory.html, accessed September 9, 2015.

[9] Denis Lamoureux, author of *I Love Jesus and I Accept Evolution* (Eugene, OR: Wipf & Stock, 2009), quoted from BioLogos interview, http://biologos.org/blog/interpreting-adam-an-interview-with-denis-lamoureux-part-1, accessed September 8, 2015.

mean? They all mean the latter, but we have to be careful to discern this each and every time we see "evolution" used because evolutionists frequently cite variation but call it "evolution." I provide examples of this later, but one now will help clarify matters.

In what is otherwise a wonderful book about biological diversity, Richard Dawkins lets creationists have it in *The Greatest Show on Earth: The Evidence for Evolution*. Claiming evolution is the "central and guiding principle of biology," Dawkins bemoans "brainwashed children" and the "woefully uninformed" for questioning the fact of evolution, calling them "history-deniers."[10]

However, "evolution" for Dawkins simply means variation, and once this fact is made clear, all his braggadocio dissipates. Dawkins defines evolution as "a systematic increase or decrease in the frequency with which we see a particular gene in a gene pool."[11] In other words, as soon as an organism bears offspring, we have "evolution."

Armed with this broad definition, Dawkins can go on the warpath against anybody who would deign to say that evolution is false or "only a theory." The intricacy of the biological world has merely "the beguiling illusion of design by a master engineer,"[12] when any good scientist knows that it all came about from genetic changes filtered through natural selection. All "reputable biologists" understand this "inescapable fact" such that "there is no longer a doubt in any serious mind."[13] "Educated priests and professors of theology" accept evolution, as do "thoughtful and rational churchmen and women," while "the woefully uninformed" deny it.[14] Thus, "evolution is a fact in the same sense as it is a fact that Paris is in the Northern Hemisphere."[15]

Those kowtowed by Dawkins's bluster and seemingly endless confidence might miss a sleight of hand that he makes. Let me take two quotations from the same paragraph in *The Greatest Show on Earth* to make my point. Here's the first: "Evolution is a fact. Beyond reasonable doubt, beyond serious doubt, beyond sane, informed, intelligent doubt, beyond

---

[10] *Greatest Show on Earth*, 4, 6.

[11] Ibid., 33.

[12] Ibid., 22.

[13] Ibid., 18.

[14] Ibid., 6.

[15] Ibid., 10.

doubt evolution is a fact."[16] As Dawkins defines "evolution," this is correct. Biological variation is real; it cannot be doubted.

However, the second quotation just two sentences later in the same paragraph is this: "It is a plain truth that we are cousins of chimpanzees, somewhat more distant cousins of monkeys, more distant cousins still of aardvarks and manatees, yet more distant cousins of bananas and turnips . . . continue the list as long as desired." Thus Dawkins's leap from variation to macroevolution. It is the only trick evolutionists possess, and as we will see, it is used with impunity.

Contrary to evolutionists, I believe God literally took dirt from the earth and formed the first man, Adam. He did not use a natural process that began with a one-cell organism and then sat back while it ran its course, eventually over billions of years producing human beings. God created everything we see in six, literal, twenty-four-hour days, making Adam on the sixth day.

Many Christians blindly accept what science says about evolution and then make their biblical understanding conform to it.[17] The aim of chapters 3 and 4 in this book is not to convince skeptics and materialists who already have their minds made up about the origin of the universe. I am concerned with Christians who feel pressured into incorporating evolutionary theory into their doctrine of origins. Evolution is bad science, and I am amazed how many evangelicals shoehorn their reading of the early chapters of Genesis into this modern view. Science by its very nature is tentative and changing; the revelation of God is immutable and permanent. Why some evangelicals force the latter into the fleeting forms of the former is beyond me.

I think the adoption of evolutionary theory into the biblical framework will, in retrospect, be one of the greatest errors in Christian scholarship from the past several centuries, right up there with those who doggedly

---

[16] Ibid., 8.

[17] The modern explosion in evangelical scholarship about the "historical Adam" is a case in point. Some scholars question the existence of a first man because it contradicts the scientific consensus that humans evolved from a population of apelike creatures. This BioLogos article lists the "big name" evangelical scholars who have devised ways to read the Genesis account with evolution in mind: http://biologos.org/questions/evolution-and-the-fall, accessed February 6, 2016.

held to a flat earth or a terra-centric solar system. The following is a brief attempt at showing why.

Theistic Evolution Is Not Good Theology

After our analysis in the previous chapter, we are left with two options for reconciling science and the Bible:

1. *Fiat Creationism*: God supernaturally created all that exists in six, twenty-four-hour days yielding a young earth, comprising the natural laws by which his creation operates and including the handiwork of a fully formed, fully functioning human being made de novo (from scratch) from the dust of the earth.
2. *Theistic Evolution*: God created an exploding singularity that ran its course through cosmological and biological evolution over billions of years. Perhaps God never intervened during this evolutionary process, or he did at certain points, or he only intervened at the final step from primate to human, but the vast majority of Adam's development came not by a divine act of creative will, but through natural selection and an accidental process of random genetic mutations.

Neither of the above will satisfy an atheist, but which one best accords with a straightforward reading of Scripture and does justice to the scientific evidence?

The theistic evolutionist is between a rock and a hard place. On one side is the evangelical like me who feels that the Christian evolutionist gives up too much of the Bible, while on the other side is the atheist who feels theistic evolution betrays proper science (which I agree with but for different reasons). In trying to appease both sides, theistic evolution satisfies neither.[18]

Regardless, there are intelligent, high-profile evangelicals who believe evolutionary theory is scientifically unassailable and must be incorporated into Christian thinking. One such evangelical is Francis Collins, who in

---

[18] Many theistic evolutionists believe that neither side understands them: http://biologos.org/blog/on-living-in-the-middle, accessed September 19, 2015.

2007 while he was the director of the Human Genome Project, founded BioLogos, a theistic evolution think tank. Two years later he was appointed by President Barack Obama as the director of the National Institutes of Health.

BioLogos is evangelical, proclaiming in its statement of faith that the Bible is God's inspired Word and Jesus is the incarnate God-man.[19] It also embraces evolution as these statements attest:

- "BioLogos invites the church and the world to see the harmony between science and biblical faith as we present an evolutionary understanding of God's creation."
- God "created the universe, the earth, and all life over billions of years."
- "We believe that the diversity and interrelation of all life on earth are best explained by the God-ordained process of evolution with common descent."
- "God created humans in biological continuity with all life on earth."

BioLogos makes it clear that Christians must abandon fiat creationism. "BioLogos exists in no small part to marginalize this view from the church."[20] The reasons for the rejection of this interpretation of Genesis rest on scientific evidence such as "the richness of the fossil data; the millions of genetic fingerprints that point to the common ancestry of all life forms; the premises of nuclear physics which allow us to date minerals in multiple ways; the heart of astronomy which tells us how stars and galaxies are still being born; and the science of geology where we can relate events that are taking place now to ancient events from the deep past." We will use BioLogos as the quintessential example of a Christian attempt to harmonize the claims of evolutionary science and Scripture.[21]

To be fair, there is considerable debate between theistic evolutionists as to how exactly God and the process of evolution interact in forming all life on the planet. While some believe that God used natural processes but

---

[19] See http://biologos.org/about, accessed September 19, 2015.

[20] Darrel Falk, "On Living in the Middle," BioLogos, http://biologos.org/blog/on-living-in-the-middle, accessed September 20, 2015.

[21] "No serious biologist today doubts the theory of evolution to explain the marvelous complexity and diversity of life" (Collins, *The Language of God*, 99).

acted supernaturally at certain points (called "directed evolution"), others believe this is not faithful to genuine science and prefer "planned evolution," where life comes about entirely via natural processes.

Directed Evolution

Some Christians think directed evolution is the best balance between Scripture and science because they believe the problems with evolutionary theory can be overcome by invoking God whenever needed. For example, they might respond to typical objections against evolution in the following ways:

- "The odds are too great for life on earth to pop out of the pre-biotic soup." That's okay, God was the one throwing the dice.
- "Human intellect could not arise from accidental processes." That's okay, God made the final leap from primate to human.
- "A process whose only mechanism for new information is genetic mutations could not produce new machinery or overcome the law of entropy." That's okay, God stepped in at each necessary point to add new information.
- "There are too many obstacles for a water-based organism to move to dry land and thrive enough to reproduce." That's okay, God supernaturally intervened and granted that organism the ability to overcome what it could not naturally overcome.

The above would be necessary, but a self-respecting Christian evolutionist knows this is not good science. That is why the majority have God starting the process (the Big Bang) and then sitting back and allowing it to run its evolutionary course all the way to human beings, with whom God then made a covenant, metaphorically or mythically represented by the biblical Adam.

Although there is disagreement among theistic evolutionists as to what the "first Adam" was, generally speaking, they believe that through roughly three billion years of evolution, a primate that was the ancestor of Adam developed. There were tens of thousands of these primates living when God took one or even many, making the first representative "man" from the group. The modifications made to this pre-existing hominid may have included the endowment of spiritual consciousness and a genetic upgrade (God filling the "missing link" gap), which explains why humans are superior to all other animals. However, at the time of Adam there already were other, very similar hominids roaming the earth.[22]

We saw above the scientific reasons given by BioLogos for rejecting fiat creationism. This means that every shortcoming of evolutionary theory must be owned by the theistic evolutionist. He cannot invoke God whenever the scientific process he is beholden to cannot do what his atheistic compatriots claim it can do, otherwise he contradicts the very scientific process that makes him different from a fiat creationist. As such, directed evolution must be rejected on its inconsistent approach to science.

Directed evolution also suffers theologically, relegating God to a "god of the gaps" who patches up the holes in evolution as needed. He gets the ball rolling and then whenever a problem presents itself in this clunky process, he intervenes. After three billion years he finally has a being he can endow with his image. This is not a creative mechanism worthy of the biblical God. It sounds more like a being who isn't sure what he wants or how to get it.

A process that requires the constant intervention of God to get things moving in the proper direction is not a scientifically acceptable mechanism, nor does it correspond with the biblical God who touts his own creative genius (e.g., Job 38–41). For this reason, directed evolution must be rejected on both scientific and theological grounds.

Planned Evolution

BioLogos leans toward the more scientifically consistent position of planned evolution. Francis Collins states, "God intentionally chose the same mechanism [evolution] to give rise to special creatures who would have intelligence, a knowledge of right and wrong, free will, and a desire to seek fellowship with him."[23] "Adam" represents these special creatures.

---

[22] There is considerable disagreement among theistic evolutionists on how inherited sin transfers to all other humans, when there were creatures similar to Adam during his time.

[23] The Language of God, 201.

Nonetheless, the god of theistic evolution is not the God of the Bible. Well-meaning Christians who combine Darwin's 160-year-old scientific theory riddled with substantial, scientific problems with the ageless truths found "in the beginning" unwittingly undermine everything Genesis communicates about the nature of the Creator (something we looked at in chapter 1) and by implication the gospel.

Whereas God is depicted as the sovereign, purposefully engaged Lord of all that is made, evolution places the mindless, directionless, purposeless mechanism of natural selection in his role. Whereas death is a punishment meted out by a holy God, in evolutionary theory it is the grease that gets the system flowing. Without death there is no natural selection, and without natural selection you cannot have Darwinian evolution. The elegant beauty of an intelligent Maker who merely speaks and the world obeys is replaced with a blind mechanism that takes billions of years to spit out what God did in an afternoon.

In the previous chapter we noted the cosmological proof for the existence of God. Another classic argument for God's existence is the teleological proof, from the Greek *telos*, meaning goal or purpose. It is the recognition that the creation has a self-evident design. The problem with theistic evolution is that it muddles this design. Things inadvertently turned out like this; they were not specially designed by God. How can God declare his special design of the ostrich or the horse or the behemoth or the leviathan (Job 39–41), and yet these creatures are the product of accidental mutations undirected by God?

The Bible depicts an engaged, active Creator. Just as post-Enlightenment Christians in the eighteenth century reformulated their theology into the watchmaker god of deism—distant and disinterested in what he has made—theistic evolutionists compromise on the biblical view of the Creator as he sits back and "creates" through blind, accidental processes. The biblical picture of a systematic, organized God revealed in Genesis 1 is entirely at odds with random, haphazard evolutionary theory.

Fiat Creationism Does Justice to the God of Scripture

The theological problems of theistic evolution stem from ignoring an important reason for God to create in the first place. God does not create for the fun of it. He creates in order to reveal something about himself to his creatures (Isa. 43:7). This self-revelation of God through what he has made is muted with theistic evolution.

Everything God does is a form of self-revelation. By its very nature, the creative act is a revealing act. This is why the *how* of creation is as important as the *who*. Theistic evolutionists think that by proclaiming the *who* of the Bible they have done justice to the biblical message, but their *how* of creation contradicts everything the *who* of Scripture proclaims. There is a disconnect between the purposeful God of Genesis and the clunky randomness of evolution.

Conversely, fiat creationism maintains the connection between the character of God and how he creates. When God said, "Let us make man in our image," he did not take a dumb apelike creature and brush it up. The Genesis account does not read like the theistic evolutionist portrays it. Adam is not the end product of a random, violent, disease-ridden, three-billion-year process.[24] He is made in God's image from the start, endowed with the beauty of his Creator and all that image implies. Only with this view can human dignity be maintained, something we will explore in chapter 5.

The traditional view of Adam's de novo creation who, as the father of subsequent humans affects all his progeny when he sins, is an interpretation that has serviced the church well for two thousand years. To abandon the truth of an historical Adam and the related doctrine of inherited sin, all to accommodate evolutionary theory, is a pill too bitter to swallow.

Fiat creationism is more in step with the character of the biblical God. Nothing is impossible for him; no plan of his can be thwarted; what he wants he gets as the omnipotent, sovereign Lord. Mice are mice because God designed them that way. On the fourth day of creation God made the sun in its mature state, capable of sustaining life on earth. Most important, humans are humans because God formed them in the beginning, in his image from the start.

Theistic evolution does not do justice to the biblical teaching concerning death as a punishment for sin, a shared shortcoming of progressive

---

[24] Some Christians say, "Genesis does not tell us how God made humans." I could accept this if the Genesis account merely said, "In the beginning, God made Adam and Eve." But it doesn't. It tells us how God made Adam, by taking dirt and breathing life into it, and how he made Eve from Adam's rib.

creationism. That God declares his creation "very good" (Gen. 1:31) seems peculiar if suffering, violence, and death were part and parcel of it, things God promises will all be overcome in the new creation. It is only after the curse (Gen. 3:16–19) that death enters the equation.

However, despite some Christians adopting theistic evolution, one thing that amazes me is how difficult it has been for evolutionary theory to capture the American imagination, despite the incredible amount of publicity and propaganda it has enjoyed for nearly a century in our country. Gallup polls over the past three decades show belief in atheistic evolution is *decreasing*.[25]

One reason is that the Christian ideal of God still permeates our society, and it is obvious that evolution contradicts it. It also has to do with the way humans are specially made in God's image, and despite the deluge of evolutionary propaganda that has gone into our public schools—where dissenting voices are often not allowed in the science classroom (a case of poor science)—Americans mostly embrace the biblical notion that humans are unique. It is this commonsense approach that keeps atheistic evolution largely at bay.[26]

As we move to the purely scientific reasons why theistic evolution is wrong, we should recognize that theistic evolution and atheistic evolution are virtually identical save for the initial impetus of God's creative act at the Big Bang. Because theistic evolutionists rely on the science that is handed to them by the secular enterprise, anything that is the weakness of this secular concept becomes the weakness of the Christian evolutionist, regardless of his claim that God kick-started the process.

Theistic Evolution Is Not Good Science

Evolutionists are constantly bombarding the public with propaganda meant to sway society from biblical creation and toward a naturalistic explanation for how we got here. We will consider several sources as we discuss major scientific weaknesses in Neo-Darwinism.

---

[25] Gallup, "Evolution, Creationism, Intelligent Design," www.gallup.com/poll/21814/Evolution-Creationism-Intelligent-Design.aspx, accessed June 2, 2016.

[26] Evolutionists expose the inherent weakness of their position when they eliminate dissenting voices in the science classroom. If their theory is truly unassailable, why go to such lengths to shut down all disagreement concerning it?

Evolutionary theory can be expressed in the following formula:

**Starting material + mutations + natural selection + time
= all speciation in the animal and plant kingdoms**

Starting with a simple organism and given enough time, through countless random biochemical mutations and a process of natural selection that weeds through them, we can move through an evolutionary process that yields all plant and animal life on the planet including complex human beings. We walk through the four components of this formula in this chapter and the following one.

Starting Material

The fundamental assumption of Darwin's theory is that you begin with an organism that can reproduce. Creationists are rather gracious in allowing the evolutionist to start with this "simple" entity because a major deficiency in evolutionary theory is how the initial reproducing organism existed in the first place. It is one thing to ask a person to build an automobile once he is granted the basic structure, but quite another when an explosion of elements is meant to create a chassis on which he then can construct his vehicle.

There is a problem with the idea of a "simple" organism. Granted, a one-cell amoeba is simpler than *Homo sapiens*, but do not be misled. Even one cell is incredibly complex, far too intricate to have popped up from inanimate materials. Richard Dawkins notes, "There is enough information capacity in a single human cell to store the Encyclopedia Britannica, all thirty volumes of it, three or four times over."[27] This has caused one biologist to exclaim, "The human cell is the most complex machine known in the universe."[28]

Even a modest organism has millions of parts at the atomic level, and any living cell requires DNA that stores the plans for building the organism, RNA to read the information and transport it to protein assembly stations, and various other components to make this all work. In fact, while

---

[27] *The Blind Watchmaker*, 116.
[28] Jerry Bergman, "Biology," in *In Six Days: Why 50 Scientists Choose to Believe in Creation*, ed. John F. Ashton (Green Forest, AR: Master Books, 2005), 42.

RNA is required to read DNA, the coding for making RNA is in the DNA, making this a classic "which came first?" dilemma. Both have to be there simultaneously for life to exist.[29]

This is all assumed by the evolutionist. For example, consider the BBC article from 2015, "How Do We Know That Evolution Is Really Happening?" that presents a usual approach for portraying evolutionary theory to the public.[30] The article axiomatically states:

· "The first simple life gave rise to all the huge diversity we see today, from bacteria to oak trees to blue whales."
· "All modern life has descended from a single common ancestor, the 'last universal ancestor,' which lived billions of years ago."

The assumption of biological evolution is a "common ancestor" for all plant and animal life. Knowing this, atheists posit cosmological evolution (gases from the Big Bang cooled and coalesced, producing planets), but that still does not account for the starting material for the Big Bang.[31] Claiming science has all the answers, as atheists regularly do, is preposterous in the face of no viable explanation for how the original "stuff" appeared in order for the Big Bang to bang.

We have three options. First, the universe has always been here (infinite in existence); second, the universe created itself; and third, the universe was created. The Big Bang theory has effectively eliminated the first option, which we previously noted was the dominant naturalistic explanation until the middle of the twentieth century; science now agrees with theists that the universe had a beginning.

---

[29] Enzymes used to catalyze reactions and repair DNA are also encoded in the DNA, another "chicken and egg" problem. Dawkins recognizes this: "The 'Catch-22' of the origin of life is this. DNA can replicate, but it needs enzymes in order to catalyse the process. Proteins can catalyse DNA formation, but they need DNA to specify the correct sequence of amino acids" (*The Greatest Show on Earth*, 420).

[30] Chris Baraniuk, "How Do We Know That Evolution Is Really Happening?" BBC Earth, www.bbc.com/earth/story/20150803-how-do-we-know-evolution-is-real, accessed September 21, 2015.

[31] This relationship between cosmological and biological evolution prompted one Christian evolutionist to write: "Nearly all the atoms in your body were once cooked in the nuclear furnace of an ancient supernova—you are truly made of stardust" (Collins, *The Language of God*, 68).

God's Created Order and Evolutionary Theory: A Theological Perspective 81

That leaves the other two possibilities. Which makes better sense of the available data before us? A self-creating universe is about as absurd as a self-creating toy. Science, which is nothing more than the search for intelligibility in the universe, is best performed in a theistic worldview that not only discovers this intelligibility, but predicts it.

Christians believe God created every contingent thing in the universe. Atheists, though, are left with Stephen Hawking's expectation that the universe created itself, something that is hardly scientific. Or they state, "We don't know," which is a rather large gap in their worldview. This is why creationists accuse evolutionists of having misplaced "faith."

A key battleground in this debate is in public schools, where a creationist understanding of origins (usually portrayed as "intelligent design") has consistently been shut out. One influential piece of evolutionary propaganda has been the colorful, eighty-eight-page publication *Science, Evolution, and Creationism*, compiled by the NAS and distributed across the country.

On the objection that evolutionary theory requires faith, the NAS states on page 50:

> On the contrary, an important component of religious belief is faith, which implies acceptance of a truth regardless of the presence of empirical evidence for or against that truth. Scientists cannot accept scientific conclusions on faith alone because all such conclusions must be subject to testing against observations.[32]

Yet this is precisely what atheists do: begin with the unprovable assumption that life arose from inanimate matter (called "abiogenesis"). This is a rather large postulation, and any derogatory comments from atheists about the faith of creationists must always be taken in light of their own leap. Life on earth is so complex that some atheists posit the idea of "panspermia," that life was seeded throughout the universe by asteroids, or at least brought to the earth by aliens.[33] This kicks the proverbial can down

---

[32] Forgetting my quibble with their understanding of "faith," evolutionary theory does not even conform to their definition of "science" since their assumptions about the origin of life cannot be observed and tested.

[33] Megan Gannon, "Did Earth Life Come from Space? Tough Algae Suggests Panspermia Possibility," Space.com, www.space.com/22880-life-from-space-panspermia-possibility.html, accessed September 29, 2015.

the road, as any second-grader will inevitably ask: where did the aliens come from?

The Odds of Abiogenesis

Even if we grant cosmological evolution, we still have the problem of animate life appearing from inanimate processes. Evolutionists assume that the random collisions of amino acids in a primordial soup eventually produced the correct combination of molecules to create life. Through the decades, evolutionists have argued that given the proper, initial mix of chemicals and conditions, animate life inevitably arose, despite the phenomenal odds against it. After all, they imply, isn't life just a bunch of elements thrown together?

The problem is that life is more than chemistry; it is information: specified, organized, intricate, precise. The meaning of this sentence is not to be found in the chemical properties of ink molecules in the letters, but in their arrangement into words. The atheist expects to empty an inkwell onto a piece of paper and produce a map of North America, given enough time, but an intelligence must be behind the ink, organizing it in a way that communicates a message.[34]

There is much bickering over what exactly the odds are for life to spontaneously emerge from a primordial soup. I have seen numbers ranging from 10^{30} to 10^{8000} or more.[35] To put this into perspective, the odds are thinner than a person flipping a coin and it turning up "heads" 100 times in a row. Trying to guess a 2,000-digit ATM code is a better bet.

However, the final number is immaterial. Life is so complex and ordered as to defy a natural explanation. If I handed you an old deck of cards and all four suits were arranged from ace to king, what would you assume: that this occurred by randomly shuffling the deck, or by someone organizing the cards in this fashion?

To get an idea of how improbable it is for life to arise accidentally,

---

[34] If a windswept tree beside my house consistently tapped out on my window the following message in Morse code, "BUY A PORSCHE," we would immediately know that something was up. Random events do not dependably produce intelligent information.

[35] Jerry Bergman, biology professor at Northwest State College in Ohio, has noted: "The probability of the required order in a single basic protein molecule arising purely from chance is estimated at 10^{43}" ("Biology," 39).

consider how scientists look at odds in other areas when attempting to determine if an observation is a heretofore unknown law or a statistical fluke. In experiments with the Large Hadron Collider in Geneva, anomalies are often observed at the quantum level, and the physicists must determine if they are random events or evidence of some unknown law of quantum mechanics.

To quantify such probabilities, scientists speak of a "4-sigma" certainty level, meaning they are 99.993% certain this is not a statistical fluke. Only when an observation reaches a 5-sigma level will scientists declare this a new discovery. At 5-sigma the odds are 1 in 3.5 million that the observation was not a statistical fluke, thus requiring a rethink of the current laws of quantum physics.[36] The irony is that many of these same scientists adhere to a materialistic worldview that posits that life sprung up from odds monumentally thinner than this.

You might find an evolutionist, undeterred by such odds, stating that in shuffling a deck of cards, a random sequence always appears, the odds for which were astronomically small. Yet it happened. It is the same with abiogenesis.

The fallacy of this argument is that with a deck of cards, a sequence *must* be produced, no matter how improbable it may be for any particular sequence to appear. Shuffle the cards again, and another equally improbable sequence appears. It is inevitable. However, life via random events was not inevitable.

Evolutionists reason that despite the odds, our existence proves their theory is plausible. This "just so" reasoning has the advantage of being disprovable. No matter what argument you use against it, they can always answer, "It must have happened because here we are!"

Popular author Bill Bryson displays this kind of reasoning when he writes:

Whatever prompted life to begin, it happened just once. That is the most extraordinary fact in biology, perhaps the most extraordinary

---

[36] This article discusses certainty levels with measurements of lepton (part of an atom) behavior: Tia Ghose, "Could Physics' Reigning Model Finally Be Dethroned?" Yahoo! News, http://news.yahoo.com/could-physics-reigning-model-finally-dethroned-111736279.html, accessed September 28, 2015.

fact we know. Everything that has ever lived, plant or animal, dates its beginnings from the same primordial twitch.[37]

This is an example of confusing fact and theory, something we noted in chapter 1. The fact is our existence, the theory involves how we got here. It is circular reasoning to say your theory of origins must be right because you are here as proof of it. With that logic, any theory can be true. Unfortunately, this is how evolutionists argue, especially when faced with incredible odds that work against them. This is why Stephen Hawking can call abiogenesis "the ultimate lucky break."[38]

Of course, biblical creationists invoke a supernatural Being to get things going, which is hardly a scientific theory. Yet, there is nothing any more scientific about evolutionists who propose an unknown process in unknown conditions in an unobservable, distant past—a process of abiogenesis that goes against all observed evidence that life only arises from life. Christians should not be fooled by the scientific-sounding veneer of what is for evolutionists an act of religious faith against observed facts.

Given the assumption of life arising from inanimate material, evolutionary theory is riddled with inconsistencies. Why do secular scientists look for laws, mathematical formulas, and ordered processes when they believe everything happened by random occurrence? The laws of physics are compelling evidence for a Lawmaker. The expectation of order in the universe is a leftover from the scientific enterprise produced by the presuppositions of Christian theology, but it is nonsensical for an atheist to subscribe to it.

Randomness cannot compete with intelligence. I cannot take a container of 250 toothpicks, empty it on the floor, and expect a facsimile of the Eiffel Tower to appear, no matter how many times I do it. However, if you walked into my living room and found a model of the Eiffel Tower made of toothpicks, you would immediately understand that somebody built it.

This is self-evident, such that Paul can write that those who reject the Creator and prefer to worship created things are without excuse (Rom.

---

[37] Bill Bryson, *A Short History of Nearly Everything* (New York: Broadway Books, 2003), 293.

[38] Stephen Hawking's Universe, part 1, Channel 4, UK, September 18, 2010. Transcript at www.springfieldspringfield.co.uk/view_episode_scripts.php?tv-show=into-the-universe-with-stephen-2010&episode=s01e01, accessed September 28, 2015.

1:20). Their rejection is not an intellectual problem, let alone a scientific one. It is a moral and spiritual deficiency.

If a Supreme Being exists who made everything, then we would expect exactly what we find through the scientific method. We discover constants, like the ones in various natural laws that govern the universe, because behind them is a rational, orderly Mind. We would also anticipate that these physical laws would be valid on earth or at the outer reaches of the cosmos, for all of it is made by the same Creator.

On the other hand, if the assumption is true that the universe exists by blind chance, we would not expect to find the rational, orderly laws that govern it. Instead, we would expect a haphazardness to everything we see, like dumping the toothpicks over and over again on the floor.

Why can NASA scientists send a probe into space and expect to find physical laws that govern its trajectory similar to the laws that operate on earth? Given an atheistic worldview, such an assumption is preposterous. This is why Albert Einstein quipped: "The eternal mystery of the world is its comprehensibility."[39]

The uniformity of nature is an assumption—a good one—but an assumption nonetheless. There is no way of knowing if the laws we observe here on earth are the same at the outermost edge of the universe.[40] In which worldview does an assumption of uniformity make the most sense: in one dictated by an intelligent Maker, or in one where randomness is the order of the day?

The telltale sign of a supreme Mind is organized, orderly design. This orderliness is the assumption that drives the scientific enterprise, and it can only exist in a theistic worldview. Ironically, an atheist practices science by first adopting the presuppositions of a theistic worldview—all the while denying theism.[41] Atheists chuck out any intelligence in the cosmos, replacing it with inanimate matter and endowing *it* with "intelligence."

The atheist inconsistently expects a random, mindless process to produce the mental acuity of human beings. Even if we granted evolution

---

[39] Quoted in McGrath, *A Fine-Tuned Universe*, 105.

[40] This assumption stands in respect to both location (here versus another galaxy) and time (today versus in the past or in the future).

[41] "Most scientists aren't mad, although many fashion for themselves a kind of split personality wherein they act as if the universe is knowable, as if it has intrinsic meaning that they are discovering in the data, even while they proclaim that the universe is ultimately meaningless" (Wiker and Witt, *A Meaningful World*, 25).

in the animal kingdom, there is nothing in that process that hints at the quantum leap of intellectual ability humans possess. Yes, Bingo the chimp can recognize fifty hand signs, but this is nothing compared to humans who calculated a half century ago how to travel to the moon using a slide rule.

Lastly, as noted in chapter 2, with a theistic worldview we expect to find a universe that is contingent. Because the cosmos exists solely by God's creative act, it stands to reason that everything in it is conditional; that is, every component relies on something outside itself for its existence. And as everything within the cosmos is contingent, the cosmos itself must also be contingent.

Suppose I placed a computer on the table and asked you to come up with a completely naturalistic explanation for its origin. Apart from assuming somebody made it, you must explore other possible ways the computer exists. I imagine you wasting a fair amount of time going through this worthless exercise.

Is this not what atheistic evolutionists do every single day? They tell us that belief in a Maker impedes science, but we will see in the following chapter that evolutionary theory obstructs scientific advancement.

Theistic evolutionists seem to have this problem addressed in their belief that God made the original "stuff" from which the Big Bang exploded. Yet, just because they throw God into the equation, the problems with biological evolution are not resolved.

CHAPTER FOUR

God's Created Order
and Evolutionary Theory:
A Scientific Perspective

Grant a simple Archetypal creature ... with five senses and
some vestige of mind, and I believe natural selection will account for the
production of every vertebrate animal.

—CHARLES DARWIN[1]

IN THIS CHAPTER WE continue to work through the evolutionary formula:

**Starting material + mutations + natural selection + time
= all speciation in the animal and plant kingdoms**

Christian evolutionists, despite their belief in God, have all the following
scientific problems atheists have when it comes to evolutionary theory.

Mutations

Assuming starting material, evolutionists believe that new information for
evolving organisms is produced via random genetic mutations. Mutations
are copying errors in the genome that allegedly produce previously
non-existent behavior or body parts. Natural selection is the mechanism by
which positive mutations are favored, thus allowing a creature to advance.
Throw in enough time and you can produce just about anything.

The brilliance of Darwin was his tedious observations about plant and

---

[1] Quoted in Dembski and Kushiner, *Signs of Intelligence*, 144.

animal life, meticulously cataloguing his findings over several decades. He recognized something in life that generates amazing adaptations. Darwin came upon the genius of God. Unfortunately, he allowed his philosophical and anti-Christian inclinations to get the better of him. He ran beyond variation within a kind to big-picture evolution. He stumbled upon the fingerprints of God, but instead of acknowledging the Creator, he devised a way for a blind mechanism to supposedly make God obsolete.

Darwin did not know how the information was produced, he only reasoned that it must somehow be this way. That is why today we refer to Darwin's theory ("descent with modification"), coupled with discoveries in genetics, as "Neo-Darwinism."

Evolutionists claim their theory is self-evident, but there are leaps in logic that make it untenable. Here are a few problems:

1. Mutations introduce variations within a kind but are unable to create entirely new kinds.
2. The vast majority of an organism's mutations are either deleterious or inconsequential, not beneficial.
3. Mutations add up over time and will eventually result in the failure of the creature's genome.
4. The step-by-step process proposed by evolutionists cannot account for irreducibly complex systems or body parts.

The BBC article cited in the previous chapter begins in typical fashion: "For scientists, evolution is a fact. We know that life evolved with the same certainty that we know the earth is roughly spherical, that gravity keeps us on it, and that wasps at a picnic are annoying."[2] By "evolution" the author means the big-picture kind, but then he uses numerous examples of variation to prove his point.

This is a precarious leap in logic. Small changes within limits do not imply unlimited change. Baraniuk's example of the Lenski research team's laboratory test with *E. coli* ("The world's longest-running evolution experiment") bears this out. The bacteria were placed in a special chemical

    [2] Chris Baraniuk, "How Do We Know That Evolution Is Really Happening?" BBC Earth, www.bbc.com/earth/story/20150803-how-do-we-know-evolution-is-real, accessed September 21, 2015.

environment and one of the populations developed a new trait after 31,500 generations. No biblical creationist is amazed at such a development, though, as God's creation has adaptation abilities built in.[3]

Nevertheless, the bacteria are still bacteria. The author's examples of speciation within finches, different strains of wheat, and the breeding of domesticated animals are variations within a kind.[4] Again, biblical creationists do not object to this. But a biblical creationist does not expect a farmer, through successive stages of breeding swine, to incredibly transform a pig into a whale.

When Baraniuk makes these typical evolutionist statements, he is being disingenuous:

- "breeders work just like Darwin imagined evolution worked"
- "breeding, Darwin argued, is essentially evolution under human supervision"
- "you might think that breeding can only make a few changes, but there seems to be no end to it"
- "our oldest domesticated animals are still capable of rapid improvement or modification"

Observations of incremental changes observed over short periods of time are extrapolated over long ages: "Evolution takes a long time to make big changes." The author argues that small changes witnessed over thousands of years will translate into humans who are "descended, through countless generations, from a worm."[5]

Given enough time, these changes mount up and lead to the appearance of new species and new types of organism, one small

---

[3] 31,500 generations is a very long time to make one change in an organism. If we assume an average generation to be 20 years for humans, this represents 630,000 years to make one change. The changes necessary to move from an apelike creature to *Homo sapiens* would involve a timeframe much greater than evolution has.

[4] The NAS brochure makes similar leaps, using variations within fly and guppy populations. Theistic evolutionist Denis Alexander does the same thing in *Creation or Evolution* with worms, dogs, gulls, peppered moths, mosquitos, fish, anteaters, and salamanders. He calls these "evolution in action" (82), but they are variations within kinds, not changes from one kind to another.

[5] The use of "countless" is misleading. The number of generations is finite.

change at a time. Step by step, worms became fish, fish came onto land and developed four legs, those four-legged animals grew hair and—eventually—some of them started walking around on two legs, called themselves "humans" and discovered evolution.

The comment about breeding—"there seems to be no end to it"—is a misleading statement. Yes, breeders create dogs that are faster and smaller and more specialized than before, but clearly there is an end to it. These breeders have not taken a dog and made a sea creature. Should we believe that farmers through directed breeding could transform a worm into a human being? Why should we believe that a blind, unintelligent evolutionary process can do it, given enough time? In quoting a university biology professor from the United Kingdom, the author inadvertently makes my point: "It's a series of mistakes that build up . . . It's inevitable." However, it is not inevitable unless you assume it is. This is not science, this is faith.

The author implicitly recognizes how absurd evolution is when he consistently "apologizes" for it. The article is peppered with comments like these:

- "it is hard to accept"
- "this can be hard to believe"
- "it is much harder to accept"
- "still, you may not be convinced"
- "may seem extremely unlikely"
- "this may seem odd"
- "human evolution has always been a concept difficult for some to stomach"

The BBC article ends where it begins: "What we do know is that evolution is a fact of nature." All the author does, though, is show variations within kinds, and with a sleight of hand substitute big-picture evolution.

The National Academy of Science (NAS) booklet makes similar claims for mutational advancement on page 24: "A person writes, a cow walks, a whale swims, and a bat flies with structures built of bones that are different in detail but similar in general structure and relation to each other." This is used as proof of descent from a common ancestor, in this case a small mammal about one hundred million years ago.

After first noting three kinds of mutations—beneficial, harmful, and neutral—the NAS states on page 50, "Most mutations do not change traits or fitness. But some mutations give organisms traits that enhance their ability to survive and reproduce, while other mutations reduce the reproductive fitness of an organism." The article makes it appear that the rates for beneficial and harmful mutations are similar, but this is far from the truth. We know that the vast majority of mutations are either deleterious or inconsequential, and this is the problem with the evolutionist's scenario.[6] Organisms are, over time, accumulating more and more copying errors in their genomes that produce no advantage, and this overall accumulation will eventually cause their genomes to break down.

The problem with quantifying the distribution between the three types of mutations is that a beneficial mutation in one environment could be harmful in another. Another difficulty is that it requires a long-term study over numerous generations. Mutation rates also vary across species; they are much higher in viruses than in humans.[7] Whatever the actual distribution is, virtually everybody agrees that beneficial or advantageous mutations are rare.[8] This is borne out by common sense and experience. No parents in a delivery room hope for a mutation with their soon-to-be-born child! Mutations that create some heretofore nonexistent advantage is the stuff of Marvel Comics superheroes, not reality.

This is why the proposed evolutionary process cannot do what is claimed, no matter how much time is granted. In fact, time is not a positive

---

[6] Collins notes that "most [mutations] will be deleterious, and only a rare such event will provide a selective advantage and be retained during the evolutionary process" (*The Language of God*, 130). Alexander agrees: "The great majority of genetic changes, if not neutral, are likely to be deleterious for the organism" (*Creation or Evolution*, 82). He states that beneficial mutations would be "few."

[7] Collins estimates one mutation for every 100 million base pairs in the human genome, or roughly 60 mutations per generation (*The Language of God*, 131). There are approximately 10,000,000,000,000 cells in the human body (Alexander, *Creation or Evolution*, 63). How many beneficial mutations, all working in unison, are required to move from a one-cell organism to a human being?

[8] Japanese theoretical population geneticist and evolutionist Motoo Kimura's (1924-1994) *Neutral Theory of Molecular Evolution* (Cambridge: Cambridge University Press, 1983) argues that most mutations are invisible to natural selection. One study on virus mutations by Kimura yielded a beneficial mutation rate of less than 2%. Nearly 40% of the mutations were lethal (Wikipedia, "Mutation," https://en.wikipedia.org/wiki/Mutation, accessed October 15, 2015).

element to the equation but a negative one because the more generations an organism moves through, the more genetic mutations it accumulates.[9] Ultimately, these accumulated mutations will result in the organism's failure, not advancement. Given the long ages of evolutionary theory, it is a wonder that any organisms are still around.[10]

A Fish out of Water

Even in granting Darwinists their initial, reproducible, water-based organism, there are problems with their theory. Evolutionists teach that an organism came onto dry land, from which all land and sea mammals evolved. The scenario is:

fish (no lungs) → [out of sea] → amphibian (lungs) → reptile (lungs)
→ land mammal (lungs) → [back to sea] → porpoise (lungs)

Granted, when considering the existence of amphibians, this scenario might seem plausible, especially for those looking for naturalistic explanations. However, amphibians are creatures that already have the tools necessary to live both in water and on land. We have to go back to the original organism that moved from water to land—all by random mutations—and then we see how unlikely this is.

A tremendous number of factors work against this scenario:

· *larger body weight* — On land, the organism carries its full body weight. This requires solid muscles, a stronger skeleton, and more energy.
· *new way of breathing* — Obtaining oxygen from the air is a different process than obtaining it from water. The organism must already develop this ability *before* crawling onto land, or else it will immediately die.
· *eating and digesting different food sources* — What the organism ate in the

_____

[9] Those interested in more technical explanations can read John Sanford's *Genetic Entropy*.

[10] One reason why people lived incredibly longer before the flood than they do today is because individuals like Methuselah had acquired fewer mutations; they were genetically fitter.

water probably does not exist on land; the organism would have difficulty trying to catch some new food source on land.

- *the problem of evaporation* — An organism that spent its entire life in water will find crawling out on land a drying experience. The skin of the organism must prevent desiccation.

- *large temperature fluctuations* — Underwater, temperatures remain relatively constant over a twenty-four-hour period, but on land, large temperature fluctuations occur. The organism must be properly suited for such extreme conditions.

These adaptations must occur via random mutations in the genetic makeup of the water organism *before* it sets "foot" on dry land. They could not be done in a piecemeal fashion because the organism could not exist on land without them all. Further, any of these land-dwelling adaptations make the water-based creature unviable. What would it do, for example, with a much heavier skeletal structure, other than sink?

Irreducible Complexity

Biblical creationists speak about "irreducible complexity." This describes a system that involves numerous parts that all must be functioning at the same time or the system will fail. Creationists point out that a complex organ like the human eye could not have evolved incrementally because the various parts of the eye must be there simultaneously for it to function. This is a powerful argument against the incrementalism of Neo-Darwinism.

Evolutionists retort that the eye could have formed in stages. Theistic evolutionist Denis Alexander provides a diagram ostensibly showing how a light-sensitive patch in a limpet could progress to more advanced eyes in octopi, which have "most of the components of the human eye." Alexander cites a study that proposes 2,000 necessary steps to get to the octopus eye, taking 500,000 years.[11] Of course, this would happen accidentally; there would be no divine intelligence directing it.[12] The eye also had to develop

---

[11] Alexander, *Creation or Evolution*, 145–46. The NAS booklet uses the exact same diagram (41).

[12] Evolutionists like Alexander make these leaps from primitive to complex eyes

independently along several evolutionary branches, making the scenario difficult to swallow.

There is a bigger problem with this view. It concentrates only on the eye and its components. An advanced eye is worthless unless the brain of the organism can interpret the new data. The organism's skeletal and muscular structures must be capable of supporting the new organ. Going from a patch of pigmented cells to a complex optical organ, all by random mutation, defies logic when the broader, simultaneous changes in the organism are considered. Evolutionists are too simplistic in their rebuttal of the creationist objections concerning irreducible complexity.

Vestigial Organs and Junk DNA

Evolutionists argue that as organisms evolved, previously useful body parts became "vestiges" of prior evolutionary stages—present but now unnecessary in the more developed species. Classic examples include wings on flightless birds and pelvic bones in whales that are a vestige of when these mammals (supposedly) ambulated on land.[13]

Regarding humans, in the late nineteenth century evolutionists identified dozens of vestigial organs, including the pituitary and thyroid glands, tonsils, and many other body parts that we have since discovered have important functions. Still, evolutionists continue to use the vestigial argument, with the common ones identified as the appendix, wisdom teeth, tailbone, and body hair.

If it is true that there exist body parts in humans that have no function whatsoever, then creationists have to believe either (a) God made humans with useless body parts, or (b) everything in the human design has a function, we just have not figured it out yet. Creationists opt for the latter, with

---

appear simple, but that masks the complexity of the final product. "Then there are the 100,000,000 light-sensitive cells in the human eye that send information to the brain through some 1,000,000 nerve fibers of the optic nerve. In the brain this information is sorted into various components such as color, movement, form, and depth. It is then analyzed and combined into an intelligible picture" (Ariel Roth, "Biology," in *In Six Days: Why 50 Scientists Choose to Believe in Creation*, ed. John F. Ashton [Green Forest, AR: Master Books, 2005], 88).

[13] The "Darwin Was Right" website has a typical article about this: http://darwinwas right.org/vestigial_structures.html, accessed December 15, 2015.

good reasons, one being how often evolutionists have been wrong with their vestigial argument.[14]

Recently evolutionists have subtly changed the definition of "vestigial." It used to be understood as something that had no function, period, but the term has been expanded to mean a part that does not retain its previous function from the lower evolutionary forms, but may now have a new function (e.g., the tailbone was used by our apelike ancestors for swinging from trees, but is used in humans for sitting). In this way, evolutionists continue to call the appendix vestigial despite knowing it has a function in humans. This gives the appearance of consistency in the evolutionist's argument because the appendix has been on the vestigial list for decades. However, what they have done is change the meaning of "vestigial" instead of delisting the appendix once a purpose was discovered. This is nothing more than a linguistic sleight of hand.

Evolutionary assumptions impede progress. For decades doctors were nonchalantly removing body parts deemed vestigial, slowing down progress in determining their function. Had the biblical assumption been followed that every part of human anatomy has a purpose as it was created by a purposeful, intelligent Creator, we may have saved people needless surgery and cost.

Evolutionists have not learned their lesson when it comes to vestigial organs because they are using the same argument on the genetic level. At some point in the not-too-distant past, evolutionary scientists claimed that as much as 98% of the human genome was "junk DNA."[15] The number has steadily come down as we have learned more about genetics, but I wonder how far behind we are scientifically as a result of this false assumption.

---

[14] This *National Geographic* article from 2009 appears at first to admit that the vestigial argument is fallacious, as it notes that the spleen, previously considered vestigial, has a very important function. However, by the end of the article the author argues for other vestigial body parts: Maggie Koerth-Baker, "Vestigial Organs Not So Useless after All," National Geographic News, http://news.nationalgeographic.com/news/2009/07/090730-spleen-vestigial-organs.html, accessed December 16, 2015.

[15] "Junk DNA" refers to non-protein-coding DNA, but there are many functions for this other kind of DNA, such as repairing DNA, regulating DNA transcription, and controlling RNA editing and slicing. The idea that there is "junk" in the human genome—an argument that atheists have used against the notion of intelligent design—needs to be discarded. A creationist rightly insists that everything in the design of humans has a function.

Francis Collins's book, *The Language of God: A Scientist Presents Evidence for Belief,* is something of a theistic evolution classic. It remained on *The New York Times* bestseller list for sixteen weeks during its 2006 release. In it Collins claims that "45 percent of the human genome" is "genetic flotsam and jetsam," commonly understood as junk DNA.[16] Because there is junk in the human genome similar to the genes found in other mammals, Collins is able to say, "The conclusion of a common ancestor for humans and mice is virtually inescapable."[17]

A 2012 article on the BioLogos website argues that a protein found in the human genome is used in lower species for creating egg yolk. Because humans no longer need yolk, it is a powerful proof for "non-specialists to grasp" that we have evolved from lower organisms. "Placental mammals, including humans, have a defective remnant of a gene used to make egg yolk because they descend from egg-laying ancestors."[18] This is the same faulty argument used by evolutionists concerning vestigial organs.

There is something much deeper at work here, what I call the "arrogance of implied omniscience." When scientists make such declarations, especially when we have had the human genome mapped for more than a decade, their conclusions are highly suspect. It is presumptuous to assert that we have absolute certainty here.

In engineering there is the principle of creative economy, or optimal design. Suppose you are an engineer who wants to manufacture various machines, each requiring twenty parts. Efficiency is the name of the game for a clever engineer. You might find a way to get double or even triple duty out of the same parts used in several different machines. If you can, you will be able to reduce the complexity of the manufacturing of those machines. Why is it odd if God designed in a similar fashion?

It is understandable that atheists trumpet the discovery of egg yolk in the human genome as evidence for evolution. However, Christians should

---

[16] *The Language of God*, 136–37. Collins may have changed his mind since his 2006 book was published: Jonathan M., "Has Francis Collins Changed His Mind on 'Junk' DNA'?"EvolutionNews,www.evolutionnews.org/2011/03/has_francis_collins_changed_hi044601.html, accessed April 15, 2016.

[17] *The Language of God*, 137.

[18] Dennis Venema, "Is There 'Junk' in Your Genome, Part 4," BioLogos, http://biologos. org/blog/understanding-evolution-is-there-junk-in-your-genome-part-4, accessed July 10, 2015.

know better. The genius of God as Creator is not found only in the *what* of creation, it is also found in the *how*. I am convinced that as our knowledge improves we will find a legitimate reason for why this protein is in humans. My confidence is not necessarily in our technology, but in the God who made us.

The BioLogos article makes erroneous arguments like this one: "When we see the remnants of this sequence in the human genome it is a stretch to argue that it has another, as of yet unknown function." But why? Exhaustive knowledge of the human genome is required to make this statement.

The author states, "There is no known mechanism that could create the precise, repeated pattern of shared mutations we observe between related species." This is the same problem. I can imagine an evolutionist saying the same thing a century ago concerning the thyroid gland because there was no known reason for the gland's existence. However, we now recognize that it is vital for proper metabolism. Surely scientists who are Christian need to be more circumspect when making these declarations. Have we not been consistently surprised by the genius of God's design?[19]

Theistic evolutionists do not embrace the idea of God's wondrous design. The real designer in their scheme is the random mutations, filtered through natural selection. Are humans, made in God's image, the by-product of the accumulation of billions of years of chance mutations? Scripture says that God took dirt and in one creative act made Adam, not from a pre-existing apelike creature that had come through accidental biochemical modifications. The psalmist is amazed that God made man "a little lower than the angels" (Ps. 8:5), but in theistic evolution, man is made a little higher than the apes. By demoting God, the Christian evolutionist has consequently demoted humanity.

_____

[19] An example of how presumptuous it is for any scientist to imply complete knowledge involves the recent discovery of a lymphatic system in the human brain, as reported in the journal *Nature*, "Structural and Functional Features of Central Nervous System Lymphatic Systems," www.nature.com/nature/journal/v523/n7560/full/nature14432. html, accessed November 16, 2015. They didn't just discover a new function of the brain, they discovered a new part that "overturns decades of textbook teaching!" (quote from Max Lugavere, "10 Discoveries That Made Us Healthier in 2015," Yahoo! Beauty, www.yahoo.com/health/10-discoveries-that-made-us-healthier-1325577432006710. html, accessed December 21, 2015).

Natural Selection

Natural selection is depicted as a process that, given enough time, will cause organisms to advance onward and upward as it favors new mutations.[20] However, natural selection does nothing to stop the accumulation of deleterious mutations, with more mutations occurring each generation than natural selection can eliminate.

Evolutionists speak of natural selection as if it is a creative force, but all it does is weed through existing material. It makes nothing new. It is similar to taking a deck of cards and selecting the tens on up because you want to play a game of euchre. What you have done is exclude the nines on down, and if you later want to play a game of poker, you have to reintroduce cards.

Natural selection works like this. Once the process has taken place and you have lost information, you cannot go backward without a "convenient" random mutation or breeding back in the lost genetic information.

Suppose a wild dog has six offspring: two with short hair, two with medium hair, and two with long hair. A cold spell comes through the area, causing the short- and medium-hair dogs to die before they can reproduce. The next generation of dogs will predominantly have long hair, and eventually, the short- and medium-hair genes will disappear. A subsequent heat wave will not cause those genes to miraculously reappear. They have been lost; natural selection has de-selected them. And while this process can favor a certain type of hair, it cannot explain the existence of hair, let alone dogs.

Breeders who through successive stages produce a breed of small dogs cannot later produce large dogs from the new breed, any more than by mating Chihuahuas they can hope to produce a Great Dane. They have eliminated the necessary genetic material to make large dogs. In this sense, natural selection is far from a creative force; it is akin to a destructive one, as it takes existing creatures and narrows their genetic information.

---

[20] For this reason, Charles Darwin spoke of natural selection in almost godlike terms: "It may metaphorically be said that natural selection is daily and hourly scrutinising, throughout the world, the slightest variations; rejecting those that are bad, preserving and adding up all that are good; silently and insensibly working, *whenever and wherever opportunity offers,* at the improvement of each organic being in relation to its organic and inorganic conditions of life" (*Origin of Species,* online resource, www.bartleby.com/11/4001.html, accessed December 10, 2015).

Besides, if a helpful mutation occurred in an organism, this does not assure that the organism will reproduce in time to pass it on. "Dumb luck" is more in line with what happens. It is akin to an athlete who is born with extra lung capacity, making him a superior cyclist, who gets killed by a drunk driver. Positive mutations do not automatically mean a superior population of organisms.

Natural selection occurs at the level of the *entire* organism (phenotype), not at the genetic level (genotype). It does not select genes, it selects whole creatures. A small genetic mutation in one creature does not mean that the creature passes it on to its progeny, or that the creature even survives to reproduce. The entire creature goes with the mutation. This means all the genetic information, not just part of it, is selected out.

Sections of a genome are coded to perform multiple tasks (what we call "optimal design"), which is bad for natural selection because in selecting for one gene, it inevitably affects countless other functions in the organism.[21] The idea that *one* genetic mutation results in a competitive advantage and "survival of the fittest" is a fallacy, especially when there are countless other factors that determine the life of a creature.

Evolutionists observe the empirical data of variation within kinds (e.g., the varying beak sizes of Darwin's finches) and make the false conclusion that if we accumulate these limited variations we can, in time, leap from one kind to another. They mistake change within limits for unlimited change. This is why the fossil record and the animal kingdom are littered with examples of variation, but evidence of (macro) evolution is nowhere to be found.

This is the failing of Richard Dawkins, for example, who elaborates on numerous examples of variation within kinds, then throws in enough time to supposedly yield humans. "If so much evolutionary change can be achieved in just a few centuries or even decades [through selective breeding], just think what might be achieved in ten or a hundred million years." Thus he can conclude, "It becomes rather easy to accept that evolution could accomplish the amount of change that it took to transform a fish into a human."[22]

---

[21] Dog breeders see this, where an improvement in strength or speed yields something detrimental, like weaker hips in German Shepherds.

[22] *Greatest Show on Earth*, 37, 82.

One common example employed by evolutionists (an "evolutionary icon" because it is used so often)[23] involves the giraffe. We are to suppose that a population of deer or antelope found themselves in an environment where competition for food was harsh. The longer-necked animals had a competitive advantage for leaves higher up on trees, and in a few generations, the long-neck mutation was favored via natural selection. The process continued until giraffes emerged. "It is the result of a long chain of little changes," says the BBC article.

The problems with this scenario are manifold. For starters, there are no fossils of giraffes with short necks, but the gradual lengthening of the neck would surely be reflected in the fossil record. Next, it assumes no foliage at lower levels, but this would eventually involve the death of every short animal in the area. We know that female giraffes are about a meter shorter, on average, than males, implying that all female giraffes lose out too (and what about young giraffes who have no height advantage for many months?).

The biggest shortcoming to this theory is similar to the supposed evolution of the human eye. A tremendous number of other factors must concurrently evolve along with neck length, such as a larger heart for pumping the blood higher, a unique blood valve and vein system so the giraffe's head doesn't explode from the pressure when it bends down to drink water, and a proportionate body frame (muscles, skeleton, etc.) so the giraffe is not top-heavy. These genetic mutations must conveniently coincide with the environmental changes that make the mutations advantageous, otherwise nothing would "evolve." This handy coincidence has to happen over and over again. In short, the heart of the evolutionary formula, "mutations + natural selection," cannot do what evolutionists claim it can do.

Lastly, natural selection cannot explain the existence of instinct in animals, like the accurate migration routes of sea turtles, birds, insects, butterflies, and fish, some over thousands of miles. How do beavers know they need to put an air vent at the top of their lodge once it is built, to avoid suffocation? Web design (no, not for the Internet!) with spiders and nest design with birds are other examples. The malleefowl of Australia instinctively creates an incubation chamber for its clutch of eggs, maintaining a constant temperature of 33°C by opening and closing air vents in the nest.

---

[23] See Jonathan Wells's *Icons of Evolution*.

Are we to believe that these instincts randomly arose, and if so, how did the creatures survive before these life-preserving features existed?

Natural selection has a limited ability to favor small changes within kinds, but it does not enjoy the almost godlike capacity evolutionists make it possess as it transforms worms into human beings.

Time

The evolutionist mantra is "All you need is enough time," but given the process proposed by evolutionary theory, no amount of time will suffice.[24] Back to our toothpick analogy. Given an infinite amount of time, dumping 250 toothpicks on the floor will never produce a facsimile of the Eiffel Tower, any more than throwing a pig an infinite amount of times in the air will cause it to sprout wings and fly because the laws of nature work against it. Only when intelligent design is coupled with the toothpicks can the model be produced; time plus randomness will never yield rational, organized structure. I will grant evolutionists all the time they want because the process they propose is inherently flawed.

I have heard Christians say the earth cannot possibly be six thousand years old, but why not? I assume they have bought into the evolutionary story of long ages, that rocks take forever to form, that animals evolve incrementally over millions of years, and so on. But all of these are assumptions that can be disproved by the evidence.

A clarification should be made about the creationist position. Biblical creationists are accused of believing that every species must have been directly created by God. One Christian evolutionist writes, "If we assume that evolution is impossible, then the creation of a new living species can only happen by a supernatural act."[25] This confuses macroevolution with variation. A creationist can expect the arrival of new species within kinds through variation, and still object to (macro) evolution.

There is also the problem of confusing the biblical "kind" with "species." The latter is a scientific category with some subjectivity attached to it.

---

[24] Nobel Prize winner George Wald put it this way: "Time is the hero of the plot. Given enough time anything can happen—the impossible becomes probable, the probable becomes certain." George Wald, *The Physics and Chemistry of Life* (New York: Simon & Schuster, 1955), 12.

[25] Glover, *Beyond the Firmament*, 186.

While a biological species is normally understood as an animal that cannot or will not reproduce outside its own species, this measure cannot be used for fossil "species." We have no idea if an extinct animal could reproduce with a living animal with similar characteristics. Fossils are categorized largely by physical appearance and nothing more, yet are often called new "species."[26]

Genesis speaks of God making "kinds"—"God made the wild animals according to their kinds, the livestock according to their kinds, and all the creatures that move along the ground according to their kinds" (1:25)—so that basic body designs were created by God. There was a canine kind from which the hundreds of varieties ("species" and "breeds") of canines came; the feline kind has its own distinct design too; humans are called "mankind" or "humankind."

Biblical creationists do not invoke God's special creative act every time a breeder creates a new form of poodle. We believe that God designed the genetic makeup of living things such that variation takes place in limits within each kind. A kind can become isolated from its parent group, vary, and ultimately become another "species" (i.e., speciation) according to the modern use of that term. Yet, it remains the same "kind."

Evolutionists happily point out that if the creationist scenario is true, then variation has occurred since Noah's time at a far greater clip than even proponents of evolution expect. Indeed, creationists are left with the task of arguing against one form of evolution (macro), while arguing for a more rapid process (variation) while the wide spectrum of genetic material is weeded down through the selection.

Biblical creationists believe God has placed within creatures adaptive power through variation, so that the incredible varieties we see within kinds took place over several thousand years. If you begin with the different kinds of Genesis, each adapting into other varieties of the same kind, you can fill the whole planet in a relatively short period of time.

The evolutionary assumption that variation and speciation require deep time is contradicted by examples where it occurs rapidly.[27] Consider modern

---

[26] About ten thousand new species are classified each year, with an estimated two million in existence (Alexander, *Creation or Evolution*, 103).

[27] Alexander provides numerous examples of rapid speciation (ibid., 94–101) but does not believe that all species seen today arose in ten thousand years (159).

accounts of twins who appear to come from different families, one white and the other black.[28] Dogs come in an incredible array of shapes and sizes, yet they have been domesticated relatively recently by modern humans. Rapid variation occurs in bacteria, viruses, and a variety of other creatures. Do an Internet search for rapid variation in mosquitoes, mice, wingless beetles, and blind cave fish, just to name a few. However, the beetles always remain the beetle kind, and mosquitoes always remain the mosquito kind.[29]

One other issue concerning evolutionary deep time is worth noting. Christians who deny macroevolution will often ask why we do not see it today. "We've had animal breeders for centuries. Why can't a dog breeder eventually change his poodle into a porpoise?" they rightly ask, to which an evolutionist will invariably answer, "Because evolution moves at such a slow rate that we cannot see such changes."[30] And yet, evolutionists also claim that evolution occurred too rapidly in the past to allow for the millions of transitional forms we would expect to find in the fossil record were evolutionary theory true.

This contradiction in evolutionary thinking has caused one creationist to lament, "Today evolution is moving at such a slow rate that it cannot be observed, but in the past it moved at such a rapid rate that it left no evidence in the fossil record."[31] I share this author's agitation.

Interpreting Old Bones

Have you ever assumed that people were older or younger than they are? Your suppositions are usually based on superficial things like the amount

---

[28] Here are two examples: Gillian Fuller, "These Twin Sisters Actually Could Not Look Any More Different," Elite Daily, http://elitedaily.com/news/world/twin-sister-could-not-look-more-different/952327/, accessed October 11, 2015, and Susan James, "Parents Give Birth to Ebony and Ivory Twins," ABC News, http://abcnews.go.com/Health/twins-white-black-born-biracial-parents-stirs-issues/story?id=12984334, accessed October 11, 2015.

[29] Richard Dawkins elaborates on a Russian experiment in the twentieth century that involved taking wild foxes and breeding for tameness. In just thirty-five generations, nearly 80% of the experimental fox population had been domesticated (*Greatest Show on Earth*, 73–76). Unfortunately, Dawkins believes that this is evidence that by adding enough time, natural selection can transform a worm into a human being.

[30] For example, see Dawkins, *Greatest Show on Earth*, 16.

[31] Luther Sunderland in *Darwin's Enigma*, 55.

of hair on their head or wrinkles on their brow. I went online and had my "biological age" determined.[32] The website asked how many hours I sleep each night, if I smoke or consume alcohol, and how regularly I exercise. Their software determined that I am biologically four years younger than my actual age.

There are assumptions behind the factors used to determine this. Some are generally true but not always. Would you prefer to know my age based on the website's questions, or by consulting my actual birth certificate that provides an accurate historical record?

The former is what evolutionists do. They dig up a bone and determine its age based on certain assumptions. They want us to believe their conclusions are "fact," but this is highly misleading. Whereas the Bible offers an accurate historical record, providing an outside age limit for humanity, evolutionary theory is based on inaccurate assumptions.

The fossil record is claimed as a chief support for both sides of this debate, but I think it is a major strike against evolutionary theory and its predictions. To begin with, it is horribly incomplete. The vast majority (about 95%) of fossils are from marine invertebrates (i.e., mostly shellfish). The finds of hominid remains get the biggest press, but they account for a measly one-quarter of 1% of all fossils. What we have is hardly a complete picture of the past.

Evolutionists imply that the fossil record is ordered as their assumptions predict, but this is inaccurate. There are fossils that are out of place, with the record looking more random all the time.[33] Most fossils are found in sedimentary rock, and the long-standing assumption of evolutionary theory is that these rocks are formed over long ages. Therefore, fossils within these rocks are likewise assumed to be very old, but if one assumption is wrong, so is the other.

Fossilization is actually quite rare. The vast majority of creatures that die are eaten by scavengers, decompose, or disappear in some other way long before the processes of fossilization can preserve them. The best

---

[32] At www.biological-age.com (accessed May 3, 2015).

[33] These two online articles from Creation Ministries International provide numerous examples: Gary Bates and Lita Cosner, "Are There Out-of-Sequence Fossils That Are Problematic for Evolution?" http://creation.com/fossils-out-of-order, accessed October 16, 2015, and John Woodmorappe, "The Fossil Record: Becoming More Random All the Time," http://creation.com/the-fossil-record, accessed October 16, 2015.

way to create a fossil is through catastrophic occurrences, like sedimentation caused with a flood, where the creature is rapidly preserved whole. Creatures have been discovered that were fossilized in the middle of eating another creature and even giving birth.

The lack of fossil evidence was a thorn in the flesh for Darwin. Whereas the fossil record should contain tons of incremental changes moving fluidly from species to species (something Darwin expected but whose absence he bemoaned), it is dominated by either stasis (long periods of geological time where organisms basically stay the same) or grand leaps where whole species appear out of nowhere (e.g., the Cambrian Explosion). It also shows evidence of mass extinctions. This data fits much better into a biblical framework than an evolutionary one.

Evolutionists have worked double time trying to find transitional creatures, frequently dubbing the latest discovery an important "missing link," but were later forced to dial back their exuberance. I will highlight one fossil from the animal kingdom, and then speak about something closer to home, the evolution of *Homo sapiens*.

Recall the evolutionary scenario: sea creatures made it to dry land and became tetrapods (four-legged creatures). We have noted scientifically how unlikely this is, but biblically speaking it is easily contradicted. Genesis says God made fish according to their kind (1:21); humans were made in God's image, a special "kind." There is no hint that the fish kind became the human kind.

Regardless, evolutionists have searched in the fossil record for a fishlike organism that has four appendages that could have served as a precursor to mammalian legs, and they claim to have found a candidate in *Tiktaalik roseae*.

Tiktaalik is a poster child for evolution, showing up virtually everywhere the fossil record is discussed. It is mentioned in six different places in the NAS booklet. Discovered in northern Canada in 2004, with other pieces of the creature uncovered in subsequent years, this "missing link" gained widespread praise from evolutionists who felt their theory was vindicated.[34] Alexander describes it as "about the size of a crocodile, with scales like

---

[34] Here's an example from Live Science: Bjorn Carey, "Fishy Land Beast Bridges Evolutionary Gap," www.livescience.com/4025-fishy-land-beast-bridges-evolutionary-gap. html, accessed October 23, 2015.

a fish but also fins like limbs and an elbow joint that could push the animal off the ground."[35]

Evolutionists claim *Tiktaalik*'s mixed features make it a missing link, but there are many creatures that have mixed features (called "mosaic" animals), the duck-billed platypus perhaps being the most famous. Besides, the pelvic girdle of *Tiktaalik* doesn't connect with the vertebral column, making walking impossible. Further, an entire specimen of the creature has not been found; part of the hindquarters remains missing.[36]

Evolutionists have been wrong on missing link claims before. Consider the so-called living fossils, those transitional creatures assumed dead in evolutionary thinking, only to be discovered alive. The coelacanth was presumed to have died out sixty-five million years ago, yet was found off the coast of Madagascar in the twentieth century. Before its detection, evolutionists thought it used its lobed fins for walking on the sea floor and ultimately on land, similar to *Tiktaalik*. However, upon witnessing a live coelacanth in action, we know that the fins are used for maneuvering while swimming and have nothing to do with walking.

If evolutionary theory is true, we should find transitional creatures all over the place, but we have not.[37] That is why there is so much ballyhoo when one supposedly is discovered. If they were commonplace, as evolutionary theory predicts, then evolutionists would not be so thrilled about finding one. Their exuberance reveals their theory's weakness.

Homo Sapiens

Much of the debate about the human fossil record rests on how to classify bones. There is simply no definite way of knowing if the skeletal remains of hominids actually represent new species, or just different body designs within the same species. Paleontologists argue about this, divided into "lumpers" (those who throw lots of hominid remains into

---

[35] *Creation or Evolution*, 128.

[36] The University of Chicago has tons of information on *Tiktaalik*: www.tiktaalik.uchicago.edu.

[37] With about two hundred million fossils collected by museums worldwide, there is no want for material.

one species) and "splitters" (those who divide the remains into lots of different species).[38]

I wonder what would happen if the skeletons of a twentieth-century pigmy from Central Africa and someone akin to NBA basketball player Yao Ming from China were discovered one thousand years from now. Would evolutionists assume both to be the same species? I have a sneaking suspicion that if evolutionists wanted to find similarities, they would find similarities, and if they wanted to find differences, they would find differences.

What if the remains of a St. Bernard and a Chihuahua were dug up a millennium later? I have a hunch the same (false) assumptions would apply about these creatures being different species (and possibly identifying the Chihuahua as an alien lifeform)!

Determinations made about hominid discoveries are based on physiology and morphology (e.g., the cranium looks more apelike with a protruding brow or elongated jaw). And despite all the media attention, there are few complete skeletons or skulls for these supposed transitional species. In many cases, a transitional species is asserted based on a handful of bone fragments or in one case a single tooth.

Skull shape and size are affected by diet and climate, as well as age and postmortem factors. Compare the skull shape of a twenty-year-old man with his skull sixty years later. If the biblical record of early humans living for hundreds of years is accurate, their long lifespans affected physical appearance.

Hominid discoveries are usually accompanied by incredible fanfare and the evolutionary tale is spun through various outlets. Darwin's "descent of man" is a well-known evolutionary icon, emblazoned in the minds of numerous generations.

When I was growing up, my mother would say in a disgusted tone, "Don't act like a Neanderthal!" It wasn't that long ago that Neanderthals were painted as stumpy, brutish, apelike hominids that dwelled in caves and had very limited cranial ability. Recent depictions of Neanderthals, though, have them living in wooden structures, with sophisticated weapons, using cooking implements, body jewelry, and musical instruments (had I known this in my childhood, I could have refused piano lessons

---

[38] "Both lumpers and splitters are looking at the same evidence—but making different interpretations" (Roberts, *The Incredible Human Journey*, 3).

Human form during the stages of evolution

based on my mother's admonition against acting like a Neanderthal!). This suggests they were humans, nothing less. They even had 27% more brain capacity than modern humans.

In fact, through DNA analysis, we now recognize that Neanderthals interbred with modern *Homo sapiens*, so they must have been the same species.[39] Yet, how many children were dogmatically taught that Neanderthals were a link between apes and humans?

Enter Lucy

Evolutionary history is replete with discoveries of so-called missing links that later were overturned. A famous one is "Lucy," a skeleton discovered in Ethiopia in 1974, presumed to be 3.2 million years old and dubbed *Australopithecus afarensis*, a species that scientists claimed was a direct ancestor of modern humans.[40] Lucy was touted for more than three decades as

[39] Rebecca Morelle, "Neanderthals and Humans Interbred '100,000 Years Ago,'" BBC News, www.bbc.com/news/science-environment-35595661, accessed March 14, 2016.

[40] Ker Than, "'Lucy' Kin Pushes Back Evolution of Upright Walking?" National Geographic News, http://news.nationalgeographic.com/news/2010/06/100621-lucy-early-humans-walking-upright-science/, accessed March 16, 2016.

a "missing link" in the early stages of human evolution, but now is seen as another variety of knuckle-walking ape.[41]

In 2013, my daughter was told in her science class that Lucy is a missing link, this long after evolutionists themselves debunked this claim. Thus the evolutionist propaganda machine works. When a supposed "missing link" is discovered, there is incredible fanfare. However, when it is found to be an error, there is virtual silence in the public arena. Unfortunately, school textbooks continue to use it as an example of evolution; teachers who do not upgrade their own research on the topic photocopy lecture material using dated information.

Below is an artistic rendering of Lucy from the website of *National Geographic*.[42] What was discovered was 40% of the body, including the lower jaw bone and four, small fragments from the rest of the head. Everything else is imagination. Nothing was discovered from the cheek and brow area, yet the artistic rendering makes Lucy look apelike, with hints of humanity. If the newfound hominid is thought to be a missing link between apes and humans, then the paleoartist's rendering will make it look just like that.[43]

In 2015, the world was introduced to a hominid find in South Africa, this one dubbed *Homo naledi*. The remains of about 1,500 bones from at least 15 individuals have been uncovered. Remains of the elderly, young adults, juveniles, and infants were found, with three fragmented craniums, making it a substantial find.

Whatever *H. naledi* turns out to be, the announcement came with incredible fanfare like with Lucy decades earlier. I wonder, as more tests and studies are conducted, if this latest missing link will also quietly disappear. Another discovery will take its place, and the whole cycle will be repeated.

---

[41] Evolutionists had previously estimated that it took about five million mutational events over three million years to move from Lucy to modern humans.

[42] "What Was Lucy? Fast Facts on an Early Human Ancestor," http://news.nationalgeographic.com/news/2006/09/060920-lucy.html, accessed March 16, 2016.

[43] See Lubenow's *Bones of Contention* for examples of how paleoartists have misled the public with their evolutionary depictions ("Paleoanthropology's Debt to Artists," 38–41).

Misplaced Faith in Bad Science

Evolution has numerous "leaps of faith," yet schoolchildren throughout
the world are taught this theory as the only viable explanation for the origin of the species, complete with inventive artistic renderings making it
appear reasonable and straightforward.

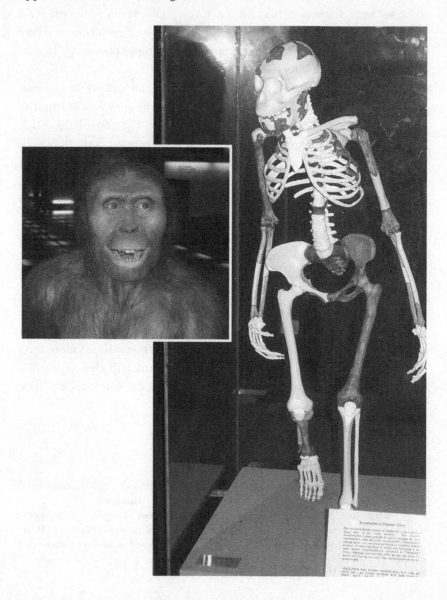

Some Christians object that arguing against evolution is wasted time: "Who cares how things came to be, as long as you believe in Jesus?" From a biblical point of view, though, if a position does not accord with God's self-revelation in his Word, then it must be discarded. As already noted, smuggling evolutionary theory into our Christian doctrine can have negative consequences for our understanding of human nature, sin, and the character of God. Genuine believers who adopt evolution are our siblings in Christ. However, they must be shown how theologically and scientifically vacuous theistic evolution is.

Huge amounts of money and effort are wasted every year on evolutionary research that could be spent on more worthwhile projects. Evolutionary theory impedes good science due to the following:

· False assumptions about long ages resulting in two centuries of neglecting to look for soft tissue in dinosaur bones (noted in chapter 2)
· False assumptions about "vestigial" organs resulting in needless removal of "useless" body parts in humans, and neglect for properly studying their function
· False assumptions about "junk DNA" setting back genetic research, perhaps by decades
· False assumptions about "cavemen" blinding evolutionists to obvious conclusions about other hominids, such as Neanderthal intelligence and creativity
· Wasted time searching for supposed transitional organisms when the fossil record is devoid of them
· Wasted time and research on how purely naturalistic causes can create intelligent information
· Wasted time and research on how inanimate material can yield animate organisms
· Unreasonably optimistic beliefs that random mutations can move organisms across kinds

Driven by false assumptions about what constitutes "science," evolutionists have dumbed-down schoolchildren by limiting access to other viable explanations for how life arose and adapted on the planet. All the while, atheists claim religion kills science, when history flatly contradicts this notion.

The hyperbole from the evolutionist camp concerning people of faith is quite alarming.[44] Consider this comment by an evangelical Christian: "If these claims [young earth creation] were actually true, it would lead to the complete and irreversible collapse of the sciences of physics, chemistry, cosmology, geology, and biology."[45] I find this incredible since these sciences have Christians at their founding. Perhaps loyalty to the philosophical materialism that underlies much of these enterprises today would happily melt away, and we could get back to studying God's creation as God made it.

Lastly, there are significant moral consequences if we adopt an evolutionary worldview. There is a vast difference between the belief that humans are made in the image of God, as opposed to humans as advanced animals. Significant harm to humanity has occurred when the latter has been assumed, as we will see in the following chapter.

[44] Like this Live Science article: "Intelligent Design: The Death of Science," www.livescience.com/9361-intelligent-design-death-science.html, accessed September 3, 2015.

[45] Collins, *The Language of God*, 174.

CHAPTER FIVE

God's Created Order
and the Sanctity of Life

No one really knows how humans got to be so clever.

—STEPHANIE PAPPAS[1]

"WHY IS THERE SOMETHING rather than nothing? This contradiction is the most perplexing problem in fundamental physics." So opened a 2015 TED (technology, entertainment, design) talk by particle physicist Harry Cliff, who works on the Large Hadron Collider at the European Organization for Nuclear Research (CERN) in Switzerland.[2] TED talks cover a fascinating spectrum of topics and are a popular way of discussing practical implications of science and culture.[3]

On the one hundredth anniversary of Einstein's general theory of relativity, Cliff noted that the strengths of two fundamental energy fields are so finely tuned that "if they were different even by a tiny bit, then the universe as we know it would not exist."[4] We live in a "Goldilocks universe" because things are neither too hot nor too cold; they are just right.

Stephen Hawking has similarly observed that "if the rate of expansion one second after the Big Bang had been smaller by even one part in a

---

[1] Stephanie Pappas, "Is Stephen Hawking Right about Hostile Aliens?" Yahoo! News, http://news.yahoo.com/stephen-hawking-hostile-aliens-111403178.html, accessed December 3, 2015.

[2] "Have We Reached the End of Physics?" TED, www.ted.com/talks/harry_cliff_have_we_reached_the_end_of_physics#t-130343, accessed December 29, 2015.

[3] There are 2,400 free talks available on TED's website, www.TED.com.

[4] These fields are the Higgs Boson energy field, from which fundamental particles get their mass, and the strength of dark energy. If the strength of the Higgs field were too weak, no matter could form, and if the strength of dark energy were too strong, it would tear everything apart.

hundred thousand million million, the universe would have re-collapsed before life had a chance to form."[5] The very existence of the universe is ridiculously improbable given blind mechanisms.

I am fascinated when evolutionary scientists conclude what Christian scholars have known for centuries: we live in an exceptional place in the cosmos, designed especially for our survival. Scientists opposed to Christianity note this, even as they deny God's existence.

Secular scientists believe that eons ago an asteroid collided with the earth, breaking off bits of the globe that merged and formed the moon. It is an amazing coincidence, then, that the moon is four hundred times smaller than the sun, but is also four hundred times closer to the earth, so that the moon's disk perfectly creates an eclipse for human observation. The beauty of this is not simply the dazzling display. During an eclipse, scientists can analyze the sun in ways they could not do otherwise. Which are we to believe: that the moon's relative distance is completely accidental, or that it was specially designed for us to study God's handiwork?

The nearly circular shape of the earth's orbit, plus its optimal distance from the sun, create temperatures on the planet's surface that stay within a tight range—not too hot and not too cold—for life to exist. The fine-tuned atmosphere that engulfs our planet, as well as the perfect balance between oxygen and nitrogen in the air, allow life to thrive. Increase the amount of oxygen, and combustion becomes a constant problem; decrease it too far and large mammals would struggle to breathe. The atmosphere is thick enough to guard the earth from harmful cosmic rays, but not too thick to prohibit the necessary amount of light to enter.

Then there is water, that elixir of life. Astronomers consistently look for signs of water on other planets because without it, life could not exist. Not only does water serve as a temperature moderator for the planet, but it possesses an amazing array of properties suited for multiple functions.

Consider this. Most substances contract when they freeze (and expand when heated up), and water behaves this way as it gets colder. That is, until it gets close to freezing when, voila! it begins to expand. Why is this important? If water did not behave in this manner, during winter the surface of a lake would freeze and contract, sinking to the bottom. The new surface would then freeze, and this cycle would continue until

---

[5] Hawking, *A Brief History of Time*, 291.

the entire lake was frozen solid from top to bottom. All life in it would cease.[6]

Then there are these tiny details about the creation that I share for fun:

- If all the DNA in a human body were stretched out, it would reach to the moon and back eight thousand times.
- If the amount of information stored in our genome were typed out, the three billion base pairs of nucleic acids in our DNA would easily fill eight hundred English translations of the Bible.
- There are 10^{11} neurons in the human brain, and 10^{14} connections between them, which is more than all the atoms in the human body.
- Water, which can put out fire, is made of two combustible elements, hydrogen and oxygen. Was God just having fun when he invented it?

We must believe that everything is accidental and human life just so happens to exist, or, in the words of the psalmist, "we are fearfully and wonderfully made" (Ps. 139:14), and the creation is designed so that this wonderfully made human body can thrive. Which position you take will have profound implications for how you treat life.

In chapter 4 we noted that evidence of design implies a Designer, but not everybody agrees with this perspective. Atheists often point out deficient "design" in creation, so that theists are left to admit either (a) things happened by accident, or (b) God is a poor designer.

For example, astrophysicist Neil deGrasse Tyson humorously claims poor "design" in the human pelvic region. "There's like a sewage system and entertainment complex intermingling. No engineer of any intelligence would have designed it that way."[7] But where would Tyson have human waste exit the body? I note that a car's fuel intake and exhaust are in the same area. Is this also evidence of poor design?

I expect nothing less from atheists, but when Christian evolutionists use the same arguments, I am quite surprised. Francis Collins mentions the

---

[6] There are many amazing details about the properties of water, as well as other fine-tuned elements of our planet, in Wiker and Witt, *A Meaningful World*, especially chapters 6 and 7.

[7] Kelly Dickerson, "Neil deGrasse Tyson Has a Hilarious Reason for Not Believing in Intelligent Design," Business Insider, www.businessinsider.com/neil-degrasse-tyson-god-religion-2015-11, accessed January 17, 2016.

wisdom teeth, the supposedly non-optimal design of the human spine, and the appendix as defying "the existence of truly intelligent planning of the human form."[8] Christian evolutionist Gordon Glover claims, "The human body also shows many signs of suboptimal 'design' that only make sense in terms of evolutionary history."[9] Examples include a "yolk sac" accompanying the human embryo, and the human backbone that could have been designed to avoid back pain.

At the heart of these arguments is that the objector knows better. However, this perspective ignores the thousands of interrelated factors in the design. Changing one affects countless others. A person must have exhaustive knowledge—divine omniscience if you will—of the human body before he could claim to design it better.

The *Imago Dei*

One biblical clue that humans are special is that only after they are fashioned does God call his creation "very good" (Gen. 1:31). Up to that point, he simply proclaimed it "good" (e.g., 1:9, 12, 18). This intensification of God's proclamation suggests that humans are the zenith of the six days of creation. Making huge balls of burning gas is one thing; crafting a creature that reflects the image of its Maker is quite another. Such a magnum opus deserves a superlative descriptor.

Another clue that humans are special is found in the intimate way God made them. "Then the LORD God formed a man from the dust of the ground and breathed into his nostrils the breath of life, and the man became a living being" (2:7). We know that afterward God formed a woman from the man's rib. In both instances, there is a closeness in the description, as if God used his own hands when he made humans into a wondrous work of art. The psalmist claims that God knit him together in his mother's womb and created his inmost being (Ps. 139:13). The language is special.

A third indicator that humans are unique is how they are described.

> Then God said, "Let us make mankind in our image, in our like-
> ness, so that they may rule over the fish in the seas and the birds in

---

[8] Collins, *The Language of God*, 191.
[9] Glover, *Beyond the Firmament*, 205.

the sky, over the livestock and all the wild animals, and over all the creatures that move along the ground." So God created mankind in his own image, in the image of God he created them; male and female he created them. (Gen. 1:26–27)

What does it mean to be made in God's image? While Christian scholars over the centuries have debated the details, the *imago Dei* appears to consist of the following attributes:

· *Spiritual Traits*: Humans have a soul capable of spiritually communing and relating with God, who is spirit.
· *Moral Traits*: As God in his holiness has a moral nature, humans possess a conscience capable of moral choices.
· *Rational and Emotional Traits*: Humans are creative, emotional beings adept at rational thought and discourse.
· *Relational Traits*: God exists in an eternal relatedness in the Trinity, and humans can relate both with God and with others bearing his image.
· *Volitional Traits*: Humans exercise their will, with moral and spiritual consequences.
· *Rulership Traits*: God gave humans dominion over the creation.[10]

This chapter lays the foundation for the arguments used in the remainder of the book, especially as the image of God impinges on the way we live.

Clash of Worldviews

Sociobiologists like Edward Wilson recognize that conflict exists between the moral underpinnings of religion and those of secular (atheistic) science. Wilson believes that evolutionary biology will eventually clarify all human life and behavior, thus eliminating religious explanations. He notes, "If religion, including the dogmatic secular ideologies, can be systematically analyzed and explained as a product of the

---

[10] I deal with how through Christ the fallen image is renewed in chapter 12 of *The Language of Salvation: Discovering the Riches of What It Means to Be Saved* (Bellingham, WA: Lexham Press, 2018).

brain's evolution, its power as an external source of morality will be gone forever."[11]

Similarly, evolutionary philosopher Michael Ruse believes that "morality is a collective illusion foisted upon us by our genes."[12] We can see the problem this presents to a Christian understanding of ethics. This is why I spent four chapters on science and its implications. Unless science is put in its proper place, in service to theology, Christian morality will go the way of the dodo bird. An evolutionary framework, where death is the key mechanism, can never be life affirming. Biblically speaking, death is a curse to be overcome, not something we encourage and affirm, or use as a means of cure or escape.

Whenever we allow Darwinian thinking to filter into our biblical interpretation, we move from humans as the acme of God's creative activity to being accidental by-products at the end of a meandering evolutionary process that took billions of years. Evolutionary thinking encourages the demotion of humanity and with it the promotion of a variety of social ills that corrupt and destroy God's masterpiece.[13] All approaches to ethics that ignore the *imago Dei* will fail. All value and values come from this; evil derives from a rejection of this image.

Darwin's "descent of man" has indeed resulted in our descent. Evolutionary theory devalues human life. In fact, it is inherently racist, portraying various "species" of humankind as more evolved than others. It is easier to slaughter humans when they are depicted as nothing more than advanced animals. Evolutionary theory is not just bad science, it is very dangerous science.

Only the biblical worldview balances a healthy view of God with a healthy view of humanity. The foundational, biblical truth of *imago Dei* must inform our respect for human life, race relations that dog us in our clashing cultures, and a personal Christian ethic that calls us to love our neighbor. Abortion and euthanasia are two obvious examples of sanctity of life issues, but we ought not forget related matters like stem cell procurement, fertility procedures that result in embryo

---

[11] Quoted in Barbour, *When Science Meets Religion*, 124.

[12] Ibid.

[13] "There is no way to describe how offensive the idea is to mainstream evolutionists that we humans are 'special' in the eyes of God—separate and distinct from all animals" (Lubenow, *Bones of Contention*, 185).

destruction, and genetic research that may eventually yield human cloning.

God became a human being, not a turtle or a chimpanzee, in order to bring salvation to his image bearers. Yet, humanity has consistently found a way to butcher and maim the pinnacle of God's creation.

Another Holocaust

One in three American women will have an abortion. Annually, one-fifth of all pregnancies end in abortion. Nearly sixty million Americans have been aborted since the procedure was legalized, and even though the annual numbers are falling, in 2011, the most recent year statistics are available, just under 1.1 million abortions were performed in the United States, or a little more than two abortions every minute. These statistics are well known.

The pro-choice Guttmacher Institute employs about one hundred people to produce its detailed statistics on domestic and international abortions. They state that half of American women who have an abortion have already had one or more previously, and that 59% of American women who have an abortion already have at least one child.[14]

The numbers are staggering. Since legalizing abortion, the United States has aborted the entire population of South Africa. Can you imagine waking up one morning to news reports that everybody in South Africa died? What effect would that have on our corporate human psyche?

Over a 5-year period during the Iraq War under George W. Bush, 4,000 American soldiers lost their lives. We were told this was a tragedy comparable to the Vietnam War. Yet in that same 5-year period, we exterminated 6 million American lives through abortion. Those are Holocaust levels. While two American soldiers were killed in Iraq every day, back home we were aborting 3,287 babies every 24 hours. In two days we killed more American lives in American hospitals and clinics than were killed by enemy combatants during 60 months. If this were done in any other context, the outcry would be severe and unremitting.

---

[14] Guttmacher Institute, "Induced Abortion in the United States," September 2016 Factsheet, https://www.guttmacher.org/fact-sheet/induced-abortion-united-states#3, accessed October 29, 2016.

When we add abortions worldwide, the dead bodies pile up.[15] A May 2016 BBC report pegs the number at 56 million annually.[16] Since 1960 somewhere between 1.6 and 2 billion (that's with a "b"!) abortions have taken place. The past half century has been a death camp where Auschwitz is a small blip on the landscape. In the words of Pope John Paul II, we truly have created a "culture of death." We are not as moved as when we see mass executions on a Nazi scale because with abortion it is done quietly, one baby at a time, in the privacy of a women's "health" facility. In the heart of every abortion advocate exists an Auschwitz.

Abortion is cloaked in the language of personal rights and women's safety, but it is nothing less than the brutal, barbaric butchering of nascent human life. The sanctuary that is the woman's womb has become the political ground on which radical feminists push their agenda. "Abortion on demand," at any time and for any reason (or no reason at all), is what feminists mandate as a right. Anything short of this goal is not good enough.

Everybody knows what happens in an abortion. The child is either burned to death with a saline solution, or chopped up piece by piece, or suctioned out like one might vacuum unwanted lint from the carpet. A beating heart is terminated for the sake of convenience. Human life is evacuated and thrown in the trash. And God is not pleased:

> There are six things the LORD hates, seven that are detestable to him: haughty eyes, a lying tongue, hands that shed innocent blood. (Prov. 6:16–17)

Pro-life proponents are regularly castigated for showing "tasteless" graphic images of what is involved in an abortion, but why? If the procedure is perfectly acceptable, how can images from the procedure be less than acceptable?

Abortion supporters feed on the nebulous notion that what is in the womb is not a human being. However, put arms and legs and a beating

---

[15] Because of China's "one child" policy, 330 million lives have been aborted, a little more than the entire population of the United States (Simon Rabinovitch, "Data Reveal Scale of China Abortions," *Financial Times*, www.ft.com/cms/s/2/6724580a-8d64-11e2-82d2-00144feabdc0.html#axzz43Y9QAo8u, accessed June 1, 2016).

[16] Smitha Mundasad, "Abortion Study: 25% of Pregnancies Terminated, Estimates Suggest," BBC News, www.bbc.com/news/health-36266873, accessed June 1, 2016.

heart on that image, and this sly notion is immediately exposed for the lie that it is. Abortion kills a human being. No amount of Orwellian Newspeak is going to change that fact.

The Womb Is under Attack

I read about an actress who appeared on a late-night talk show seven months pregnant, aglow with that prenatal look and showing off her "baby bump." The article spoke about how wonderfully she was "holding her fetus" in a picture. Holding her fetus? What normal person says something like this about a pregnant woman? "I hope your little zygote is healthy." "Have you decided on a name for your embryo?" No one talks this way because everybody knows that a pregnant woman is carrying a baby. Human life. Not undifferentiated cells. Not a parasite or lump of flesh, as some in the pro-abortion camp are wont to categorize things.

The author of the article was making a political point when she referred to the baby as a fetus. It is another attempt to desensitize us to the truth: pregnant women, no matter what stage of their pregnancy, carry human life.

There has been a steady, unrelenting attack on women in our world the past half century, which is rather ironic. If you compare the state of women from the 1950s to today, you would think that women have, in the words of that famous cigarette ad, "come a long way, baby." Women's rights have been a consistent social theme in the Western world since my childhood when the Equal Rights Amendment movement was in full force, to today where women lead nations.

Nevertheless, in this steady stream of women's rights has come an onslaught on women as created by God.[17] It is a feminist assault on a woman's womb and with it her femaleness: an attack on women as women by women. Abortion advocates typically use the following arguments (after which my comments follow):

1. A woman has a right to privacy and can do what she wants with her body.

---

[17] In countries like China where male children are preferred, abortion disproportionately kills female babies.

2. Women's health is at issue, and without the availability of safe, legal abortions, women will resort to dangerous self-induced abortions or "back alley" clinics.
3. The fetus is not a person.
4. It is preferable to abort because the quality of life for the child and mother will be pitiable, especially if the baby has a genetic defect or is born into squalor.

1. A Woman's Right to Privacy

The pro-choice camp has done well framing abortion as a women's rights issue, but this position can hardly withstand close scrutiny. If a woman has the right to do with her body as she desires, then prostitution and drug usage should also be legal for her. If the woman can terminate the human life in her womb (and even the father of the child is not allowed a say), she should be free to sell her body for sex. Once a woman's right to abortion on demand is granted, I cannot see any reason why the state could prohibit a woman from doing anything else with her body. Why demonize a woman who drinks alcohol or smokes during pregnancy, while claiming she has the right to do whatever she wants with her body?

Despite the success of the women's rights angle, feminists like U.S. Supreme Court justice Ruth Bader Ginsburg recognize that the privacy right is not constitutionally solid. She argues for abortion from the right to gender equality.[18] Prohibitions against abortion are unconstitutional, on the basis that legislation cannot single out one gender. The radical nature of the feminist agenda wipes out any and all distinctions between the genders.

Pro-life advocates retort that any rights the mother may have to privacy or equality pale in comparison to the right the unborn child has to life. This is a powerful argument. Killing a human being is clearly worse than the temporary inconvenience of carrying a baby to term.

---

[18] "Equality and Abortion Rights," University of Chicago Law School Faculty Blog, http://uchicagolaw.typepad.com/faculty/2007/04/equality_and_ab.html, accessed May 17, 2016.

2. Women's Health

One emotional argument used by abortion advocates is that if abortion is illegal, women will find a way to do it anyway, putting themselves in grave danger of permanent injury. Granted, I can well imagine the desperation that floods over a young girl who contemplates a back alley solution to her problem. The health risks are enormous, but I cannot be swayed by "they'll do it anyway so we might as well legalize it." This reasoning can be used to justify virtually anything.

There are a lot of situations that are uncomfortable and inconvenient in life, but when attempting to avoid them constitutes illegality, there is no excuse. My difficult financial struggles do not entitle me to rob my neighbor to make ends meet. My traumatic life experiences do not sanction my drug or alcohol abuse. The ends can never justify the means if one or both are sinful.

A prime example of this play on emotions comes from the abortion-rights advocacy documentary *Trapped* (a play on words for so-called Targeted Regulation of Abortion Providers [TRAP] laws), which won the Sundance Film Festival's "Special Jury Prize" for documentaries in 2016.[19] In the film, a thirteen-year-old rape victim is told she will not be able to get an abortion in her state. A clinic worker sarcastically notes that the teen will be "sentenced to motherhood." This is a telling portrayal of the attitude many abortion supporters have concerning motherhood and child bearing. I am struck by how cold-hearted the feminist position is. Pregnancy is seen more as a disease or illness in their worldview, not the joyous, life-giving, life-affirming gift from our Creator.

While the right to abortion is touted by pro-choice supporters as a necessary protection for women, right-to-life adherents note that many women suffer incredible emotional harm from the procedure. Far from positive, abortion has very negative effects.

This emotional harm argument has been consistently assailed by abortion supporters. For example, a recent study done by the University of California, San Francisco School of Medicine showed that an overwhelming number of women who have had an abortion in the United States

---

[19] Internet Movie Data Base, www.imdb.com/title/tt5259692/?ref_=fn_al_tt_3, accessed May 5, 2016.

do not regret it. Of the six hundred women interviewed over a three-year period, more than 95% of them had no remorse.[20]

In the abortion case that came before the U.S. Supreme Court in early 2016, dozens of women filed briefs with the Court to give testimony of how abortion was good for them.[21] An article on Mashable.com, "I Am Sick of Being Silenced," highlights fourteen women who are proud they aborted, and movements like #shoutyourabortion aim to help women overcome the shame of getting an abortion.[22]

We must not miss how the pro-abortion propaganda machine spins statistics such as the ones reported above. For example, a 2011 Danish study of more than 350,000 women found that "having an abortion does not increase the risk of mental health problems, but having a baby does."[23] However, a closer look at the statistics tells a different story. Fifteen per 1000 women sought psychiatric help before they had an abortion, and a similar proportion did afterward, but whereas only 4 per 1,000 women sought psychiatric counseling before giving birth, 7 per 1,000 did afterward. Thus, the study concludes that giving birth is more harmful to a woman's mental health than having an abortion.

However, over twice as many women who had an abortion sought counseling than those who gave birth. The *USA Today* article reporting the findings of the study could have just as easily been titled, "Women who have abortions twice as likely to seek psychiatric treatment than women who give birth." But if the reader does not dig into the actual statistics, the title of the article makes it appear that getting an abortion is a rather benign activity.

Even more troubling is what is entirely missed in the findings. It appears that women who have abortions are more mentally unstable than women

---

[20] Maria Caspani, "Overwhelming Majority of U.S. Women Don't Regret Abortion: Study," Yahoo! News, http://news.yahoo.com/overwhelming-majority-u-women-dont-regret-abortion-study-141323478.html., accessed April 28, 2016.

[21] Adam Liptak, "Eyes on Kennedy, Women Tell Supreme Court Why Abortion Was Right for Them," *The New York Times*, www.nytimes.com/2016/03/01/us/politics/abortion-supreme-court-women-explain-choices.html?_r=2, accessed May 28, 2016.

[22] Rebecca Ruiz, "'I Am Sick of Being Silenced': 14 Women Share Their Abortion Stories," Mashable.com, http://mashable.com/2016/03/06/abortion-stigma-women-stories/#gTJv3WcZ3gqF, accessed May 27, 2016.

[23] *USA Today*, "Study: No Higher Mental Health Risk after Abortion," http://usatoday30.usatoday.com/yourlife/health/medical/mentalhealth/2011-01-26-mental-health-abortion_N.htm, accessed October 29, 2016.

who give birth. The article notes that women who get abortions have problems with "debilitating anxiety, severe stress and depression," but how often is this reported in the media? On the other hand, women who give birth have increased stress associated with "changes in hormone levels, sleep deprivation and other demands associated with having a baby." The article then wryly notes, "By contrast, women who have an abortion don't experience similar changes." Of course they don't! They killed the baby. Thus the researcher who led the Danish study can say, "A woman should know that her risk of having a psychiatric episode is not increased." This is the cold-hearted message daily broadcast by abortion advocates as they parse words and splice statistics.

Conservatives often push for mandatory ultrasounds before women have an abortion, hoping they will change their minds once they see the sonograms. While this occasionally helps, the majority of American women having abortions already have children, and half have already had at least one abortion. They already know what their wombs produce. We can hardly expect regret from women who have made the trip to the abortion clinic multiple times already.[24] These statistics tell us that getting an abortion is not so much a matter of convenience as it is a heart issue. A sinful heart is the problem, for which the only cure is the gospel.

3. The Fetus Is Not a "Person"

Abortion advocates claim that the unborn child is not a "person." For instance, the authors of a *Journal of Medical Ethics* article argue that both the unborn and the newborn are "potential persons." Therefore, it is acceptable to kill a newborn infant if it survives an abortion attempt or suffers a serious abnormality during delivery. The authors oxymoronically call this "after-birth abortion," claiming it is not properly deemed "infanticide."[25]

---

[24] According to this study, more than 98% of women who viewed an ultrasound still terminated their pregnancy: "Relationship between Ultrasound Viewing and Proceeding to Abortion," *Obstetrics and Gynecology,* http://journals.lww.com/greenjournal/Abstract/2014/01000/Relationship_Between_Ultrasound_Viewing_and.13.aspx, accessed May 29, 2016.

[25] Alberto Giubilini and Francesca Minerva, "After-Birth Abortion: Why Should the Baby Live?" http://jme.bmj.com/content/early/2012/03/01/medethics-2011-100411.full, accessed May 28, 2016.

They further argue that because the rights of actual persons supersede any supposed rights of potential persons, adoption is unwarranted. The mother may "suffer psychological distress from giving her child up." This is shocking reasoning. Killing a newborn is quite acceptable, but putting it up for adoption is too traumatic.

The unborn are not "potentially human." There are no degrees of "humanness," and believing in such opens the door to unbridled racism of the worst kind. Life begins at conception, and any abortion after that point terminates human life. It is difficult to assail this consistent position, which if not embraced forces a person to create an arbitrary point for when the fetus is deemed a "human person." This may be when the fetus feels pain, or when it reaches "viability" and can survive outside the womb. This is why abortion advocates choose their words carefully when discussing abortion. They prefer "terminate a pregnancy," not "abort a child."[26]

Yet organizations like Planned Parenthood, the largest abortion provider in the United States, still recognize the value of human body parts. Abortion is their business, and 92% of pregnant women who go to Planned Parenthood abort their babies.[27] They claim the fetus is not a person, but they are all too willing to make a buck selling fetal parts used in research for degenerative neurological diseases, brain tumors, and spinal cord injuries—in human beings. If a *part* of the being is deemed human, certainly the whole being must be too.

Many states have instituted abortion restrictions based on how far along the pregnancy is because after a certain point the baby feels pain. Not surprisingly, abortion advocates reject these arguments.[28] The pain

---

[26] Hillary Clinton, an ardent supporter of abortion rights, mistakenly called the product of the womb a "person" and a "child" during the presidential primaries. She was castigated by Planned Parenthood for the snafu, despite its earlier endorsement of her campaign (Alan Rappeport, "Hillary Clinton Roundly Criticized for Referring to the Unborn as a 'Person,'" *The New York Times*, www.nytimes.com/politics/first-draft/2016/04/04/hillary-clinton-roundly-criticized-for-referring-to-the-unborn-as-a-person/, accessed April 16, 2016).

[27] Planned Parenthood has aborted more than seven million American lives since 1970. Mercedes Schlapp, "Raise the Curtain on Planned Parenthood," *US News*, www.usnews.com/opinion/mercedes-schlapp/2015/10/02/dont-let-planned-parenthood-hide-behind-womens-health-curtain, accessed April 16, 2016.

[28] This article attempts to debunk the notion that a twenty-week-old fetus feels pain:

argument has particularly been key, though, in laws restricting "partial birth" abortions.

Can there be anything more despicable than partial birth abortions? A human life, as yet unsullied by the world and its depravity, rests peacefully in the sanctuary of its mother's womb. Little does it know that its safety is at odds with the "reproductive rights" touted by the "right to choose" camp who would, if given the chance, drag this child prematurely out by its legs until it is 80% out of the womb, and then drive a medical instrument into the base of its skull to evacuate its brain. Radical feminists and those on the political left have vehemently opposed restrictions even on this barbaric procedure.

4. Poor Quality of Life

Some Christians who oppose abortion on demand allow for abortion in special cases. These are (a) when the mother's life is in jeopardy; (b) if the quality of life of the baby will be greatly compromised, like in the instance of severe handicaps; and (c) when the woman is pregnant as a result of rape or incest.

For the first situation, we must choose between the mother's and the baby's life. For example, with a tubal pregnancy there is no chance that the fetus will develop in the fallopian tube. However, given enough time it will kill the mother. In such cases, most evangelicals rightly believe that abortion is justified.

On quality of life, abortion advocates contend that it is morally unacceptable to bring an unwanted child into the world who will most likely be unloved and abused. In this case, abortion is the compassionate thing to do. But who determines "quality of life"? This argument requires prescience to be valid. There are plenty of people born into poor environments who have become valuable contributors to society. Nobody has a crystal ball.

Also, if it can be argued that abortion is necessary because of the *potential* the child will have for poor quality of life, then we might as well terminate someone who *actually is* enduring a poor quality of life.

David Levitan, "Does a Fetus Feel Pain at 20 Weeks?" FactCheck.Org, www.factcheck.org/2015/05/does-a-fetus-feel-pain-at-20-weeks/, accessed June 15, 2016.

The compassionate reaction is not death, and who better to know than people who have survived failed abortions? According to The Abortion Survivors Network, there are currently 44,000 people in America who have survived an abortion attempt.[29] Such realities get little press, but their stories are inspiring.

A progressive political agenda in America that began in the early decades of the twentieth century is flourishing today as our country moves farther away from its Judeo-Christian roots. This agenda was thriving in America in the eugenics movement even as Adolf Hitler was making similar arguments in Nazi Germany. Margaret Sanger, the founder of Planned Parenthood, advocated nearly a century ago for the elimination of "unfit" people in our society, and the organization she founded is still doing so today.[30]

Do we want a society that safeguards and affirms the handicapped, the infirm, and the disadvantaged? Or do we want a culture that eliminates them? Granted, pregnancies do not always occur in affirming environments. Some come from abuse and rape. Still, can we proclaim that our society is better now that human life is so much chaff to be discarded whenever we feel like it?

Speaking of quality of life, not only is abortion a black spot on the collective soul of America, but it has yielded unforeseen negative consequences as well. The predicted bankruptcy of Social Security has resulted in part from carving out millions of lives from a segment of society that was meant to pay into the system's coffers. At least ten million of those abortees would be in their prime earning years today.

Lastly, in the instances of rape and incest, I do not want to downplay this horrible situation. Whether a young girl falls pregnant due to promiscuity or by force, the church must respond compassionately. Yet, we can never compromise on what are biblical truths, and taking the life of the unborn child, even in a situation as heinous as rape, cannot be justified.

Less than 1% of aborted pregnancies are from rape and incest.[31] These

---

[29] www.theabortionsurvivors.com/index.html, accessed June 17, 2016.

[30] Read Sanger's *The Pivot of Civilization* (Lenox, MA: Hard Press, 2006; originally published in 1922) for chilling suggestions on how to weed out the "feeble-minded" in our society.

[31] According to the Guttmacher Institute, 0.4% of abortions are for girls age fourteen and under, and less than 1% occur due to rape and incest.

examples are frequently exploited by abortionists to emotionally sway the argument, and then smuggled in for the ride are the rest of the abortions. However, the vast majority of abortions are for nothing more than convenience and cannot be justified.

The Church's Response

Some of my overseas Christian friends are shocked that abortion is used as a litmus test for American political candidates. Evidently their political systems are much more enlightened than our own since the issue rarely comes up. My reply is a simple one: how can any Christian not object to this practice?

If Jesus was willing to internalize murder, saying that hatred is subject to God's judgment (Matt. 5:22), what would he say about the termination of human life in the womb? When hatred harbored in the heart can receive harsh treatment from our Lord, how much more will the tearing apart of a human baby? If the standard of judgment according to Jesus is that "every careless word" (Matt. 12:36 ESV) will be judged, would he not condemn the intentional intervention into the womb in order to terminate human life?

One clue to understanding how Jesus would have thought about the issue is to look at the Old Testament Law. While there is little dealing with unborn life, there is something on which to build a case.

A law in Exodus 21:22–25 deals with men who inadvertently harm a pregnant woman while fighting. If the woman gives birth prematurely but the baby is uninjured, then a fine is imposed on the men. However, if the baby is killed during the fight, then the law of retaliation (*lex talionis*) is invoked: "Life for life, eye for eye, tooth for tooth." This is the only case in the Mosaic Law where the death penalty is prescribed for an accidental death. This indicates that God cares deeply about unborn life and the women carrying it.

In the Mosaic Law, God's people were commanded to care for the downtrodden and less fortunate because God, who "shows no partiality[,] . . . defends the cause of the fatherless and the widow, and loves the foreigner residing among you, giving them food and clothing" (Deut. 10:17–18). This is why Proverbs says, "Speak up for those who cannot speak for themselves, for the rights of all who are destitute. Speak up and judge fairly; defend the rights of the poor and needy" (31:8–9).

Later, when Israel turned its back on God's covenant, the Lord chastised the people: "Your hands are full of blood! Wash and make yourselves clean. Take your evil deeds out of my sight; stop doing wrong. Learn to do right; seek justice. Defend the oppressed. Take up the cause of the fatherless; plead the case of the widow" (Isa. 1:15b–17). What segment of our society comes close to the defenseless unborn?

The church's first reaction to this issue should be preventative. Christians must teach celibacy before marriage. Abstain from action the consequences of which you cannot endure. If you are not willing to bear a child, don't be involved in activities that will produce one.

This approach butts up against our culture's preoccupation with the right to sexual freedom. A large segment of our society is aghast whenever it is suggested that people forgo sex. We will see this in more detail in chapters 8 and 9.

Still, encouraging abstinence will not solve all the problems. People do not heed sound advice and unwanted pregnancies result. The church's response to unwanted pregnancies is tricky. On the one hand is the pre-teen girl who cannot bear the thought of giving birth to her rapist's child. On the other hand is the rabid feminist who will go to any lengths to win approval for women to abort at any time and for any reason. For any believer who publicly declares abortion evil, keep in mind there may be women in your audience who have had an abortion and are overcome with guilt. The church must navigate this moral problem with great care.

During a Saturday morning ethics seminar I taught, several social workers attended who were from a Cape Town clinic. One woman was particularly vocal against my position on abortion. She snorted, "I have seen twelve- and thirteen-year-old pregnant girls who could not possibly bear the responsibilities of a child. Are you saying they should be forced to give birth?" She was indignant.

Please understand me. I feel my emotional heartstrings pulled by such cases. I cannot imagine how devastating it is to have a perverted uncle take advantage of you. I do not minimize the difficulty that is faced with this decision, and any Christian response needs the truth spoken in love. However, killing the unborn child is a short-sighted solution.

A fellow member of the church we attended in Namibia had a teenage daughter become pregnant when she was seduced by her older cousin. The shame was tremendous, and the problems were similar to the social work-er's objections. "Will my daughter have to drop out of high school? Who is going to look after the child? Can our family bear this shame?"

My counsel to the teenager's mother was simple: "While this is a devas-tating experience now, there will come a time when you cannot imagine life without your grandchild." Her daughter eventually gave birth to a beau-tiful girl and, as predicted, neither the mother nor the grandmother can imagine life without her.

One typical evangelical answer to abortion is to implore the mother to put her child up for adoption, but adoptions in the United States are at their lowest in decades. According to the U.S. Department of Health and Human Services, roughly 400,000 children are in foster care. And about one-fourth of those are awaiting adoption, but in the most recent year sta-tistics were available, only 12% were adopted.[32]

Critics of evangelicals have flippantly exclaimed, "If you don't want babies aborted, then why aren't you adopting the ones available?" There is some validity to this accusation. It seems hypocritical of Christians to decry abortion but do nothing for unwanted children in our society. More emphasis in our churches on adoption is warranted.

However, Christians *are* doing something about unwanted pregnancies, but it gets little press. Crisis pregnancy centers outnumber abortion clinics throughout the United States by five to one.[33] This is a grassroots move-ment that has generally kept the public's opinion about abortion surpris-ingly leaning toward the pro-life side.

The right to life movement also pushes heavily on the legislative side by curbing access to abortions. Since 2011, thirty states have enacted nearly three hundred laws limiting abortion.[34] Restrictions include reducing the

---

[32] U.S. Department of Health and Human Services, "The AFCARS Report," no. 22, July 2015, www.acf.hhs.gov/sites/default/files/cb/afcarsreport22.pdf, accessed June 2, 2016. For comparison, this report catalogues adoption rates in the United States for 2007 and 2008, which were incredibly higher than those of today.

[33] Warren Richey, "Inside the 'Pro-Life' Answer to Abortion Clinics," *The Christian Science Monitor*, www.csmonitor.com/USA/Justice/2016/0229/Inside-the-pro-life-answer-to-abortion-clinics, accessed June 2, 2016.

[34] Patrik Jonsson, "Plunging Numbers of Texas Abortions: Are Clinic Closings be-hind Decline?" *The Christian Science Monitor*, www.csmonitor.com/USA/2016/0319/Plunging-numbers-of-Texas-abortions-Are-clinic-closings-behind-decline, accessed June 2, 2016.

number of abortion clinics, requiring sonograms that occasionally persuade women to not abort, and reducing government funding.

These are positive steps to protect unborn life, but they deal with the symptoms, not the source. The problem is not simply pragmatic, it is spiritual. Hence, despite the laws and programs that conservatives create, the best way to combat a woman's desire to terminate the life of her unborn child is by changing her heart. She must, as must we all, be transformed into the image of Christ, who cares for the downtrodden and abused.

For the remainder of this chapter, we will briefly cover some related "life-and-death" issues.

Capital Punishment

Evangelicals appear inconsistent on the issue of capital punishment. If the argument against abortion is that we should not take human life because we are made in God's image, then how can a conservative Christian support capital punishment?

The Catholic Church maintains that it is always wrong to take human life. Even the Vatican's ban on birth control has this assumption at its root. Therefore, the Catholic Church equally opposes abortion, euthanasia, and capital punishment.

The problem with this position is that "Thou shalt not kill" is not an inviolable rule. In the same Mosaic Law that prohibits the taking of human life, capital punishment and warfare are prescribed by God (e.g., Lev. 24:21). The Law codified what God had said centuries earlier to Noah after the flood: "And from each human being, too, I will demand an accounting for the life of another human being. 'Whoever sheds human blood, by humans shall their blood be shed; for in the image of God has God made mankind'" (Gen. 9:5b–6). Even animals that take human life must be put to death. Because we are made in God's image, it is an offense against God whenever we violently take human life.

While it appears contradictory that the punishment for taking human life is to take human life, it makes perfectly good sense. If a person has chosen to wantonly take another's life, that person is unfit for human society. This is the most compelling reason for capital punishment, to preserve society from heinous crimes.

There is both good and bad when it comes to the lengthy legal process that accompanies the death penalty in America. Because it can take decades before a person is actually put to death, the natural deterrent that comes with capital punishment is greatly reduced. On the flipside, no legal system is perfect. There have been cases where a person given the death penalty was later found innocent and "saved" by the protracted process.

If there is a guarantee that a life sentence means being in prison the rest of your life, and that reasonable safeguards are in place so the criminal cannot harm others, then I won't push for the death penalty. Nevertheless, I reject the opinion that capital punishment is beneath our first-world sensibilities. There is biblical justification for it as well as practical benefits for society.

Euthanasia

The word "euthanasia" comes from the Greek for "good death." Many arguments used in support of abortion are employed for euthanasia, including quality of life and what defines personhood. However, the issue that trumps them all is dignity. What would you prefer: dying a slow, painful death where your mental acuity disappears and you are left a drooling individual, or to die quickly in the dignified way you have predetermined? I have a hunch the vast majority of people would choose the latter.

This makes euthanasia a thorny issue. I recall the controversy in the 1990s surrounding "Dr. Death." Dr. Jack Kervorkian assisted dozens of people in taking their own lives as he championed a patient's right to physician-assisted suicide. Eventually imprisoned for second-degree murder, he served eight years before being released on parole. Since then, several states have legalized physician-assisted suicide, including Washington, Oregon, Vermont, and California.[35]

In my estimation, euthanasia is a more difficult issue than abortion. With abortion, you are snuffing out human life in its nascent stage—and quite often for no other reason than convenience—while with euthanasia you are taking a life that is usually near its end, regularly accompanied with great pain and suffering. Is euthanasia not the merciful thing to do in these instances?

---

[35] Five European countries have legalized it (Winston Ross, "Dying Dutch: Euthanasia Spreads across Europe," *Newsweek*, http://europe.newsweek.com/choosing-die-netherlands-euthanasia-debate-306223?rm=eu, accessed May 29, 2016).

Here are some key terms to help us navigate this complex issue:

1. *Voluntary versus involuntary*: Voluntary euthanasia occurs when the person requests it; involuntary euthanasia happens when the person is put to death without requesting it or granting permission.
2. *Active versus passive*: Active euthanasia involves purposefully taking a life; passive euthanasia is the withholding or refusing of treatment necessary to sustain life.
3. *Direct versus indirect*: When the individuals themselves carry out the act it is direct euthanasia (suicide), whereas if someone else does it, it is indirect.
4. *Ordinary versus extraordinary means*: This refers to how a person is kept alive. Ordinary means are air, food, and water, while extraordinary means involve being hooked up to a machine that does the breathing for you.

Many Christians support voluntary, passive, indirect euthanasia when the means are extraordinary. In other words, the person is allowed to die an "ordinary" death. Things, though, are rarely this neat and tidy. What if a perfectly healthy person wants to end his life due to some emotional trauma?[36] It is one thing to unhook a person in a vegetative state from a life support machine, but quite another for someone to euthanize himself because his girlfriend just dumped him. For this reason, most Christians oppose euthanasia except in extreme circumstances.

At this point, there is no country in the first world that supports involuntary euthanasia. There is a fear, though, that when the state controls

---

[36] Deaf Belgian twins, age forty-five, who were slowly going blind, opted to be voluntarily euthanized in 2012 by lethal injection (*USA Today*, www.usatoday.com/story/news/world/2013/01/14/deaf-belgian-twins-going-blind-euthanized/1834199/, accessed September 6, 2016). According to the article, a spokesman for the Catholic Church stated, "It is troubling that doctors who swear an oath to do no harm are carrying out these procedures." Unfortunately, we may begin to see similar things in the United States. In Vermont, for example, many doctors are opposing a state law that appears to require them to tell their patients about euthanasia ("Doctors Push Back against Assisted Suicide," Patheos, www.patheos.com/blogs/geneveith/2016/08/doctors-push-back-against-assisted-suicide/?utm_source=feedburner&utm_medium=feed&utm_campaign=Feed%3A+geneveith+%28Cranach%3A+The+Blog+of+Veith%29, accessed September 6, 2016).

healthcare, the elderly will be eased into the next life for the better of soci-ety. What would you rather do given limited funding: spend the money to help Grandpa live six more months into his eighties, or help ten pri-mary school children with a curable illness? These are not easy questions to answer.[37] However, all people are made in God's image, regardless of race, color, gender, or age. There is no difference between taking unborn life or octogenarian life.

You may be thinking, "Okay, I get it. The state does not have the right to take people's lives against their will, but what I do with my own life is my business." But in the strictest sense, your life is not your own. We are made to glorify God. Once we ignore this, it becomes much easier to pre-tend that we can do with our lives as we see fit. Paul tells Christians, "You are not your own; you were bought with a price. Therefore honor God with your bodies" (1 Cor. 6:19b–20). As with abortion, the Christian response to euthanasia should be to preserve life.

Three years ago, a Christian friend of mine died from bone marrow can-cer. He was in excruciating pain. The cancer metastasized and his bones became so brittle that he broke his arm just trying to open a window. Yet, he consistently greeted people with a smile. In great agony he exuded joy. He died with dignity. This is the way Christians should die. Even in our death we should glorify God. In this sense, only Christians can have a "good death."

Related Medical Issues

Do you know who Louise Brown is? She was the first "test tube" baby, born in 1978. Since then, in vitro fertilization (IVF) has become common-place and is used in the conception of 1% to 2% of babies in the Western world. With IVF comes "embryo wastage." This is when multiple eggs are

---

[37] Five percent of Medicaid beneficiaries account for almost half of program spend-ing (Peter Sullivan, "5 Percent of Medicaid Patients Account for Half the Program's Costs," The Hill, http://thehill.com/policy/healthcare/241491-5-percent-of-medicaid-patients-account-for-50-percent-of-costs, accessed January 16, 2016) while half the population uses 3.1% of the money (Jeffrey Young, "The Top One Percent of Patients Ac-count for More Than 25% of Health Insurance Costs," The Huffington Post, www.huffing-tonpost.com/2012/02/28/health-insurance-costs_n_1306862.html, accessed June 22, 2016). These disparities tempt some to support euthanizing the most costly patients.

fertilized, they begin to develop in the lab, and then a few are chosen for implantation. The rest of the embryos are cryogenically frozen, donated for research, or discarded. This presents a moral dilemma for Christians, who believe life begins at conception. While in the natural practice of intercourse embryos can be discarded (miscarriages), this does not warrant their voluntary creation and destruction.

Similarly, intrauterine devices (IUDs) that prevent a fertilized egg from implanting in the womb are also unethical. However, most IUDs prevent the egg from being fertilized so no human is created and discarded.

Lastly, if we do get to that "brave new world" of cloning humans to harvest their body parts, may God have mercy on us. I have no objection to artificially generating body organs for transplants, but any life conceived by natural or artificial means creates a person with a soul, a human being made in God's image. It is as morally objectionable to clone humans for research or consumption as it would be to take living individuals and kill them for their organs.

While these life-and-death issues can cause us considerable angst, the Christian response must be life affirming. We are made in God's image and with that come responsibilities both to ourselves and to the creation around us. It is to this topic that we now turn.

CHAPTER SIX

God's Created Order
and the Environment

> We, in the Green movement, aspire to a cultural model in which the killingofaforestwillbeconsideredmorecontemptibleandmorecriminalthan the sale of 6-year-old children to Asian brothels.
>
> —CARL AMERY[1]

PERHAPS LIKE ME, YOU see the news reports about the climate changing. You hear Hollywood stars and musicians and politicians and diplomats say that the earth is heating up and if we don't act right away, hundreds of millions of people will perish. You read recent studies by top scientists from key think tanks and international committees all saying that humans are creating a global catastrophe. Yet something rings hollow about the whole enterprise.

Maybe you can't put your finger on why. Few of us sit in a position to test the scientific data being reported. If "experts" say the earth has heated up over the past century, who am I to disagree? Still, the fear-mongering and threats that go with this "science" cause me to hesitate. I feel like I am at a used car lot and the salesman is laying it on a bit too thick.

I ask my evangelical readers, is it just me, or is something afoot in the climate change hysteria that we daily face? Are you put off by the rhetoric from climate change advocates, such as their claims that the evidence is unequivocal and if anybody disagrees (they are called "deniers") with this incontestable science, they have a screw loose?

If you surf the net looking for information that global warming is a

---

[1] Carl Amery of the Green Party, quoted in Richard O'Leary, *Environmental Mafia: The Enemy Is Us* (New York: Algora Publishing, 2003), 13.

hoax, you will find loads of data. If you look for information that global warming is *the* social issue of our day, you will find loads of data too. Thus the problem. As a Christian and a lover of science who cares about our responsibilities as God's tenants on this planet, I want to weigh the evidence carefully and make sure I am not getting sold a rotten bill of goods.

Few of us own a weather satellite to verify the climatologists' statistics. Still, I can test the assumptions underlying the science of global warming much like I do when the scientific community tells me that we evolved from apelike creatures, or that the earth is 4.54 billion years old.

In this chapter we will take a look at the data reported by global warming alarmists and weigh that against what Scripture says about the planet God created. We need a level-headed, Christian approach to climate change that navigates between the hubris of "saving the planet" (and the consequent elevation of humanity to godlike status) and the complete disregard for God's creation that can potentially come with an evangelical perspective. We will then take a brief look at animal rights.

The Global Warming Argument Examined

Climate change alarmists argue that the earth is getting warmer primarily from human activity, which will result in more polar ice melting. In this sense, "global warming" and "climate change" mean the same thing, so I will use the terms synonymously. The earth is heating up, humans are to blame, and if we don't do something to stop it, the entire ecosystem will melt down.[2]

There are conflicting reports as to the extent of the warming, if it exists. We will consider the data, but I will grant that the earth has warmed up roughly 1°F (0.6°C) since the late 1800s. This is a typical claim by climate change advocates. However, I am more concerned with the reasons given for this increase, especially as they relate to anthropogenic (i.e., manmade) factors.

To set the stage, here is a comment by the American Geophysical Union:

---

[2] I find the term "climate change" nebulous and nondescript. Of course the climate is changing; it always changes. "Global warming" is more helpful. However, "climate change" is better for those arguing that humans are damaging the environment because no matter what happens to the climate, these alarmists can claim they are right.

The earth's climate is now clearly out of balance and is warming. Many components of the climate system—including the temperatures of the atmosphere, land and ocean, the extent of sea ice and mountain glaciers, the sea level, the distribution of precipitation, and the length of seasons—are now changing at rates and in patterns that are not natural and are best explained by the increased atmospheric abundances of greenhouse gases and aerosols generated by human activity during the twentieth century.[3]

We will look at the science behind four key arguments in the climate change position. I have drafted the following synopsis to get us started.

There are too many humans on the planet producing dangerous levels of greenhouse gases, increasing the earth's temperature to the point where melting glaciers and polar ice will cause the seas to rise to catastrophic levels. The best way to combat these problems is to regulate human behavior on a global scale and institute means to dramatically decrease population growth rates.

(1) *Human Population Explosion*: The earth's population is growing at such a rate that we will not be able to produce enough resources to sustain it.

In his 1968 book *The Population Bomb*, Paul Ehrlich proposes vast distribution of contraception, forced sterilization, abortion on demand, and withholding food aid to countries that cannot sustain themselves, until their population reaches an acceptable equilibrium. This is necessary to keep at bay runaway world population growth that will result in resource depletion and environmental degradation. The effect of Ehrlich's book on a generation already raised to believe that the earth is in jeopardy from catastrophes like massive asteroids, nuclear holocaust, and even alien invasions cannot be overestimated.[4]

---

[3] Union of Concerned Scientists, www.ucsusa.org/global_warming/science_and_impacts/science/scientific-consensus-on.html#.V3FC5o0VgkI, accessed March 14, 2016. I must admit, I get a chuckle out of the notion that whatever the earth does is not "natural."

[4] Ehrlich built on arguments going back hundreds of years, most notably those by Thomas Malthus in the late eighteenth century. Thus, arguments for population control are often called Malthusian. How a man living in the 1700s could have known the

A more recent report by the Worldwatch Institute pegs the optimal global population for sustainability at around two to three billion.[5] Only a "colossal reduction" in population will save the earth. I shudder at the thought of how they propose we get the population down to that figure.

Is it any wonder that anti-human rhetoric from fanatical environmentalists is commonplace? Here's an example of this bombast: "Until such time as Homo Sapiens should decide to rejoin nature, some of us can only hope for the right virus to come along."[6] Or consider the musings of British naturalist Sir David Attenborough: "If we [humans] disappeared overnight, the world would probably be better off."[7]

At times, fanatical environmentalists make it sound like humans are just so many cockroaches crawling around the surface of the planet, and squashing them is the best way to save Mother Earth. Every cold front, heat wave, change in sea level, blustering hurricane, torrential monsoon, drought, or blizzard is our fault.

However, after a half century of hearing that the earth is over-populated, the tune is starting to change. Fred Pierce's 2011 offering, *The Coming Population Crash*, argues that the world's population is starting to peak and will soon reverse course, bringing numerous challenges.[8] The United Nations predicts that the world's population, now around 7.4 billion people, will be 6.2 billion by 2100 if current birth and death rates continue.[9]

Christians need to weed through the conflicting reports and stick with Scripture, which elevates humanity, made in God's image, above everything else in creation. Any suggestion that we must exterminate humans to save

---

earth was in danger of over-population, when much of it had yet to be discovered, is beyond me.

[5] www.worldwatch.org/node/563, accessed June 27, 2016.

[6] David M. Graber, National Park Service biologist, in a review of Bill McKibben's *The End of Nature* (New York: Random House, 1989) in the *Los Angeles Times Book Review*, October 22, 1989, 9.

[7] *New Scientist*, November 10, 2005, 10.

[8] Aurora Xu, "The Coming Population Crash: Investigating the Aftermath of a Population Implosion," Yale Scientific, www.yalescientific.org/2013/05/the-coming-population-crash-investigating-the-aftermath-of-a-population-implosion/, accessed March 3, 2016. This article is based on Pierce's book (Boston: Beacon Press, 2011).

[9] "The Looming Population Implosion," Science 2.0, www.science2.0.com/news_articles/looming_population_implosion-108334, accessed March 4, 2016.

the planet can be rejected outright. The biblical view is that by redeeming humankind, God will also redeem the planet (Rom. 8:19–21).

(2) *Carbon emissions are at dangerously high levels*: Through the burning of fossil fuels, humans are producing greenhouse gases, especially carbon dioxide, at rates too high for the earth to process, leaving the gases suspended in the atmosphere and trapping the sun's heat.

Carbon dioxide (CO_2) is a nasty, toxic gas, at least according to many environmentalists. This impression is certainly unfair to carbon dioxide. Without greenhouse gases the earth could not support life. Higher carbon dioxide actually improves plant growth and fruit production, which is why greenhouses practice "carbon dioxide enrichment" by increasing the level of carbon dioxide. In fact, increases in food production over the past century can be directly tied to higher carbon dioxide levels in the atmosphere, which is good given the growing human population.

Still, carbon dioxide is consistently trotted out as the bad guy, with human production of the gas the chief culprit. However, per the fifth assessment report of the Intergovernmental Panel on Climate Change (IPCC), nature emits about twenty times more carbon dioxide than humans.[10] IPCC claims, though, that the earth consumes roughly the same amount it produces, leaving the human-produced carbon dioxide remaining. I admit my skepticism on how scientists precisely figure out what part of the gas comes from human activity and what part from the planet, let alone how the planet is absorbing *only* the carbon dioxide it produces. Yet these reports largely determine global policies for climate change and control.

My disbelief is driven by the data acquisition methods used to produce the charts scattered throughout such studies. On page 673 of the IPCC report is a chart covering the ozone layer. The years 1850 to 2000 are the "modeled past," while the years 2030 to 2100 are the "modeled projections." In other words, a small slice of the chart is built on actual observed data; the rest is guesswork.

On page 680 the report admits to a "low confidence" in pre-industrial ozone observations, but even this is hedging. Regardless, what do you most remember: the chart with the dramatic slope detailing the drop in ozone

---

[10] The latest IPCC report drove the conclusions of the 2015 United Nations Climate Change Conference in Paris. It can be accessed here: www.ipcc.ch/report/ar5/wg1/ (accessed March 6, 2016).

content, or the comment in the margins that there is low confidence in the data from the past?[11]

It is impossible to measure how much atmospheric carbon dioxide is the result of human activities versus natural activities. How can we determine that X amount of carbon dioxide in 1925 came from automobiles and Y amount from decaying trees in the rainforest?

Four graphs that track anthropogenic gases for the past 160 years are shown on page 677. The fourth graph shows a dramatic increase in the rate of change of "radiative forcing" of greenhouse gases, but pay attention to the y-axis scale. What looks like a shocking rise in anthropogenic gases since 1850 is in fact tracking a miniscule change from 0.00 to 0.03, in other words, three-hundredths of a difference.

Based on evolutionary assumptions that drive the modern science of climate change, climatologists estimate that 440 million years ago, carbon dioxide levels were 1,200 ppm (parts per million) yet the earth was much colder.[12] Today the level is roughly 400 ppm but the earth is considerably warmer. How is this possible, especially when we are told that increased greenhouse gases are the main reason why the earth is heating up?

The report claims that past higher levels of carbon dioxide were counteracted by the sun being 4% weaker, but this defies the reasoning of the report itself. If the sun has virtually nothing to do with global warming as the report states (pp. 392–93), then a slightly weaker sun in the past would have little part to play in an environment where carbon dioxide concentration was three times the current level yet the earth was *cooler*. Inconsistencies like this cause me unease about the IPCC report and the global policies built on it.

This is no minor concern. Virtually every nation on the planet participated in the United Nations Climate Change Conference in Paris at the end of 2015, and the conclusions are meant to be binding worldwide.[13]

---

[11] Pay close attention to the terms used throughout the report when speaking about data from the past or projected into the future, like "very likely," "very low confidence," and so on. This is a clue we are not dealing with hard science, mainly because there is not enough trustworthy data. Terms like "very low confidence" are euphemisms for "we really don't know" and "this is our best guess."

[12] See page 395 of the IPCC report.

[13] This hotlink provides access to numerous articles from *The New York Times* about the Paris conference: www.nytimes.com/news-event/un-climate-change-conference (accessed March 5, 2016).

Eventually, individual nations are going to be told what they can and cannot consume, given the protocols created by the Paris conference.[14]

Little island nations like Tuvalu in the South Pacific have a forum in which they can demand that industrialized countries like the United States only produce a mandated amount of carbon emissions, lest the seas rise and inundate their homelands. As the seas inevitably rise, these nations will demand reparations from industrialized countries for causing the problem.[15] The Climate Vulnerable Forum, currently with twenty member states, was founded in 2009 to address this issue.[16] Climate change is being used as an effective social hammer to erode the sovereignty of individual nations.

My concern is that false assumptions drive these erroneous conclusions. In 2006, NASA produced a computer simulation of carbon dioxide levels in the atmosphere based on the assumption that most of the gas came from the industrialized Northern Hemisphere.[17] However, there is a striking contrast between the simulation and the actual data reported by the Orbiting Carbon Observatory 2 (OCO-2), a satellite NASA launched in 2014 specifically designed to measure carbon dioxide levels. While the Northern Hemisphere produced loads of carbon dioxide in the simulation, the satellite data shows a vastly different story.

The first year of satellite measurements is available in a time-lapse video.[18] The majority of carbon dioxide emissions during the year came from

---

[14] Details of the accord's goals are here: Coral Davenport, "Inside the Paris Climate Deal," *The New York Times*, www.nytimes.com/interactive/2015/12/12/world/paris-climate-change-deal-explainer.html?rref=collection%2Fnewseventcollection%2Fun-climate-change-conference&action=click&contentCollection=earth&region=rank&module=package&version=highlights&contentPlacement=1&pgtype=collection, accessed March 16, 2016.

[15] The issues are not limited to sea levels rising. Developing nations that experience abnormal drought or flooding or erratic rainfall can also blame industrialized nations for the calamity (John Vidal, "Climate Change Compensation Emerges as Major Issue at Doha Talks," *The Guardian*, www.theguardian.com/global-development/2012/dec/03/climate-change-compensation-doha-talks, accessed March 14, 2016).

[16] Wikipedia, "Climate Vulnerable Forum," https://en.wikipedia.org/wiki/Climate_Vulnerable_Forum, accessed June 1, 2016.

[17] View the simulation here: www.nasa.gov/press/goddard/2014/november/nasa-computer-model-provides-a-new-portrait-of-carbon-dioxide/ (accessed June 16, 2016).

[18] YouTube, https://www.youtube.com/watch?v=_UEZqyGU5RU&feature=youtube, accessed June 16, 2016.

the Southern Hemisphere, not the Northern Hemisphere. There is only a three-month period where the Northern Hemisphere produced more carbon dioxide. Unfortunately, the inaccurate NASA computer simulations were key features in climate change policies over the past decade, despite their false assumptions.

When plants are dormant in wintertime, carbon dioxide builds up in the atmosphere, but come spring and summer, plants rapidly consume it.[19] One of the maps from NASA's satellite shows carbon dioxide levels during October and November 2014, when it is springtime in the Southern Hemisphere. Rainforests and tropical forests of South America and Africa produced the most carbon dioxide in the atmosphere, not the industrialized North. Whom should tiny island nations sue for reparations when the seas rise?

Also, the scale in the NASA maps for carbon dioxide concentrations measures from 390 ppm to 405 ppm. That means that over the entire year carbon dioxide levels deviated by just 1% to 2%.

In summary, carbon dioxide concentration was much higher in the earth's past, dropping dramatically to today's levels. We know that nature itself produces far more carbon dioxide than humans do.[20] Since 1978 space-based measures have been possible, meaning that past calculations are not nearly as precise. Obviously, any claims of increased carbon dioxide levels are only as accurate as both present and past measurements. Lastly, we know that water vapor far outstrips carbon dioxide in its ability to trap heat.[21] When will we begin saving the planet from too much water?

Common sense dictates that the earth's carbon dioxide levels naturally fluctuate over the course of time. What reasons are there for humans to spend trillions of dollars to attempt to stop what naturally occurs in

---

[19] "NASA's Spaceborne Carbon Counter Maps New Details," www.nasa.gov/jpl/oco2/nasas-spaceborne-carbon-counter-maps-new-details, accessed June 16, 2016.

[20] Sometimes with dramatic consequences, like in 2010 when Iceland's Eyjafjallajökull volcano began an eruption phase that shut down European air traffic for six days.

[21] These two NASA webpages provide information on water vapor trapping heat in the atmosphere: NASA Earth Observatory, http://earthobservatory.nasa.gov/Features/WaterVapor/water_vapor2.php, accessed June 16, 2016, and "Water Vapor Confirmed as Major Player in Climate Change," NASA, www.nasa.gov/topics/earth/features/vapor_warming.html, accessed June 16, 2016.

the earth's cycles? Could that money be better spent on more worthwhile projects?

(3) *Earth's temperature is too high*: The planet is hotter than it has been in the past 150 years, and the temperature is increasing faster than at any time in recorded history, resulting in drastic climate changes that jeopardize humanity.

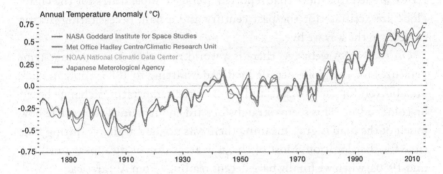

This chart from NASA's Earth Observatory website shows the average global temperature change from the start of the industrial revolution to today.[22]

The graph's steep increase is because the measurements along the vertical axis are so small. From 1880 to the present represents an increase of merely three-fourths of one degree.

Also, consider from where these measurements have come and when they were taken. They are reported by four global locations: NASA, the National Oceanic and Atmospheric Administration (NOAA), the Japan Meteorological Agency, and the Met Office Hadley Centre (United Kingdom). While all four graphs relatively track together, in some places the variance between one record and another is as much as a quarter of a degree. Given the overall scale, that is quite a variance. Still, there is an upward trend reported by all four agencies.

However, the chart gives the impression that temperature measurements for 1890 are as trustworthy as measurements from today, but there was no way to attain the precision of climate measuring in the 1800s that we have today. Further, it is impossible to say with any certainty that the average

---

[22]   http://earthobservatory.nasa.gov/Features/WorldOfChange/decadaltemp.php, accessed March 14, 2016.

temperature of the entire planet in 1872 was a whole degree less than today. One-tenth of the number of weather stations we have today were in use then, with most only in the United States and Europe.

Wikipedia has a map of the 7,280 fixed temperature stations in the Global Historical Climatology Network and a record of how long they have been recording data.[23] Much of the world had no coverage fifty years ago, yet we are led to believe that reported average temperatures for the entire globe are accurate for the past century and a half, necessitating drastic changes in the way we live.

On the NASA webpage, there is a world map that shows average temperatures for the globe decade by decade starting in 1885. You can click on a button for each decade and see how the temperatures change based on color coding. This seems straightforward enough, until you realize how much of the map is gray, meaning there was no data available during that time for that location. Most of the gray areas do not disappear until the mid-1950s, when we finally have decent readings from Antarctica.

Antarctica plays a key role in climate change theories. The continent has 90% of the world's ice and about 70% of the fresh water, which makes it crucial when speaking about global warming and potential sea level increases. Because humans arrived in Antarctica in the early nineteenth century, we only know what past temperatures were on the continent via proxy measurements like ice cores, which I will cover shortly.

Antarctica is one and a half times larger than the United States. Currently there are about a dozen locations on the continent that record temperatures. Where would you place twelve thermometers in America to get the average temperature? Suppose we placed one thermometer each in California, Arizona, Texas, Montana, North Dakota, Iowa, and half a dozen states east of the Mississippi River. Could we really get an accurate average temperature of the entire United States from merely twelve locations? Should we have a thermometer in Death Valley? How about on Mount Whitney, the highest peak in the continental United States? Keep in mind that average temperatures in reports from IPCC are measured in fractions of a degree.

---

[23] 226 stations, a little more than 3%, have kept records for the past 150 years (Wikipedia, https://en.wikipedia.org/wiki/Global_Historical_Climatology_Network, accessed June 16, 2016).

Antarctica has an incredibly diverse terrain. The highest mountain is 16,000 feet (higher than Mount Whitney), and it is home to more than seventy lakes. Throughout any given year, temperatures can drop 120°F (-84°C) below freezing and can rise to a balmy 60°F (16°C) at the coast.

In October 2014, NASA reported that ice on the continent reached record levels since scientists began satellite measurements. Yet, a senior scientist at NASA claimed this was a sign of "global warming."[24] This is the beauty of the climate change position. No matter what happens, it is proof they are right. Thus the problem. How trustworthy are the reports from "experts" who appear to have their own agenda?

Even figures for the United States are questionable. One study looked at hundreds of weather stations run by the National Weather Service. It found a majority of them in poor repair or with gages that were near other heat sources, skewing the readings. The report asks, "If the temperature reported for a single town is not truly representative of that town, then how is the global average of such temperatures representative of the entire world?"[25]

There is also the problem of what is used as a benchmark for comparison. From the same NASA website we read:

> Global temperature records start around 1880 because observations did not sufficiently cover enough of the planet prior to that time. The period of 1951–1980 was chosen largely because the U.S. National Weather Service uses a three-decade period to define "normal" or average temperature. The GISS [NASA's Goddard Institute for Space Studies] temperature analysis effort began around 1980, so the most recent 30 years was 1951–1980.

While we need a benchmark for comparisons, note how it was chosen: the GISS analysis, begun in 1980, covers the previous thirty-year period. But who is to say that temperatures during that period were "normal"? Besides, what is the optimal temperature for the earth anyway?

---

[24] "Antarctic Sea Ice Reaches New Record Maximum," NASA, www.nasa.gov/content/goddard/antarctic-sea-ice-reaches-new-record-maximum, accessed June 16, 2016.

[25] Anthony Watts, "Is the U.S. Surface Temperature Record Reliable?" Heartland Institute, https://www.heartland.org/sites/default/files/SurfaceStations.pdf, accessed March 15, 2016.

Looking again at the NASA chart above, the earth's temperature varies within a degree or two over a long period of time. The earth's elliptical orbit, the variance over time in its tilt, and the degree that the planet wobbles around its axis create times of exceptional chilliness or warmth in the earth's history.

This is confirmed by another NASA chart showing the average temperature of the United States since 1880. Temperatures fluctuated within a narrow range of two degrees on average, and the hottest years in the past century were in the 1920s and 1930s.[26]

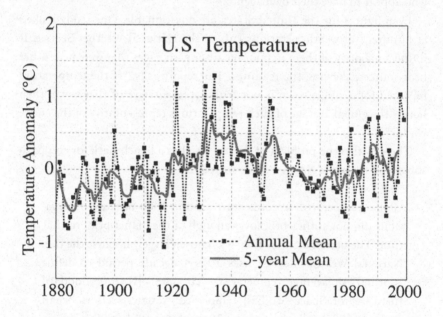

By the way, in the mid-1950s scientists were predicting global *cooling*, based on trends at that time. You can see why, as the average temperature dropped by about one degree in that decade. Over the next forty years, it warmed up to roughly the same temperature before the drop.[27]

---

[26] http://earthobservatory.nasa.gov/Features/GlobalWarm1999/Images/1999_fig3.gif, accessed June 16, 2016.

[27] Do an Internet search for magazine covers from *Time, Newsweek,* and *National Geographic* to see that global cooling was being predicted in the 1970s and 1980s, based on the trends at that time. For example, a *Newsweek* article from April 28, 1975, began with what sounds exactly like what is being said today by climate "experts": "There are

However, there is a limit to what average temperatures can tell you. The average for any given twenty-four-hour period in the desert (with its dramatic highs and lows) may be the same as the average for a location close to the sea (where the temperature stays fairly constant). How helpful is it to average the temperatures of Hawaii and Antarctica, Australia and Greenland? When we are told what the supposed average temperature for the entire planet was 150 years ago, this tells us very little about the actual climate.

We know that about five hundred years ago there was a "little ice age" in Europe, but this does not mean that temperatures elsewhere in the world were lower too. It simply means that in one part of the world the temperatures dropped a little lower than usual. This makes good sense because the earth naturally cycles between warmer and cooler periods. If it did not, we could not have seasons and ecological cycles.

NASA claims, "Global temperature is warmer now than it has been in the past 1000 years," but such statements are virtually impossible to verify.[28] What was the average temperature of the planet, say, five hundred years ago? Not many people were concerned enough to take measurements, nor was the technology available.

Proxy Measurements

In the absence of actual human observations of climate in the distant past, climatologists use "proxy measures." We will briefly consider two of these: ice core samples and tree rings.

Ice Cores. Greenland and Antarctica are the most popular places from which to pull ice cores. Climatologists claim they have a record of the past 650,000 years of the earth's history. Obviously, this assertion is based on evolutionary assumptions of deep time.

The idea seems simple enough. You pull an ice core and see distinctions

---

ominous signs that the earth's weather patterns have begun to change dramatically and that these changes may portend a drastic decline in food production—with serious political implications for just about every nation on earth" (64). This was a warning concerning "The Cooling World."

[28] "How Is Today's Warming Different from the Past?" NASA Earth Observatory, http://earthobservatory.nasa.gov/Features/GlobalWarming/page3.php, accessed March 15, 2016.

from one layer to the next. Materials trapped in the ice can be analyzed and a picture of the climate for each layer can be discerned.[29]

Core sampling, though, is by no means an exact science. Because climatologists use oxygen and beryllium isotopes to determine age, the same problems we noted previously with radiometric dating methods exist. Major assumptions are built in before conclusions are made. For example, it is usually assumed that each layer in the ice represents a specific year, but "sub-annual" layers can occur when several storms in any given season each create a layer. Skeptics of the procedure object that years do not create ice rings, temperature differences do, and there have been cases where core samples taken from nearby areas produced vastly different results.[30]

Core samples have been pulled from as deep as 3,500 meters, but the deeper you go, the more compressed the layers become, making accurate measurements nearly impossible. Lastly, a major drawback of these measurements is that they only record the climate where the ice is. An ice core from the Antarctic cannot tell us what the weather was like in Canada.

Tree Rings. Dendroclimatology is the study of tree rings to track growth patterns and discern environmental conditions during the life of the tree. Narrow rings reflect cooler temperatures and wider rings hotter ones. Studies have noted that, on average, tree rings are wider in the twentieth century than in previous ones. However, there is no way of determining what the cause is, and warmer weather is one of many factors. Variations in soil quality, wind, sunlight, precipitation, number of trees in the area competing for nutrients, carbon dioxide levels, pests, herbivore activity, and a hoard of other factors affect a tree's ring width. Also, older trees do not grow as quickly as younger ones.

These studies have additional limits. They can show climate effects during growth season, but not during dormant periods like deep winter, and stressed trees from a particularly harsh winter might take a season or two to recover before growing again.

Lastly, trees do not cover the whole earth. A tree in Siberia will not tell

---

[29] This webpage details the science behind it: Holli Riebeek, "Paleoclimatology: The Ice Core Record," NASA Earth Observatory, http://earthobservatory.nasa.gov/Features/Paleoclimatology_IceCores/, accessed March 23, 2016.

[30] Cores taken in Greenland had this problem. M. J. Oard, "A Tale of Two Greenland Ice Cores," *Journal of Creation* 9, no. 2 (1995): 135–36.

us about the climate in Antarctica let alone in the middle of the Atlantic Ocean. Correlations with other methods are attempted, but these have a host of problems too.

The next time you see a report on climate change with a graph reaching back thousands or even millions of years, keep in mind that proxy measurements are extremely inconsistent and inaccurate.

Climate change warnings are usually coupled with the projected disintegration of social and ecological systems, and human health and security. Fanatical alarmists talk about major cities disappearing from the face of the earth. However, if it is true that increased temperatures on the earth will result in the destruction of everything we know, why, when the temperature has gone up in the past century, have things generally gotten better? Ask yourself: would you prefer to live in 1890 or 1990?

(4) *Rising Sea Levels*: Due mainly to human activity, ocean levels are rising at an alarming rate and will eventually inundate major coastal cities around the world.

The negative effects of global warming are vast: increased hurricane activity in both frequency and severity, droughts and flooding, scorching summers and colder winters.[31] Nonetheless, the threat that trumps them all is sea levels rising from the melting polar ice caps and glaciers. Similar to doomsday prophets in religious garb, climatologists sound rather apocalyptic with their predictions. Consider these comments from 2016 presidential-hopeful Bernie Sanders's website:

- "Climate change is the single greatest threat facing our planet."
- "If we do nothing, the planet will heat up five to ten degrees Fahrenheit by the end of this century. That would cause enough sea level rise from melting glaciers to put cities like New York and Miami underwater."[32]

The science here is straightforward. As the earth warms up, ice at both poles melts into the oceans, causing them to rise. The issue, though, is if

---

[31] The demise of polar bears is one of the "ecological icons" of global warming. Polarbearscience.com tracks all the studies from around the world about the furry creatures, which are enjoying a healthy increase in population despite popular depictions of the white beasts "stranded" alone on floating patches of ice, as if they could not swim.

[32] BernieSanders.com (accessed April 25, 2016).

this melting is caused by anthropogenic sources, or is simply a natural occurrence in the earth's ecological cycles.

In his 2006 blockbuster *An Inconvenient Truth*, Al Gore warned that the arctic ice cap would completely disappear by 2014, and he repeated that prediction over and over again as late as 2009.[33] However, the ice actually increased. A decade after Gore's prediction, ice volume remains higher.[34]

Based on Antarctic research reported in the journal *Nature*, in March 2016, *The New York Times* predicted that sea levels could rise as much as six feet by the end of the century, causing major catastrophes for coastal cities around the world including London, Hong Kong, Shanghai, Sydney, and New York.[35] This is twice as bad as the worst-case scenario the United Nations reported in 2013. If given just this article, the situation appears bleak.

Nevertheless, the *Nature* article makes it clear that current ocean levels are not as high as they were before the industrial revolution, which raises the question: how are these scientists sure that humans are to blame? Their conclusions are predicated on "future greenhouse gas emission scenarios" that are guesswork, as previously noted. These emissions are claimed to be the "dominant driver of ice loss," but I find this claim unconvincing. They take a tiny slice of earth's history and extrapolate it into the future using "computer models" and "simulations," but who writes the programs? As with everything else, the programmers are driven by assumptions and presuppositions.

Consider this analogy. Suppose you take a five-second measurement of the burn rate of a foot-long candle on your dining room table. How

[33] Douglas Stanglin, "Gore: Polar Ice Cap May Disappear by Summer 2014," *USA Today*, http://content.usatoday.com/communities/ondeadline/post/2009/12/gore-new-study-sees-nearly-ice-free-arctic-summer-ice-cap-as-early-as-2014/1#.Vxu9NrMVgkI, accessed March 17, 2016.

[34] A chart from the Department of Atmospheric Sciences at the University of Illinois shows that global sea ice in terms of total area naturally fluctuates over time: http://arctic.atmos.uiuc.edu/cryosphere/IMAGES/global.daily.ice.area.withtrend.jpg (accessed March 18, 2016).

[35] Justin Gillis, "Climate Model Predicts West Antarctic Ice Sheet Could Melt Rapidly," *The New York Times*, www.nytimes.com/2016/03/31/science/global-warming-antarctica-ice-sheet-sea-level-rise.html?hp&action=click&pgtype=Homepage&clickSource=story-heading&module=first-column-region&region=top-news&WT.nav=top-news&_r=1, accessed March 21, 2016.

accurate would your predictions be for the life of the entire candle? You cannot account for variability in the wick thickness, inconsistencies in the wax, or changes in atmospheric conditions such as a breeze that comes through the door, fanning the flame. That five-second window will provide little guidance when making long-term determinations.

Now try to make predictions about the earth given a small slice of human observation and within the context of myriad variables. Weather satellites have existed for a short period of human history. We cannot treat past measurements with the same degree of veracity as present ones, especially when current readings are often proved to be inaccurate.

There is evidence that glacial ice sheets covered the Northern Hemisphere as far south as northern Illinois, New York, and Ohio, and that ocean levels rose as much as 60 meters in the distant past. These facts must be carefully considered since they happened long before humans were burning fossil fuels.[36]

Cleopatra's ancient Egyptian city Alexandria was overcome by the rising Mediterranean about 1,650 years ago, lost to history until it was rediscovered in the 1990s about twenty feet under the harbor of the modern city.[37] Vanishing completely was Heracleion, founded in the eighth century BC and in its day the main Egyptian port of entry for ships coming from the Greek world. It has since been rediscovered about four miles off the coast of Egypt, under 150 feet of water.[38] The ancient Phoenician city Tyre experienced a similar fate, as predicted by the prophet Ezekiel (26:1–21).

Underwater cities have been found off the coasts of Japan, India, China, Greece, Italy, and Peru. This suggests that the seawaters have been on the rise long before human-produced greenhouse gases could have affected them.

---

[36] There is evidence that the polar caps on Mars are also receding, which may suggest a wider solar system warming from the sun's activity (Kate Revilious, "Mars Melt Hints at Solar, Not Human, Cause for Warming, Scientist Says," National Geographic News, http://news.nationalgeographic.com/news/2007/02/070228-mars-warming.html, accessed September 5, 2016).

[37] Andrew Lawler, "Raising Alexandria," *Smithsonian Magazine*, www.smithsonianmag.com/science-nature/raising-alexandria-151005550/?no-ist, accessed March 27, 2016.

[38] "Lost Egyptian City Found Underwater after 1200 Years," Twisted Sifter, http://twistedsifter.com/2013/06/lost-egyptian-city-heracleion-found-underwater-after-1200-years/, accessed March 26, 2016.

The World Meteorological Organization (WMO), a specialized agency of the United Nations, claims to be the "authoritative voice on the state and behavior of the earth's atmosphere." Its website states that sea levels have risen at a faster rate in the past hundred years than in the previous three thousand years. To put it bluntly, there is no way WMO can know this.

When the WMO reports that 95% of global warming over the past several decades has been caused by humans, I am skeptical.[39] We do know that the oceans have risen 20 centimeters (about 8 inches) over the past century, and they rose the same amount in the century before that. If the ocean rose the same amount before and after the industrial revolution, how is the burning of fossil fuels the main perpetrator?

Sifting through Fact and Fiction

Climate change is the type of argument you cannot lose. If temperatures increase, you can say you were right in your predictions, but if they fall, you can say that your alarmist approach has stemmed the increase. Despite false predictions from the past decade (e.g., sea levels will rise to ridiculous heights, entire populations of polar bears will be wiped out, monster hurricane activity will increase), the alarmists are undeterred. No new data will dissuade them from their mantra. This approach is not scientific, it is religious.

Some Christians have jumped onto the climate change bandwagon. In 2006, the Evangelical Climate Initiative produced a statement detailing what it believed to be the proper Christian response to global warming. Signatories included dozens of high-profile pastors, deans, professors, and presidents from thirty-seven Christian colleges and universities in America.

Apparently adopting the conclusions made by the "scientific community," the statement claims, "Millions of people could die in this century because of climate change, most of them our poorest global neighbors."[40] This sounds noble, but when the call is based on flimsy science, it is

[39] WMO, "CSIRO: Burning of Fossil Fuel Causes Most Sea Level Rise," http://public.wmo.int/en/media/news/csiro-burning-of-fossil-fuel-causes-most-sea-level-rise, accessed May 12, 2016.

[40] "Climate Change: An Evangelical Call to Action," www.npr.org/documents/2006/feb/evangelical/calltoaction.pdf, accessed March 24, 2016.

pointless. My hope is that many of the signatories have taken time to recon-sider the data.

The approach that drives evolutionary "science" likewise drives climate change apologists. Dramatic declarations about the state of the planet are built on meager data and extrapolated into the future (or with evolu-tion, into the distant past). However, in time these pronouncements are found wanting as new information emerges. Both the worldviews of the evolutionist and the fanatical environmentalist are based on paltry data, with a healthy dose of imagination and (in the case of environmentalists) fear-mongering thrown in.

A friend calls global warming the "new socialism." He contends that cli-mate change is exploited as an opportunity to globally redistribute wealth by punishing developed countries with restrictive environmental controls, while allowing developing countries to run amok. In this scenario, capital-ism is the bad guy that has ruined the environment for everybody else; it must be punished.

I am admittedly swayed by my friend's notion, especially after consider-ing the data used to blame humans for rising sea levels. What has increased my suspicion is that key climate change alarmists have been caught fudg-ing the data.[41] Emails have been accessed at IPCC, for example, showing that it fiddled with data on global warming.[42]

This is no small issue; it will affect us all whether we like it or not. At the Paris talks a call was made to exclude companies from investment in state pension funds if they do not conform to stricter guidelines for carbon emissions. A primary goal of the Paris talks is to limit global warming to a 2°C increase by 2100, and carbon trading and carbon taxes will become a financial way to punish industrialized nations.

Individuals must "reduce their carbon footprint" in order to save the planet: consume less, drive less, recycle more, waste less, burn less elec-tricity, move to renewable energy sources. I haven't a problem with any of

---

[41] "Another Climate Alarmist Admits Real Motive behind Warming Scare," *Inves-tor's Business Daily*, www.investors.com/politics/editorials/another-climate-alarmist-admits-real-motive-behind-warming-scare/, accessed March 30, 2016.

[42] This U.K. website catalogues many of these emails: James Delingpole, "Uh, Oh, Glob-al Warming Loons Here Comes Climategate 2.0," *The Telegraph*, http://blogs.telegraph.co.uk/news/jamesdelingpole/100119087/uh-oh-global-warming-loons-here-comes-climategate-ii/, accessed May 3, 2016.

these suggestions. I should consume only as much electricity as I require. I should turn off the lights when I am not in the room. Why buy something brand new when I can use a recycled product? These are reasonable ideas.

My objection comes when climate change advocates micro-manage our lives according to how climate "experts" think it best to live. Some like Bill Nye, "the science guy," promote prison time for climate change deniers, based on the logic that if you repudiate global warming, you put us all at risk.[43] Environmental activist Robert Kennedy Jr. calls deniers treasonous and equates them with war criminals. The Weather Channel called for the revoking of licenses or withholding certification of skeptical meteorologists.[44] This smacks less of real science and more of political or religious ideology.

Coal and "big oil" companies are repeatedly demonized because they are seen as the main instigators of global warming.[45] After all, their products produce the carbon emissions endangering the planet. However, if we stopped using coal and oil in the United States, we would have to eliminate virtually every vehicle on the road today. Driving electric cars does not help because the electricity used to power them is often created by fossil fuel–burning power plants.

There is a certain hypocrisy here. Every time an environmentalist turns on the lights, or drives to work and back, he is hypocritically using the resources that he later demonizes in his march against carbon emissions.

Granted, renewable power certainly has benefits. Texas gets nearly half of its energy from renewable sources (wind, solar, hydro), and 13% of the nation's power grid is supplied this way. Two-thirds of the world's solar capacity was installed in the past five years, and solar installations are

---

[43] Valerie Richardon, "Bill Nye, the Science Guy, Is Open to Criminal Charges and Jail Time for Climate Change Dissenters," *The Washington Times*, www.washingtontimes.com/news/2016/apr/14/bill-nye-open-criminal-charges-jail-time-climate-c/, accessed May 3, 2016.

[44] Marc Morano, Climate Depot, www.climatedepot.com/2014/09/21/robert-f-kennedy-jr-wants-to-jail-his-political-opponents-accuses-koch-brothers-of-treason-they-ought-to-be-serving-time-for-it/, accessed March 7, 2016.

[45] There has even been an attempt to do to oil producers what was done to the tobacco industry in the 1990s, namely, to sue petroleum companies for racketeering and fraud. However, this may have backfired for now (Adam Brodsky, "The Imploding Cabal to Criminalize Climate Dissent," *New York Post*, http://nypost.com/2016/06/30/the-imploding-cabal-to-criminalize-climate-dissent/, accessed September 5, 2016).

forecast to quadruple by the end of the decade.[46] Our energy production is transforming, which is how a free market society works.[47] If this makes us more efficient and less reliant on foreign nations—especially those that support Muslim terrorists—this is welcome news.

Over the past five years, though, more than one hundred solar companies have filed for bankruptcy. The high-profile failure of Solyndra cost American taxpayers $535 million. Environmentalist pressure often results in poor fiscal decisions, wasting billions of dollars globally.

What about Animal Rights?

In 2001, Michael Vick became the first African American quarterback as the top pick in the NFL draft, becoming the starting quarterback of the Atlanta Falcons. An electrifying player with amazing quickness and agility, he appeared in multiple Pro Bowls and had endorsement deals worth millions.

Vick's downfall came when a federal investigation uncovered his participation in an interstate dog-fighting ring. Not only did Vick finance a large portion of the operation, he also hosted events at his home and aided in killing underperforming dogs by hanging or drowning. He was prosecuted and spent nearly two years in prison. Vick immediately became one of the most vilified people in America. During the trial, he was escorted to the courthouse while many animal rights advocates screamed for the death penalty. However, despite Vick's cruelty to animals, is the death of a human justified?

We saw in the previous chapter that humans are made in the image of God, endowed with characteristics superior to any other creature on the planet. We received a God-given mandate to rule over the creation (Gen. 1:26), but what should we do when humans abuse this responsibility?

---

[46] Lucas Mearian, "Solar Panels Don't Last Forever and Degradation Varies Wildly, Study Says," *Computerworld*, www.computerworld.com/article/3058270/sustainable-it/study-solar-panels-dont-last-forever-and-degradation-varies-wildly.html, accessed March 7, 2016.

[47] Naureen Malik and Harry Weber, "What Do Texas and California Have in Common? 'Negative Power' Caused by Renewables Glut," *The Dallas Morning News*, www.dallas-news.com/business/energy/20160405-what-do-texas-and-california-have-in-common-negative-power-caused-by-renewables-glut.ece, accessed April 16, 2016.

There are two equal yet opposite reactions: treating animals as if they are human beings, and treating humans as if they are animals. Abortion is an example of the latter problem; animal rights advocates make the former error. This works out in several ways.

Environmentalists claim that beef is the most environmentally damaging form of meat because cows produce lots of methane, a factor in global warming. Thus, as climate change has risen as a major social issue, so has vegetarianism.

Taking it one step further are those who adopt a vegan lifestyle, not merely for dietary reasons but for ethical ones as well. Not only do ethical vegans refrain from eating animals, they also do not use animal products such as fur, leather, silk, honey, milk, and eggs. Using beeswax and pillows stuffed with bird feathers is a definite no-no, as is utilizing animals for sports, entertainment, work, or medical research.

Living a vegan lifestyle is difficult to do in an absolute way. Household cleaning goods, building products, and toiletries such as shampoo, lip balm, and creams use animal products. If this is how vegans choose to live, I won't bicker with them. However, militant animal rights advocates go too far when they pressure everybody to conform to their worldview.

Many famous individuals sponsor People for the Ethical Treatment of Animals (PETA),[48] but several of these same people support a woman's right to abortion. They are more concerned about a young seal being clubbed or saving the eggs of bald eagles than a human life sliced and sucked out of its mother's womb.

There is a misanthropy habitually expressed by environmentalists, like the Voluntary Human Extinction Movement that hopes to phase out humanity by ceasing to breed.[49] Rabid animal rights proponents oppose God's declaration that humans are the pinnacle of his creative activity. The visceral hatred some environmentalists have for humankind is a reflection of their animosity toward God. They reject both God's sovereignty and the authority over creation of those made in his image.

Fanatical environmentalists recognize that Christianity's view of humanity is at odds with their worship of the planet. Consider these quotes:

---

[48] Look to the Stars, "PETA Celebrity Supporters and Events," www.looktothestars.org/charity/peta, accessed April 27, 2016.

[49] http://vhemt.org/.

- "Christianity is our foe. If animal rights is to succeed we must destroy the Judeo-Christian religious tradition."[50]
- "If you'll give the idea a chance . . . you might agree that the extinction of Homo sapiens would mean survival for millions if not billions of other earth-dwelling species."[51]
- "Man is no more important than any other species . . . It may well take our extinction to set things straight."[52]
- "I got the impression that instead of going out to shoot birds, I should go out and shoot the kids who shoot birds."[53]

According to the website of the Chicago Field Museum, two hundred species go extinct each day "due to factors such as climate change and habitat destruction," a not-so-subtle jab at humanity.[54] Yet the museum notes that 99% of all species that have ever existed have already disappeared from the face of the earth, recorded only in the fossil record. Mother Nature has done a far more effective job wiping out species than humans could do. This does not mean we should wantonly destroy the environment, but it does put into perspective the guilt trips that the ecologically minded place on those who do not buy into their fanatical concerns.

Still, there is no doubt that humans affect the environment. Visit Los Angeles on a smoggy afternoon, or take a gaze across the polluted horizon the next time you visit Beijing. I have a friend who teaches English in China. He uses a CPAP (continuous positive airway pressure) machine for sleep

---

[50] Australian philosopher and bioethics professor at Princeton University Peter Singer, the "father of animal rights" (Accuracy in Media, "Peter Singer," www.aim.org/wls/author/peter-singer/, accessed June 14, 2016).

[51] The Voluntary Human Extinction Movement, quoted by Daniel Seligman in "Down with People," *Fortune* magazine, September 23, 1991.

[52] David Foreman, Earth First! spokesman, quoted by M. John Fayhee in *Backpacker* magazine, September 1988, 22.

[53] Paul Watson, a founder of Greenpeace, quoted in *Access to Energy* 10, no. 4 (December 1989).

[54] The Field Museum, "How to Recover from a Mass Extinction," www.fieldmuseum.org/science/blog/how-recover-mass-extinction, accessed March 17, 2016. The World Wildlife Federation estimates that the extinction rate is much higher and it lays almost all blame for modern extinctions on humans, calling this a "very serious biodiversity crisis." However, humans have accounted for less than 1% of all extinctions throughout the earth's history ("How Many Species Are We Losing?" http://wwf.panda.org/about_our_earth/biodiversity/biodiversity, accessed June 7, 2016).

apnea. While living in Chicago, he had to change the filter once a month, but in China, he changes it weekly.

Trophy hunting has resulted in tusk size reduction in both African and Asian elephants, as well as horn size in moose and bighorn sheep. Humans have caused high-profile extinctions like the western black rhino and the dodo bird, or lesser-known ones like the quagga of South Africa and the fruit bat on Réunion Island.

Humans are quite capable of ruining a local ecosystem, or polluting an area's drinking water, at least for a period of time. The case of Easter Island and the Rapanui islanders who obliterated the tree population, throwing into chaos the entire ecosystem, has been well documented.[55] However, are humans really capable of destroying the entire planet?

A Balanced Christian Approach

Global warming is not simply a scientific or political issue, it is a spiritual one. There is an implicit paganism that forms the heart of much of environmentalism today, an idolatry that has exchanged the worship of the Creator for worshiping created things (Rom. 1:22).

For those who store up treasures on earth, earth is their only home. Jesus warned against such treasure seeking, where moths and rust and thieves can rob us of our earthly prize (Matt. 6:19). His disciples must be concerned with eternal treasures. It makes sense that those who reject the gospel fixate on the here-and-now.

Most climate science is built on an evolutionary framework where the earth's environment is the product of random events. If we take a Christian perspective, though, we immediately recognize that the planet has built-in regulators.

> When there is too much CO_2 in the atmosphere, the Earth heats up. When it heats up, plants grow more luxuriantly (both from being in a hothouse and from increased CO_2) and greater evaporation occurs. But plants breathe CO_2, thereby removing it from the atmosphere, and the greater evaporation leads to greater

---

[55] Peter Tyson, "The Fate of Easter Island," NOVA, www.pbs.org/wgbh/nova/earth/fate-of-easter-island.html, accessed March 17, 2016.

precipitation, which also removes the excess atmospheric CO_2. Things cool down. If things get too cool, precipitation decreases, and less CO_2 is removed, allowing atmospheric buildup to occur again from volcanic activity and animal respiration. Without this finely tuned thermostat continually running, Earth would be uninhabitable.[56]

This system speaks of design, not haphazard evolutionary chance. There is genius in this self-regulating scheme, created so that God's image bearers can live in it.

According to secular scientists, the earth has endured several ice ages, the eruption of numerous mega-volcanoes, mass extinctions, the bombardment of mega-asteroids, tsunamis and earthquakes galore, flooding on a massive scale from both water and lava, and numerous other catastrophes. Yet it continues to spin, sustaining life, doing everything it was designed to do. Claims that the earth is going to come apart at the seams because of human activity are pure hubris.

There is a hardiness to God's creation that is breathtaking. Devastation on an enormous scale can occur in an area, like the eruption of Mount St. Helens in the 1980s, and in less than a year life bounces back. God has built adaptability into his creatures. Consider "extremeophiles," those organisms that exist in punishing conditions like hyper-saline or acidic environments, or in the parched desert or the super-frigid ice caps.

While I believe that the claims by global warming alarmists are unfounded, I do think we need to care for the planet God has given us. Christians ought to navigate between an idolatrous obsession with the planet and a cavalier exploitation of it. The Bible provides several guidelines in this regard.

First, God owns his creation and has a right to do with it as he wills, appointing humans to be his viceroys. "God blessed them and said to them, 'Be fruitful and increase in number; fill the earth and subdue it. Rule over the fish in the sea and the birds in the sky and over every living creature that moves on the ground'" (Gen. 1:28; see also Ps. 8:6–8). I refuse to believe that God gave this command with a hidden caveat: "but don't reproduce too much. See, I've put you on a planet that won't be able to sustain many

---

[56] Wiker and Witt, *A Meaningful World*, 162.

of you." This flies in the face of the biblical account, which states that the earth was made from the very beginning to support abundant life.[57]

Second, God instituted the Old Testament priesthood. One of the priest's responsibilities was to present sacrifices of rams and goats and bulls and doves and pigeons and sheep virtually every day. There is no hint that slaughtering animals is a high crime in God's eyes. However, killing humans is. Even an animal that kills a human should be destroyed (Gen. 9:5; Exod. 21:28–32).

Biblical perspective is required. When Jesus healed the Gerasenes demoniac, he cast the demons into a herd of two thousand pigs that subsequently plunged to their death (Mark 5:13). The deliverance of one man was worth it. Any perspective that puts animal life on par with human life is demeaning both to humans and to the God who made them in his image.

Third, God gave animals for us to manage and consume (Gen. 9:3). Jesus declared all foods clean (Mark 7:19), and the apostle Paul warned Timothy about those who forced others to abstain from certain foods (1 Tim. 4:3–4). Humans have tamed, domesticated, and trained animals with incredible success. There is clearly nothing wrong with this. How people treat animals is a decent litmus test for their character. Those who enjoy abusing animals have a screw loose.

Using animals for medical experiments that save human lives is not unnecessary cruelty, it is the exercise of our God-given mandate to rule over the creation. Human life is precious to God. If we can use a mouse or a monkey to better humanity, this is worthwhile. Without animal testing, hundreds of lifesaving medical procedures and medicines would not exist today. However, this in no way means we can maliciously handle these animals; animals used for medical research must be cared for humanely.

Fourth, it was only several thousand years ago that God wiped clean the entire surface of the earth with a worldwide flood. The flood changed the climate dramatically, yet here we are. God made a promise to Noah that explicitly states that the earth will function as designed. "As long as the earth endures, seedtime and harvest, cold and heat, summer and winter, day and night will never cease" (Gen. 8:22). Clearly people will be on the planet when Christ returns. The notion that humans will destroy the

---

[57] Mining and farming appear to be the natural result of humans subduing the earth (Gen. 4:20–22).

planet is overblown. In Matthew 24:37–39 Jesus uses the flood as a paradigm of the judgment to come. Earth will experience God's judgment again, which exposes the environmentalist lie that we can "save the planet."

Nevertheless, even though we believers are told to fix our hope on our home to come, heavenly treasures do not mean abandonment of our earthly obligations. We must care for the earth. While the earth will experience God's judgment as the "elements melt in the heat" (2 Peter 3:12), this hardly justifies its ruin by humans now. No amount of theological gymnastics can rationalize trashing the place. That would be akin to saying it is alright to kill people because they are going to die anyway. While believers navigate between exploitation of the environment and worshiping it, we cannot become careless. Christians should cherish this earthly home that God has given us, even as we look forward to our heavenly mansions.

CHAPTER SEVEN

God's Created Order
and Gender Roles

Self-definitionandself-determinationis[sic]aboutthemanyvarieddecisions thatwemaketocomposeandjourneytowardourselves,abouttheaudacityand strengthtoproclaim,create,andevolveintowhoweknowourselvestobe.It'sokay ifyourpersonaldefinitionisinaconstantstateoffluxasyounavigatetheworld.

—JANET MOCK[1]

DURING MY BOYHOOD IN the summer of 1976, along with millions of Americans, I was enraptured by the epitome of maleness, the winner of the Olympic decathlon gold medal, Bruce Jenner. Fast, strong, good looking, and the quintessential athlete, Jenner became an overnight sensation and Wheaties box icon. He received the highest cumulative score in the history of the decathlon. For a lover of the jack-of-all-trades figure, Jenner was the perfect athlete.

As I began to write this book in 2015, the news broke that Bruce Jenner no longer considered himself a man. Caitlyn Jenner is the new name of choice for America's decathlon victor. While it did not surprise me that Jenner's coming out made headlines, I was shocked how often it did. It was every day for two weeks solid. "How many times do I have to see Jenner's *Vanity Fair* cover?" I asked myself in disbelief.

Many celebrities were quick to express their approval of Jenner's "new self." Jenner was awarded ESPN's "Arthur Ashe Courage Award." *Vanity Fair* proudly revealed the "authentic" Jenner to the world. And anyone who spoke out against his "transformation" was vilified and shouted down with slanderous slurs.

---

[1] *Redefining Realness*, 172.

In this area of gender roles our culture's ideals are decidedly unbiblical. Whereas in the creation account God made them male and female (Gen. 1:27), Western nations have created a dizzying array of gender identities, relying on a suspect bifurcation between "sex" and "gender." While I always thought the two terms were synonymous, apparently "sex" refers to your biology, while "gender" is your personal sense about who you are.

Laura Erickson-Schroth's *Trans Bodies, Trans Selves: A Resource for the Transgendered Community* is something of a manual for the transgender movement. Its Amazon page puts it clearly:

> There is no one way to be transgender. Transgender and gender non-conforming people have many different ways of understanding their gender identities. Only recently have sex and gender been thought of as separate concepts, and we have learned that sex (traditionally thought of as physical or biological) is as variable as gender (traditionally thought of as social) . . . There are an estimated 700,000 transgendered individuals in the US and 15 million worldwide.[2]

Two years ago Facebook instituted a new gender policy, eliminating the "binary" designations of male and female and replacing them with a myriad of options, fifty-one to be exact.[3] Among the gender selections are intersex, gender queer, two-spirit, and gender fluid. The latter term indicates people who move through genders as it feels right to them. Given the statistics from Erickson-Schroth's book, 0.2% of the United States is transgender. I find it odd that Facebook identifies forty-nine gender configurations for two-tenths of 1% of the population.

What I find more incredible in this strange new world is that for the past decade we have heard from the sexually deviant that their orientation is inborn. Now that Pandora's box is open, though, there is no orientation at all. It is simply left to how you feel on any given morning.

Transgender rights advocate Janet Mock's quotation at the opening of

---

[2] www.amazon.com/Trans-Bodies-Selves-Transgender-Community/dp/0199325359 ?ie=UTF8&*Version*=1&*entries*=0, accessed May 14, 2016.

[3] "What Each of Facebook's 51 New Gender Options Mean," *The Daily Beast*, www.thedailybeast.com/articles/2014/02/15/the-complete-glossary-of-facebook-s-51-gender-options.html, accessed June 17, 2016.

this chapter that speaks about someone's identity being in a "constant state of flux," which contradicts the "inborn orientation" argument sexual rights advocates have been parroting for years. Author of *The New York Times* bestseller *Redefining Realness: My Path to Womanhood, Identity, Love and So Much More*, Mock was born male but underwent "sex reassignment surgery" at age eighteen.[4] Mock posits that a person should determine whatever she likes, regardless of what is inborn.

> There is no formula when it comes to gender and sexuality. . . . I wish that instead of investing in these hierarchies of what's right and who's wrong, what's authentic and who's not, and ranking people according to these rigid standards that ignore diversity in our genders and sexualities, we gave people freedom and resources to define, determine, and declare who they are.[5]

As we navigate this difficult topic, we will look at how the transgender movement is affecting American society. Then we will consider the biblical understanding of the genders and the church's response.

Transgenderism Is Transforming Society

The rights battle has moved from the bedroom to the bathroom. With the explosion of cases recently in America concerning who can use what restroom, it may seem that the transgender movement is relatively new, but that is a mistaken impression.

There has been an active transgender movement for at least a generation. In 2002 the Transgender Law Center began, with the National Center for Transgender Equality starting a year later. Both lobby for laws that positively affect transgender people. While the gay rights movement took center stage, transgenderism was quietly enacting policies.

For example, in 2013, the U.S. Senate passed the bipartisan Employment

---

[4] The label "sex change operation" is no longer in vogue. While "sex reassignment surgery" is acceptable, some prefer the term "gender confirmation surgery" (Loren Schechter, "'Gender Confirmation Surgery': What's in a Name?" *The Huffington Post*, http://new.www.huffingtonpost.com/loren-s-schechter-md-facs/gender-confirmation-surgery_b_1442262.html, accessed April 13, 2016).

[5] *Redefining Realness*, 50.

Non-Discrimination Act. Fortunately, the bill never made it to the House for a vote. The bill states: "The term 'gender identity' means the gender-related identity, appearance, or mannerisms or other gender-related characteristics of an individual, with or without regard to the individual's designated sex at birth." It later speaks of a person's "perceived" gender, but this is highly subjective. I suspect it is only a matter of time before the law is passed.

A pro-transgender agenda is in the works both in America and abroad.

· In late 2015, a Chicago transgender student threatened to sue if he was not allowed to use the girls' locker room. The school board capitulated.[6]

· A similar case earlier in 2015 in Missouri involved Lila Perry, who was born a male, self-identified as gay in ninth grade, then decided he wanted to be a woman. Offered a unisex bathroom, Perry refused, saying it was discriminatory. The school relented and now Perry, a man, uses the girls' locker room.[7]

· Another case in Virginia involved female student Gavin Grimm, who self-identifies as male and underwent hormonal treatments to appear masculine. The school district granted Grimm a unisex bathroom, but the student found this stigmatizing and sued for access to the boys' facilities. Backed by the Obama administration, Grimm won a federal appeals court ruling, the first of its kind that could have dramatic ramifications for other cases.[8]

· Student activists at several universities in the United Kingdom want sanitary bins for feminine products placed in men's bathrooms.[9]

---

[6] Jason Pierceson, "This Is What Americans Think about Transgender Students in Locker Rooms," *The Washington Post*, https://www.washingtonpost.com/news/monkey-cage/wp/2015/12/21/this-is-what-americans-think-about-transgender-students-in-locker-rooms/, accessed April 17, 2016.

[7] Doug Moore, "Hillsboro High Students Walk Out over Transgender Dispute," *St. Louis Post-Dispatch*, www.stltoday.com/news/local/education/hillsboro-high-students-walk-out-over-transgender-dispute/article_be488fab-d239-5944-9733-32f569dcdc32.html, accessed May 17, 2016.

[8] "Court Overturns Virginia School's Transgender Bathroom Rule," Fox News, www.foxnews.com/us/2016/04/19/court-overturns-virginia-schools-transgender-bathroom-rule.html, accessed June 1, 2016.

[9] Jonathan Petre, "Students Call for Sanitary Bins to Be Placed in Male Toilets for Transgender Men on Their Period," Mail Online, www.dailymail.co.uk/news/article-3567616/Students-call-sanitary-bins-placed-male-toilets-transgender-men-periods.html, accessed May 18, 2016.

- High-profile cases move our society toward embracing transgenderism. Though now divorced, Brad Pitt and Angelina Jolie are helping their nine-year-old daughter Shiloh as she "works through her gender identity."[10]
- For more than two years, Germany has offered a third option on birth certificates: "indeterminate."[11] Nepal, India, Bangladesh, Australia, and New Zealand have third-gender options for official documents such as passports.[12]
- Children as young as four are being asked in the United Kingdom to choose their gender.[13]
- Back in 2008, Oprah Winfrey's show covered the "first pregnant man." Thomas Beatie was born a woman but transitioned to male with a double mastectomy and male hormone injections, but Beatie kept the uterus and was impregnated through in vitro fertilization.[14]
- MMA (mixed martial arts) fighter Fallon Fox was born male, transitioned to female, and is now thrashing women competitors.[15]
- Gender-neutral baby names (e.g., Amari, Karter, Phoenix, Reese, Parker, Sawyer) are on the rise, with BabyCenter declaring 2015 "the year of the gender neutral baby."[16]

---

[10] Jen Heger, "Sister to Brother?" Radar Online, http://radaronline.com/celebrity-news/shiloh-transgender-claims-brad-pitt-angelina-jolie-coping-daughter-gender-idenity/, accessed April 1, 2016.

[11] Bill Chappell, "Germany Offers Third Gender Option on Birth Certificates," NPR, www.npr.org/sections/thetwo-way/2013/11/01/242366812/germany-offers-third-gender-option-on-birth-certificates, accessed June 1, 2016.

[12] Kyle Knight, "Dividing by Three: Nepal Recognizes a Third Gender," World Policy Blog, www.worldpolicy.org/blog/2012/02/01/dividing-three-nepal-recognizes-third-gender, accessed June 1, 2016.

[13] Amanda Prestigiacomo, "Four-Year-Olds Being Asked to Choose Gender in Britain," *The Daily Wire*, www.dailywire.com/news/5345/four-year-olds-being-asked-choose-gender-britain-amanda-prestigiacomo, accessed June 2, 2016.

[14] *The Oprah Show*, www.oprah.com/oprahshow/First-TV-Interview-The-Pregnant-Man, accessed June 16, 2016.

[15] Glennisha Morgan, "Fallon Fox, Transgender MMA Fighter, Wins First Match since Coming Out," *The Huffington Post*, www.huffingtonpost.com/2013/05/28/fallon-fox-transgender-victory_n_3345934.html, accessed June 19, 2016.

[16] Jennifer O'Niell, "Most Popular Baby Names of 2015 Revealed," Yahoo! News, https://www.yahoo.com/parenting/most-popular-baby-names-of-2015-revealed-100040311.html, accessed January 17, 2016.

Pay attention to that quote. It does not say "gender-neutral baby *name*," it says "gender-neutral *baby*." I am not being pedantic. Our culture is moving away from gender distinctions toward a fuzzier notion of maleness and femaleness. The name is not just a label, it is a statement.

Along with this transformation of our society comes the proper terminology. Transgender people should be referred to in the plural. You wouldn't speak about "her" book when talking about Catherine, you'd say "their" book.[17] Getting this wrong, especially in our overly sensitive, politically correct culture, can bring unwanted accusations your way.[18]

Gender Roles ≠ Gender Inferiority

Jesus Christ affirmed the created order (Gen. 1:27) of male and female:

> "Haven't you read," he replied, "that at the beginning the Creator 'made them male and female,' and said, 'For this reason a man will leave his father and mother and be united to his wife, and the two will become one flesh'?" (Matt. 19:4–5)

Whatever else we may think about the gender confusion gripping Western society, evangelicals ought to affirm that God made two genders and only two. We must reject additional manmade categories. Contrary to the trans-movement, biological facts are not social constructs. The problem is seeing the issue ideologically instead of biologically.

I own a car and a computer. Both are wonderful machines that perform important functions, but when I run to the convenience store to pick up a gallon of milk, I don't strap myself into my computer. I take my automobile. This says nothing either good or bad about my computer.

Right now I am doing something on my PC that I cannot do with my car,

---

[17] Sam Escobar, "I'm Not Male. I'm Not Female. Please Don't Ask Me about My Junk," *Esquire*, www.esquire.com/lifestyle/sex/news/a43461/what-is-non-binary-gender/, accessed June 1, 2016.

[18] New gender-neutral pronouns have also been invented to rectify this problem, such as "ze" and "hir," as this article explains: Kristina C, "Ze, Hir, Hirs; He, She, They: Which Pronoun Are You?" Care2, www.care2.com/causes/ze-hir-hirs-he-she-they-which-pronoun-are-you.html, accessed October 29, 2016.

but that says nothing good or bad about my car. My computer is designed for certain tasks and my automobile is designed for others.

If I sat on my computer and tried to drive it, I would damage it. Misusing something can result in its destruction. Anybody who has used a screwdriver as a hammer can attest to this. Ultimately the tool breaks because it was never intended to do that job.

Gender is restrictive by its very nature. A man cannot give birth no matter how desperately he wants to get in touch with his "feminine side." We need to affirm equality between the genders while not falling into identity. Men and women are not clones of each other.

Men and women are made in God's image (Gen. 1:27; 5:1–2) and are equal in value and essence. Yet, we can rejoice in the different roles each gender possesses. The statement "A woman can give birth, a man cannot" does not disparage maleness. On the contrary, it celebrates the differences between male and female (and every man I know is quite happy women are the ones giving birth!). Similarly, the statement "A woman should not be an elder in the church" demarcates gender roles. It says nothing about the value of one gender over the other.

Consider the Trinity. Each person—Father, Son, and Holy Spirit—is equally God. The statement "Only the Son became a man" does not belittle the Father or the Spirit. Similarly, "The Son willingly submits to the Father's will" does not make the Son ontologically inferior to the Father. They both remain co-existent and co-eternal. Yet this does not mean that their responsibilities and functions must be absolutely identical.

The problem with the modern feminist and transgender movements, as well as the egalitarianism of much of Christianity today, is that they confuse function with value. "Submission" has become a dirty word, yet Jesus Christ was all he was meant to be precisely because he submitted his will to his heavenly Father. We can have ontological equality while also having functional hierarchy.

In the design of gender we see our Creator in the balanced role of engineer and artist. There is a functional beauty to male and female; their bodies are complementarily designed; they "fit" both physically and emotionally.[19]

---

[19] In homosexual relationships, often one partner plays the role of the opposite gender, implying that despite their perversion of sexuality, homosexual couples recognize the natural pairing designed by God in making them "male and female."

Gender-neutral trends and the hatred of male-female distinctions are nothing more than an indictment of God's design for his creation.[20]

While I will speak more in chapter 10 about the importance of gender roles in the family, suffice it for now to ask a rhetorical question: is it a coincidence that as the nuclear family has disintegrated in America, gender dysphoria is on the increase? The transgender movement's obliteration of gender distinctions will eventually undercut any notion (at least as recognized by the state or by law) of the family.

Some Christians don't realize the seismic shift that is taking place in American culture. Unfortunately, we have hurried it along. Consider where we spend our hard-earned money. Much of it goes to movie and music industries driven by counter-Christian ideals. Solid, evangelical believers won't bat an eye giving money to organizations with values entirely at odds with Christ.

North Carolina has been in the middle of the transgender bathroom drama in America. Immediately upon enacting the level-headed law that forbids people of one sex from using bathrooms designated for the other gender, rocker Bruce Springsteen canceled a concert, citing the "bigotry" of North Carolina lawmakers. I don't know why it took this long for the light to go on in my head. "Why am I paying money to listen to music from people like this?" I asked myself.

I don't mean evangelicals must tediously go down the list of businesses, only buying products from Christian enterprises. However, when Target came out with its pro-transgender bathroom policy, while Walmart maintains traditional, Christian values, why shouldn't I support the corporation with the principles I want promoted in America? Isn't it wiser to spend my money at a decidedly Christian establishment like Chick-fil-A, than at a fast food hangout run by neo-pagans?

While I have never been one to jump on the boycott bandwagon, I am changing my tune. Christians should not give money to openly anti-Christian organizations, as long as it is within reason and ability. If your electricity only comes from atheists, you don't have much choice, but if you can choose between three burger joints of equal quality, pick the one that supports Christian values.

---

[20] For a thorough treatment of the biblical perspective on gender roles and distinctions, see Sam Andreades's *enGendered: God's Gift of Gender Difference in Relationship*.

Women in Church Leadership

Christians are complicit with our culture's slide from Judeo-Christian values because many have abandoned biblical principles for church leadership. It is no coincidence that virtually all the churches that allow homosexuals to serve as pastors and elders first permitted women to do it. Denying gender complementarity is the road to rejecting sexual complementarity. The arguments for both are largely the same.

For example, the Presbyterian Church (USA) began allowing women to minister the Word and sacraments in 1956, and sanctioned openly gay ministers in 2012. The Evangelical Lutheran Church in America did the same in 1970 with women and with gays forty years later. For the Episcopal Church (US) it was 1976 and 2009. The United Methodist Church began ordaining women in 1956, and while it does not allow homosexuals in the clergy, a commission formed in 2016 to look into LGBT issues. Gay rights groups are hopeful about the outcome.

A debate within evangelicalism exists between those who believe women should be certified to do anything a man does (the egalitarian position) and those who believe that God has ordained functional hierarchy and roles for the genders (the complementarian position). Today the egalitarian position is the majority view, which is certainly a mistake.

Egalitarians argue that male headship is a consequence of the fall, but it has existed since creation and continues into the biblical institutions of marriage and church leadership. Male headship was present in Eden before Adam and Eve sinned:

- Adam was created first, then Eve. God could easily have done it the opposite way.
- Eve was created as a helper for Adam (see also 1 Cor. 11:8–9).
- Adam gave the name "woman" (Gen. 2:23) and later "Eve" (3:20) to her. In Scripture, the one who names has authority over the one who is named.
- God directly addresses Adam, not Eve, before and after the fall, signifying his headship in the relationship.
- Despite Eve eating the fruit first, Adam is held responsible; his sin is inherited by his progeny (Rom. 5:12). Adam represents humanity, not Eve.

- Jesus is called the "last Adam" (1 Cor. 15:45), showing a connection between the one who represents humanity in the fall and the one who represents us in redemption.[21]

Besides, if God had wanted to make the woman equal in every manner to the man, he would have taken another handful of dirt to form her. However, he took a rib from Adam. Paul connects this created order with leadership in the church (1 Tim. 2:12–14), and his list of requirements for elders speaks of men taking the role, not women (1 Tim. 3:1–7; Titus 1:6–9).

Egalitarians say that Paul's qualifications for elders do not expressly prohibit women. Paul never says, "A woman cannot be an elder." But if I write, "Elders must be six feet tall," someone cannot later claim that a five-foot man can be an elder because I did not prohibit five-foot men. By laying out the clear requirements for an elder, I do not have to list all the negations of those requirements.

Nor is Paul using generic language. Past societies regularly used the masculine pronoun "he" to refer to anyone, whether male or female. Only recently have we moved through the cumbersome "he or she" language of gender neutrality to a mixing of pronouns that I am sure drives English purists batty, using "they" for singular nouns. When Paul says of an elder, "He must be trustworthy," the argument goes that Paul is using the generic "he" and is open to women filling the role. However, when Paul says an elder "must be faithful to his wife" (Titus 1:6), clearly he is speaking about men.

Another typical argument against male-only eldership is that elsewhere Paul erases distinctions between the genders when he writes: "There is neither Jew nor Gentile, neither slave nor free, nor is there male and female, for you are all one in Christ Jesus" (Gal. 3:28). However, Paul is not declaring a gender-free society. The context is how people come to faith in Jesus, and in that case, there is no distinction. "So in Christ Jesus you are all children of God through faith" (Gal. 3:26). This passage has nothing to do with church leadership roles.

Recently I switched from the 1984 rendering to the 2011 translation of the New International Version (NIV). While there are definite improvements, there is one change I hesitate to applaud—the one made in Romans 16:1. In the 1984 translation, Phoebe is called a "servant" (translating the

---

[21] Consult Grudem's *Systematic Theology* (454–68) for further elaboration.

Greek *diakonos*). In the 2011 translation, though, Phoebe is called a "deacon." This is the sole instance that *diakonos* was changed from "servant" to "deacon" in the updated NIV.

I asked the translators why this change was made, and was told there have been no new discoveries in the manuscript evidence that required the replacement. For Baptists (including myself) the word "deacon" is loaded with meaning. It is an elected church office, not a generic label for someone who serves.[22]

Many evangelical churches limit eldership to men but have deaconesses in the church. I recognize that well-meaning believers are on both sides of this debate. While liberal Christians often kowtow to modern society and change their theology to fit the times, I can hardly believe that this is the motivation when evangelical Christians argue for females occupying what have traditionally been male roles in the church.

That being said, New Testament examples abound of males occupying leadership positions when capable women were available. Jesus chose men as his disciples, and the early church picked between two men to replace Judas.[23] Further, if ever there was the right place to choose women for the job—to "wait on tables" (Acts 6:2) in a male-dominated society—the selection of the "proto-deacons" was certainly it. Nevertheless, seven men were selected.

Some may think, "This is just good old-fashioned misogyny." But reveling in God's design for females does not destroy women, it liberates them. The clear, biblical mandate is male leadership in the church. Unfortunately, instead of the modern church standing against culture's warfare against God's created order for the genders, we have allowed its influence to seep into our congregations. That we are now shocked when the sexually immoral are granted leadership in our churches merely exposes our

---

[22] This is the same committee that created the gender-neutral Today's New International Version in 2002, which was almost immediately a complete failure. I cannot help but feel suspicious about the Romans 16:1 change.

[23] The argument that Jesus was forced to choose men as his disciples because of cultural pressures is weak. If there was anybody who on godly principle alone would do what was right, it was Jesus. To argue that Jesus wanted to choose women for the Twelve but was compelled not to by cultural and religious pressures ignores the numerous times Jesus did just that: flaunt the customs of the day as the kingdom of God broke into first-century life through his advent (e.g., spoke alone to a Samaritan woman, healed on the Sabbath, etc.).

spiritual foolishness. By stubbornly snubbing God's design, many churches are guilty of hurrying our society along the transgender route by confusing the complementary roles God has given men and women.

Hard versus Soft Feminism

In the chapter on the sanctity of life, I took jabs at what I call "hard feminism." These feminists pretend there is nothing different between men and women. Consequently, men are seen as redundant, and the trendy move among Hollywood actresses to have babies on their own ("I don't need a man to raise a child") is par for the course. Instead of reveling in our differences as made by our Creator, these feminists ironically ooze a visceral hatred for women, which they try to mold into the image of men. The transgender movement is also an expression of this misogyny.

The transgender community is exploiting Title IX, the 1972 federal law prohibiting educational institutions from sexual discrimination in their sports programs. Ironically, a transvestite who is genetically male is allowed to compete against genetically female opponents.[24]

Imagine a 100-meter race in the Olympics, where in the "female" category every athlete but one is genetically male. How is this fair? Men have more muscle mass than women. They are naturally stronger and faster. To call a man a woman is not only unfair in this context, it is an insult to genuine females. Plus, authentic women would be getting shut out of female events.[25]

Soft feminism, on the other hand, simply calls for the fair treatment of the fairer sex. Women occasionally encounter a "glass ceiling" in certain occupations because of their gender.[26] A woman who has the same

---

[24] Here's one example of a male allowed to compete against girls in track and field in high school: Beth Bragg, "At Alaska State Track Meet, a Transgender Athlete Makes Her Mark," Alaska Dispatch News, www.adn.com/sports/2016/05/27/at-alaska-state-track-meet-a-transgender-athlete-makes-her-mark/, accessed June 3, 2016.

[25] South African track and field athlete Caster Semenya sparked controversy at the Rio Olympics in 2016 by winning gold in the women's 800-meter race. Semenya has been diagnosed with hyperandrogenism, which means she has testosterone levels far higher than those of typical females. Many other athletes in the race complained that Semenya had an unfair advantage. In late 2015, Semenya married "her" girlfriend and even paid the "bride price" that is traditionally paid by men in South African culture.

[26] However, this is becoming more difficult to find, and because of quotas women can enjoy a competitive advantage over men.

qualifications and experience should be paid a salary equal to that of a man applying for the same job.

Recently the U.S. women's soccer team complained that they got paid anywhere from 20% to 60% less than their male counterparts, despite bringing in more revenue.[27] Female doctors make on average about 10% to 20% less than their male counterparts.[28]

I agree that women should have opportunities to compete on a level playing field with men. Still, it is sometimes difficult to distinguish between the two kinds of feminism, just as it is difficult to differentiate between two kinds of transgenderism.

Category 1: Transgenderism as Environmental

I had a difficult time writing this chapter. I began when the news broke out about Bruce Jenner, and a year later I was still writing it! Part of my trouble was due to the two kinds of transgender people that we encounter today. Let me explain.

In chapter 9, I am unambiguous: homosexuality is not inborn, it is learned. With transgenderism, though, I require a subtler argument, one that recognizes the substantial proof that some people are born with gender confusion.

There are two categories of transsexual people. One includes someone like Bruce Jenner who has no genetic or physical abnormalities. The gender they were born with is distinct and unconfused. Why they seek to imitate the opposite sex can be chalked up to environment, experiences, and personal preference. These people have been overcome by sin, which is precisely what we should label it, and we must not transform our society to accommodate them. A man wearing lipstick and a dress has emotional and psychological problems that ought to be addressed through the appropriate avenues. We cannot coddle this behavior let alone praise it.

The *Vanity Fair* cover depicting Bruce Jenner's "authentic self" is of a

---

[27] Chris Isador, "U.S. Women Soccer Players Charge Pay Discrimination," CNN Money, http://money.cnn.com/2016/03/31/news/companies/womens-soccer-equal-pay/index.html, accessed May 1, 2016.

[28] Erin Brodwin and Dragan Radovanovic, "Here's How Much Money Doctors Actually Make," Yahoo! Finance, http://finance.yahoo.com/news/heres-much-money-doctors-actually-185858177.html, accessed May 17, 2016.

65-year-old grandfather who, through a series of plastic surgeries, a large amount of makeup, the shaving of the bones in his forehead and trimming of his cheekbones, the removal of body hair, the injection of large amounts of synthetic chemicals, and the tucking away of certain body parts, was made to appear to be a woman. Jenner's gender was not changed, it was plastered over. This is not spectacular; this is spectacle.

Granted, I am concentrating on the physical aspects of Jenner's transformation. The psychological and spiritual issues are undoubtedly deep. Jenner is a sinner who has been overcome by the beast within us all. I cannot begin to relate to the series of life events that caused Jenner to undergo incredible medical procedures, but I do understand sin. The beauty of God's Word is that it tells us the truth about everybody, equally, without sugar-coating it. Paul writes that we are by nature objects of wrath (Eph. 2:3). Sin is our default mode. Each one of us, if left to our own devices, will drift toward that which is innate to us. We can do no other until God through his Holy Spirit transforms us into the image of his perfect Son.

If I take God's Word seriously, I have to believe that Jenner is deeply confused and horribly hurting, and only by God's grace found in Jesus Christ can he be repaired. Does he wake up, look in the mirror, and proclaim, "I am finally liberated!" Or does he say, "What have I done?" The media are begging us to believe the former proclamation, but I cannot help but think that the latter is more the truth.

While the Old Testament has much to say about sexual immorality and perversion, there is little that directly impinges on transgenderism. However, there is a law that speaks to the issue. "A woman must not wear men's clothing, nor a man wear women's clothing, for the LORD your God detests anyone who does this" (Deut. 22:5).

Gender confusion is evidently nothing new. Many commands in the Mosaic Law were given in the context of Canaanite practices, and this is most likely one. While the command to not "cross dress" strikes even the most ardent evangelical as outdated, keep in mind why God prescribed it. In addition to having sex with animals, bowing to idols, and sacrificing children, the Canaanites practiced transvestism and God did not want his people behaving similarly.

I wonder how the world at the time of Noah became so degenerate that it provoked God to wipe out 99.9% of the population? And what led the Canaanite nations to adopt such despicable behavior that God commanded the Israelites to eradicate them?

Perhaps a clue is given in the book of Judges. As Israel began to embrace Canaanite practices like idolatry, self-mutilation, and temple prostitution, "everyone did as they saw fit" (Judg. 21:25). This is a shocking statement, especially in light of our impression that relativism is a recent phenomenon. More than three thousand years ago the behavior of God's chosen people can be characterized in this way. This provides insight into what is currently happening in American culture.

We can expect to see more of these stories in the news as our society drifts (or runs) from God's design and toward a sinister, evil depravity the seeds of which were sown in Eden by the serpent. Will we become like the people of Noah's day, or the early inhabitants of Canaan? Will God eventually come to us and say, "Enough!"?

By the way, if it is true that despite chromosomes and DNA and gender-specific body parts I can decide to "identify" with a gender contrary to my actual configuration, then why can't I do the same thing when it comes to race? I am a Caucasian with majority Russian and German blood. Why can't I "self-identify" as a black person and qualify for scholarships reserved for African Americans? If a woman can claim to be a man, why can't a white man claim to be black?

This is not a fanciful fabrication. In 2015, Rachel Dolezal was forced to resign as president of the NAACP chapter in Spokane, Washington, because she falsely identified herself as African American despite being Caucasian.[29] This was happening at the same time as Bruce Jenner's revelation.

People in the black community were angry because Dolezal's assertion was offensive to those who are actually black, but some of these same people applauded Jenner's actions. I see little difference between Dolezal's "I identify as black" and Jenner's self-identification as a woman. If a person with male chromosomes, male anatomy, male DNA, and male hormones can claim to be a woman, why can't a white person claim to be black? After all, "self-identification" is what really matters, right?

---

[29] Dylan Stableford, "Rachel Dolezal: 'I Identify as Black,'" Yahoo! News, https://www.yahoo.com/news/rachel-dolezal-naacp-black-white-misrepresenting-interview-today-110003467.html?ref=gs, accessed August 21, 2015.

When a man says, "I identify as a woman," what can that truly mean? Is this not offensive to genuine women?[30] Castrating a man does not make him female, any more than a hysterectomy makes a woman a man. Gender is immutable. There are two of them, male and female, created at the beginning by our omnipotent Maker, wonderfully and fearfully made, man and woman, in God's image, to God's glory. Any attack on those genders is an attack on God.

The transgender movement confuses personal preference with fact. "I love apples; I don't like strawberries" is personal preference. However, "apples are a vegetable" is factually inaccurate. Similarly, a man may prefer to behave like a woman, but that does not mean he is female.

Category 2: Transgenderism as Genetic

If physical abnormalities such as Down syndrome are inborn, couldn't there be genetic abnormalities that result in transgenderism? This second transsexual category is people born with "gender dysphoria." Here the church must tread delicately.

Cases where a person's chromosomal (genetic) sex is inconsistent with her phenotypic (physical) sex may result in gender dysphoria, such as the following:

- *Intersex.* This is the umbrella term signifying births where the chromosomes and genitals are mixed and/or the genitalia are ambiguous. It is usually treated hormonally or surgically (with a choice made by the parents as to which gender they believe their child should be). There is a lot of debate on what constitutes intersex (e.g., large clitoris or small penis).
- *Hermaphrodite.* A hermaphrodite is born with both male and female organs where a clear determination cannot be made. This is extremely rare and there are no documented cases of a person having *functioning* ovaries and testicles. The term has fallen out of use in favor of the broader "intersex."

---

[30] Some feminists think Jenner's case is a subtle form of misogyny. "Germaine Greer Slams Bruce Jenner: 'Our Acceptance of Her Is Misogynistic,'" Yahoo! News, https://www.yahoo.com/news/germaine-greer-slams-caitlyn-jenner-our-083626581.html?ref=gs, accessed November 11, 2015.

- *Congenital adrenal hyperplasia.* Congential adrenal hyperplasia is the result of an enzyme gene mutation that affects the development of sex steroids, resulting in ambiguous genitalia and delayed or failed development of puberty.
- *Turner Syndrome.* This is a syndrome in which females are born missing all or part of the X chromosome, resulting in sterility and no breast development or menstruation.
- *Klinefelter Syndrome.* This is a syndrome in males caused by two or more X chromosomes, resulting in sterility, breast development, and small genitalia.
- *Various forms of gonadal dysgenesis.* Gonadal dysgenesis is hormonal failure that affects both sexes in the development of secondary sex characteristics—those traits not directly associated with reproduction yet that help distinguish between the two genders (e.g., body and face shape, breast development, facial hair in males). A reasonable estimate is that less than 1% of births exhibit some form of gender dysphoria. While thankfully a low figure, this is by no means an insignificant number.

How should the church respond? I imagine the heartbreak parents experience when faced with an intersex baby. A prudent response cannot treat this type of transgenderism similarly to the Bruce Jenner kind that involves a blatant choice to move away from one's true gender.

Responding to Transgenderism

Christian reactions usually fall on polar opposites. On the one side is shrill condemnation, as if this particular sin is the worst evil to ever befall the human race. On the other side is passive capitulation that approves the sin while piously claiming that such commendation is the "Christian" thing to do. Navigating between these two reactions is difficult.[31] I offer the following guidelines.

---

[31] The Salzburg Declaration adopted in September 2015 by the Congress of the International Christian Network captures this balance well: www.ikbg.net/pdf/Salzburger-Erklaerung-englisch.pdf.

1. Protect our children

Our culture's love affair with sexual immorality puts children in harm's way of sexual predators, as well as tempting them to personally dabble in sexual perversity. The transgender movement is no exception.

I have a friend whose twenty-year-old nephew came home and told his parents they should call him Olivia. This young man grew up in a strong, Christian home and had not, as far as his parents knew, been abused or sexually mistreated.

Yet beginning in his late teens, he became addicted to gaming. It had gotten to the point where he slept during the day and gamed all night. He became detached from reality and, through a series of events, became the "bitch" of a man he met online.

Did my friend's nephew finally "find his true self," or was he overcome by sinful influences and temptations? He had no genetic abnormalities. Let it be a warning to parents who allow their children unlimited access to media. As we will see in chapter 8, our children are under an unprecedented amount of temptation to imbibe sexually immoral material through television programs, movies, and the Internet. Christian parents who permit their children to have televisions in their bedrooms, or unlimited Internet access on their laptops or cell phones, are courting disaster.

2. Model gender roles

In 2016, the American College of Pediatricians affirmed male and female as the only gender types, while condemning any other supposed configurations as "a sign of confused thinking" and a form of "child abuse."[32] The entire statement is a must-read, but one item is important for us here. Despite gender confusion in some children, the vast majority of them naturally work it out after puberty, without any chemical or medical intervention:

> Rates of suicide are twenty times greater among adults who use
> cross-sex hormones and undergo sex reassignment surgery, even

---

[32] "Gender Ideology Harms Children," www.acpeds.org/the-college-speaks/position
-statements/gender-ideology-harms-children, accessed May 19, 2016.

in Sweden which is among the most LGBTQ-affirming countries. What compassionate and reasonable person would condemn young children to this fate knowing that after puberty as many as 88% of girls and 98% of boys will eventually accept reality and achieve a state of mental and physical health?[33]

This underlines the importance of parents modeling clearly defined gender roles for their children. God has designed family in such a way that fathers teach their boys what it means to be men, and girls learn from their mothers what it means to be women. Gay marriages, single-parent homes, homosexual adoptions, and transgenderism undermine God's design for children to grow up with healthy images of the two genders.

3. Fight the legal battles

While laws will not change a person's heart, they can protect the greater society from predators and perverts. Allowing men to use women's facilities is dangerous. Given current statistics, you are forty-five times more likely to run into a sex offender than someone who is transgender.[34] On June 2, 2016, *Christianity Today* reported that a man undressed in a women's locker room in a Seattle Parks and Recreation facility, citing his rights under Washington's transgender law.[35] In Canada, a sexual predator claiming to be transgender gained access to two women's shelters where he abused several occupants.[36] Christians who sit by and say nothing about the current

---

[33] The percentages come from the *Diagnostic and Statistical Manual* of the American Psychiatric Association.

[34] Rosslynn Smith, "Who Will Be Using Opposite Sex Bathrooms under Cover of Being 'Transgender'?" American Thinker, www.americanthinker.com/blog/2016/06/who_will_be_using_opposite_sex_bathrooms_under_cover_of_being_transgender.html, accessed June 17, 2016.

[35] Jonah Hicap, "Man Undresses in Front of Women in Seattle Locker Room," *Christianity Today*, www.christiantoday.com/article/man.undresses.in.front.of.women.in.seattle.locker.room.asserts.right.to.do.so.under.states.transgender.bathroom.policy/80262.htm, accessed March 18, 2016.

[36] Sam Pazzano, "Predator Who Claimed to Be Transgender Declared Dangerous Sex Offender," *Toronto Sun*, www.torontosun.com/2014/02/26/predator-who-claimed-to-be-transgender-declared-dangerous-offender, accessed June 2, 2016.

legal environment are granting implicit approval of the transgender desire to transform our society.

Also, it may not simply be our society that the trans-agenda wants to transform, but our churches as well. Recently the Massachusetts Commission Against Discrimination published guidelines concerning bathroom policies in places of "public accommodation," and the law that went into effect October 1, 2016 will include churches. Several churches have banded together and sued the state for infringing on their religious freedom.[37]

Much of the legal battle with transgenderism is tantamount to creating legislation against the law of gravity. It is nonsensical to create laws that negatively impinge on the greater society for a miniscule slice of the populace who are gender confused, especially when those rulings can have potentially life-threatening consequences. These laws are pushed by an unhinged, vocal, aggressive minority. Christians must take a stand.

4. Show compassion and condemnation, where appropriate

Surveys show that 41% of transgendered individuals attempt suicide at some point in their lives, nearly ten times the national average.[38] Christian educator Megan DeFranza, author of *Sex Difference in Christian Theology: Male, Female, and Intersex in the Image of God,* says the church marginalizes people with sexual development disorders. As Christians, we must care for people. Like Jesus with the "prostitutes and sinners," we need to reach out with the love of Christ.

Christians can delineate between the sexual predator who puts on a dress so he can exploit liberal bathroom laws, and the person who is born intersex and experiences gender confusion. The former deserves our condemnation, the latter our compassion.

---

[37] "Churches Sue over Massachusetts Transgender Law," *Boston Herald,* www.bostonherald.com/news/local_coverage/2016/10/churches_sue_over_massachusetts_transgender_bathroom_law, accessed October 29. 2016.

[38] Fr. Mark Hodges, "The Transgender Suicide Epidemic: Is Accepting Their Confusion Really the Answer?" Life Site, www.lifesitenews.com/news/gender-confused-suicide-rate-ten-times-national-average, accessed June 17, 2016.

CHAPTER EIGHT

God's Created Order
and Sexual Morality

Iamliterallyopentoeverysinglethingthatisconsentinganddoesn'tinvolvean animalandeveryoneisofage...I'mdownwithanyadult—anyoneovertheage of18whoisdowntoloveme.Idon'trelatetobeingboyorgirl,andIdon'thaveto have my partner relate to boy or girl.

—MILEY CYRUS[1]

A FEW YEARS AGO I learned a new word—"pansexual." An article about Texas congresswoman Mary Gonzalez caught my attention. She was elected as Texas's first lesbian House member but had since declared herself pansexual, meaning she is attracted to all gender identities. To call her bisexual is a "binary" way of thinking about sexual identity that is too restrictive.[2]

Miley Cyrus, the singer-actress best known for her childhood role as Hannah Montana on the Disney Channel, has become a controversial star. Her infamy rose with her "twerking" on the 2013 MTV Music Video Awards, and since then she has become increasingly risqué in her sexuality. She shared with *Paper Magazine* that she is "gender fluid" and "pansexual." Virtually anything goes for Cyrus, as her quote at the opening of this chapter testifies.

Christians rightly bemoan Western culture as too sexualized. With the

---

[1] Korin Miller, "Miley Cyrus Identifies at Pansexual: What Does That Mean, Exactly?" Yahoo! Beauty, www.yahoo.com/health/miley-cyrus-identifies-as-pansexual-what-does-127797473807.html, accessed August 27, 2015.

[2] Michelangelo Signorile, "Mary Gonzales, First Openly Pansexual Legislator, Explains How She Is Changing Minds in Texas," *The Huffington Post*, www.huffingtonpost.com/2015/05/29/mary-gonzalez-pansexual_n_7433432.html, accessed August 30, 2015.

rise of the "free sex" movement, what used to be a simple, biblical combination of two genders has become a pansexual free-for-all. "Gay," "lesbian," "bisexual," "transgender," "intersex," "pansexual," and "metrosexual" are just a few of the words seen daily in headlines.[3]

If the multiplicity of terms is any proof, there is a whole lot of sex going on in our culture. I wonder if this reveals sexual diversity or sexual confusion. Whereas God made them male and female, we have remade them hetero-, homo-, trans-, bi-, metro-, a-, inter-, poly-, pan-, and every other prefix we can think of.

In this chapter, we will explore how fallen humans have deviated from God's design for sex, covering perversions prevalent in our society such as pedophilia, incest, prostitution, and pornography.[4] Along the way, I will suggest how Christians should respond to a culture fixated on sexual deviancy.

Sex Is Good

Sex is an incredible gift God bestowed on humanity not only so we can "be fruitful and multiply" (Gen. 1:28), but also for our enjoyment. Long after married couples are past the age of childbearing, they can enjoy sexual fulfillment in each other. In fact, Paul sees marital sex as so important that he prohibits one partner from withholding it from the other, unless it is mutually agreed on (1 Cor. 7:5). Unfortunately, as is the case with virtually every good thing God has given us, we have a sinful tendency to warp and devalue the gift of sex.

I am concerned that as a negative reaction against our society's abuse of sex, many Christians have been programmed into thinking sex is naturally evil. There has been a long tradition of this attitude, perhaps originating with the fourth-century bishop Augustine, who believed that even sex in the context of marriage involved sinful concupiscence or lust.

Perhaps it stems from our desire to protect our children from the evils

---

[3] This *Huffington Post* article catalogues some other terms, such as "greysexual," "demisexual," and "skoliosexual": Noah Michelson, "What's a Skoliosexual?" *The Huffington Post*, www.huffingtonpost.com/entry/skoliosexual-zucchini-and-10-other-sexual-identity-terms-you-probably-dont-know_561bf841e4b0082030a35f80?cps=gravity_5043_5857459970857833095, accessed September 14, 2015.

[4] Homosexuality and adultery are dealt with in later chapters.

that come from using sex in ways displeasing to God. Often Christian parents, armed with good intentions, drum into the heads of their adolescents that a natural, biological part of them is evil. As their hormones kick in, they become repulsed by urges they know from their parents to be from the devil.

These same believers enter adulthood with the perception that sexual activity is wrong. Unfortunately, counselors hear numerous stories from Christian couples who have found sex to be a disappointment. One reason is because they have entered marriage with these negative images of sex.[5]

We should talk to our children about sex much like we speak to them about dessert. We don't demonize dessert: "Dessert is bad, dessert is evil, you should never want dessert!" Instead, we tell them that it is a good thing but only in the proper time; they must eat all their vegetables before they can enjoy it. Sex is a gift from God, given for our delight, but we can ruin it if we are not careful.

God is not a killjoy who knows that multiple sex partners are more satisfying than lifelong monogamy. He commands us to remain faithful because fidelity is more satisfying than promiscuity. However, the world repeatedly tells us that having sex with as many people as possible will bring fulfillment. This implies that the Designer of sex is ignorant of his own creation.

This is similar to the lie the serpent told Eve in Eden. He said that God was withholding something good from her and that if she ate the fruit, she would become like God, who basically wanted to keep all the goodies for himself (Gen. 3:5).

Please understand: God made sex. He designed men and women in a complementary way; we are built for each other. Any message that says otherwise is not godly. Nevertheless, sex is not solely about us. As with all things, how we use this gift from God is a barometer of our relationship with him.

Frequently, Christian debates on sex boil down to speaking exclusively about homosexuality, as if it is the chief sexual sin. Perhaps this is due to the topic becoming so politicized in our culture. After all, we do not see

---

[5] Another reason Christian couples experience disappointment with sex is because one or both spouses have unwittingly bought into the world's definition of sex, which we will look at shortly.

"pedophile pride" parades in our cities or "we're adulterers and proud of it" signs. It is natural that Christian apologetics concentrates on what is in many respects *the* ethical issue of our time. Militant homosexuals must be addressed, but other forms of sexual perversion should likewise be tackled. Pornography, prostitution, adultery, fornication (premarital sex), sodomy (homosexual and heterosexual), incest, rape, bestiality, sadomasochism, and pedophilia are some of the sexual perversions our society craves.

I say "perversion" because in the truest sense of the word, anything that warps the original intention and design of something "perverts" it. Adultery perverts God's design for marriage; incest perverts God's design for the family; homosexuality perverts God's design for the genders.

After the creation of Eve from Adam's rib, Genesis records: "That is why a man leaves his father and mother and is united to his wife, and they become one flesh" (2:24). However, sexual intercourse does not merely involve a physical union, but a mental, emotional, and spiritual union as well.

In 1 Corinthians 6, Paul writes to believers who thought "I have the right to do anything" (v. 12), warning them of the spiritual connection in mis-using sex:

> Do you not know that your bodies are members of Christ himself? Shall I then take the members of Christ and unite them with a prostitute? Never! Do you not know that he who unites himself with a prostitute is one with her in body? For it is said, "The two will become one flesh." But whoever is united with the Lord is one with him in spirit. Flee from sexual immorality. All other sins a person commits are outside the body, but whoever sins sexually, sins against their own body. Do you not know that your bodies are temples of the Holy Spirit, who is in you, whom you have received from God? You are not your own; you were bought at a price. Therefore honor God with your bodies. (vv. 15–20)

Evidently some Gentile converts in Corinth were still frequenting prosti-tutes, and one of the believers was having sexual relations with his father's wife (something "even pagans do not tolerate"), and the church put up with it (1 Cor. 5:1–2).

Paul says that sexual sin is of a unique quality, thus "whoever sins sexually, sins against their own body." God has designed human sexuality to be a powerful tool that binds a husband and a wife together. When we abuse this gift, we dehumanize ourselves; instead of intimacy we create guilt, alienation, and fear. Each time people participate in sexual intercourse, an emotional, spiritual, and psychological bond is created, not just a physical one. The beauty of the gift is that it creates "one flesh" bodily and at the very deepest levels of humanity. When individuals move from partner to partner, little bonds are created and destroyed, ripping apart the fabric of their soul.

This is why sexual sin is so damaging. Christians are regularly castigated for their apparent fixation on sex, but it is God who is concerned most about this precious gift. Sex is misunderstood, misused, and abused, to our harm. Knowing this, God warns us. People who jump into bed with anybody and everybody are tearing themselves apart spiritually and psychologically, even if for a moment they enjoy it physically. Because the world narrowly views sex as solely physical, the other aspects of sexuality are ignored. Yet, the individual is still affected at those profound levels of intimacy.

Christianity has historically been opposed to premarital sex, despite being told today that it is of little consequence. "Friends with benefits" is a familiar slogan referring to someone with whom you have casual sex, even though you are not in a relationship. This is why one Christian ethicist can write, "It is seldom assumed that premarital or extramarital sex is morally wrong and in need of curtailment. It is only portrayed as foolish if you get caught without protection."[6]

This attitude produced a commercial some years back on Namibian television during afternoon programming for young people. The scene began with a man waking up and looking around. He didn't know where he was or who the woman was sleeping next to him. He searched desperately around the room until he found his used condom from the night before. He then laid back down next to the woman, with a peaceful, relieved look on his face. The message was clear: he was a fool if he failed to use protection, but it did not matter that he had had sex with an unfamiliar woman. Consider the message this "public safety" commercial communicated to Namibian youth.

---

[6] Feinberg and Feinberg, *Ethics for a Brave New World*, 429.

Why do Christians encourage their children to abstain from sex until they are married? Because with each sexual encounter, indelible marks are left on their soul. It stands to reason that the more sexual partners you have in your life prior to marriage, the less likely you will remain faithful during marriage. Usually youth are the most damaged in a society that moves toward greater sexual freedom because they do not have the emotional and mental maturity to handle it. However, adults can be likewise affected by misappropriated sexual pleasure.

Are We a Sex-Crazed Society?

A disparate range of people view pornography as a blight on our society. Whether conservatives or liberals, Republicans or Democrats, evangelical Christians or radical feminists, a varied segment of our society finds pornography to be demeaning to women. It distorts our views on what is lovely and pure about sexual fulfillment as God intends it.

I frequently hear numbers thrown around for the amount of Internet traffic devoted to pornography. The figures vary wildly depending on how the number is calculated (e.g., by number of websites, or webpages, or data downloaded, or unique click per visitor per site, etc.). *Forbes* reports that the largest adult site in the world "gets around 32 million visitors a month, or almost 2.5% of all Internet users." [7]

The Indo-Asian News Service puts the figure at about 30% and notes a report from the *Daily Mail* that only Google and Facebook surpass the single largest pornography site in terms of unique visits per month. [8] According to *The Huffington Post*, the highest Internet traffic is on Netflix, Amazon, and Twitter, but porn sites are more than all three combined, [9]

---

[7] These articles explain the difficulty: Julie Ruvolo, "How Much of the Internet Is Actually Porn?" *Forbes*, www.forbes.com/sites/julieruvolo/2011/09/07/how-much-of-the-internet-is-actually-for-porn/, accessed August 17, 2015, and Mark Ward, "Web Porn: Just How Much Is Out There?" BBC, www.bbc.com/news/technology-23030090, accessed August 17, 2015.

[8] "30 Percent of Global Web Traffic Is Porn—Study," http://gadgets.ndtv.com/internet/news/30-percent-of-global-web-traffic-is-porn-study-223878, accessed August 17, 2015.

[9] "Porn Sites Get More Visitors Each Month Than Netflix, Amazon, and Twitter Combined," www.huffingtonpost.com/2013/05/03/internet-porn-stats_n_3187682.html, accessed August 22, 2015.

and *The Guardian* reports, "Only 'arts and entertainment'—a category that is boosted by Google's video site YouTube—and search engines were bigger, at 9.5% and 15.7% respectively."[10] Throw in novels like the *Fifty Shades of Grey* trilogy, which features explicit sex and has sold more than 125 million copies in 52 languages (spinning off a movie trilogy whose first installment grossed more than $560 million worldwide), and this confirms an apparently insatiable desire for smut and perversion in our society.[11]

Pornography poses a real threat to perceptions about human sexuality, but it has a disproportionate effect on young people who are susceptible to these distorted images. Unfortunately, modern technology has made access to pornography as easy as buying a toothbrush online. In the past, young people had highly limited access to porn. Buying a dirty magazine or renting an X-rated video involved looking someone in the eye when you made the purchase. Today, however, nobody has to know about it; it's just a click away. With this increased accessibility to pornography comes the enticement to embrace other forms of sexual deviance.

Previously, people who participated in perversion hid in the darkness. Now they march on the streets demanding their rights. They employ lobbyists and utilize public media to disseminate their depravity. Nevertheless, this should not surprise those who are familiar with the Bible's teaching about sin.

The Seeping Silica of Sin[12]

Before we speak about other forms of sexual sin, we need to establish a biblical understanding of how sin works, and this takes us to the beginning. After Adam and Eve fell, the very next picture of sin recorded in Genesis

---

[10] Charles Arthur, "Porn Sites Get More Internet Traffic in UK Than Social Networks or Shopping," *The Guardian*, www.theguardian.com/technology/2013/jul/26/porn-sites-internet-traffic-uk, accessed August 22, 2015. The report did not differentiate the video content viewed on YouTube, which can include "soft porn," and search engines are frequently used to locate pornography.

[11] The most popular translation of the Bible, the New International Version, has sold about 650 million copies worldwide since its release more than three decades ago. *Fifty Shades of Grey* sold about one-fifth that many in just one year.

[12] About a decade ago, Rev. Jim Johnston preached a sermon in my home church where he used a phrase similar to this. Any elaboration on the metaphor comes from me.

is Cain killing his brother Abel. Two chapters later we have Noah and the flood, with the entire world corrupted. Sin's spread was rapid and thorough.

When Cain presented an unacceptable sacrifice to God, he was told to correct himself and offer a proper sacrifice like his brother Abel. God warned Cain: "sin is crouching at your door; it desires to have you, but you must rule over it" (Gen. 4:7). We know the rest of the story. Instead of doing what was pleasing to God, Cain lured his brother into the fields and killed him. But murder was not Cain's first or primary sin. It was a stubborn refusal to follow the way God had prescribed.

The same can be said for the Israelites, who conquered Canaan but eventually succumbed to the depravity of its inhabitants. They turned their back on their covenant with God, who had warned them about sin and its ravenous appetite.

A superb analogy of the deadening effects of sin comes from geology, where an object subjected to highly mineralized (silica) water or another medium such as lava can be petrified. Petrification involves two processes. The first is permineralization, when the cavities and pore spaces of an object are filled by silica, while a large amount of the original material remains. The second step, replacement, goes deeper, where the original substance is gradually substituted by the silica at the microscopic level. Over time virtually nothing is left of the original material.

Paul describes the process of sin in a similar way when he writes to believers in Ephesus:

> So I tell you this, and insist on it in the Lord, that you must no longer live as the Gentiles do, in the futility of their thinking. They are darkened in their understanding and separated from the life of God because of the ignorance that is in them due to the hardening of their hearts. Having lost all sensitivity, they have given themselves over to sensuality so as to indulge in every kind of impurity, and they are full of greed. (4:17–19)

Paul envisions four stages of the seeping silica of sin: (1) darkness, (2) hardness, (3) deadness, and (4) recklessness.[13] A person's perspective on

---

[13] John Stott notices a similar four-fold progression in *The Message of Ephesians* (Leister, England: Inter-Varsity, 1979), 177–78.

life—why she is here and how she should live—will produce either a life that is worthwhile and pleasing to God, or one that is driven by futile thoughts. The author of Ecclesiastes calls it a "chasing after the wind" (1:14). Once a person has lost an eternal perspective on reality, the temporal becomes devoid of any real value.

This is why Paul begins with futile thinking (v. 17) and darkened understanding (v. 18). As with Cain, those who do not submit to biblical truths about sex will be mastered by their sinful inclinations, thus becoming "separated from the life of God." This is what the godless men of Jude's day did when they took "the way of Cain" (Jude 11), which led to polluting their own bodies (v. 8). It is why Paul writes elsewhere about the need to renew our minds (Rom. 12:2) lest we conform to the world's standards. All godly action begins with godly thinking.

An example of darkened thinking involves Belle Knox (a pseudonym), who revealed that she was paying for her university fees by working as a porn star. She has become something of an evangelist for the porn industry, telling Piers Morgan on CNN that being a porn star is "liberating and freeing" because she can "make decisions about my own body."[14] Why does Knox believe she is free when she sells her body to pornography peddlers?[15]

From this darkness of mind comes hardness of heart. The Greek word for "hardness" is *poros*, which literally means "hard as marble." It is the same Greek word used in the Gospels to refer to those in the synagogue who wanted to kill Jesus after seeing him heal the man with the withered hand (Mark 3:5–6). Despite the great miracle Jesus performed right before their eyes, their hard-as-marble hearts produced murderous thoughts.

Is this not comparable today to those who have rejected biblical truth and in turn attack Christians who speak up for godly morality? Peter recognized this same attitude in his first-century context: "They are surprised that you do not join them in their reckless, wild living, and they heap abuse on you" (1 Peter 4:4).

Next come people who have "lost all sensitivity" (Eph. 4:19). In the

---

[14] Maria Shiavocampo, "Teen Porn Star Bella Knox Will Return to College Despite Threats," ABC News, http://abcnews.go.com/blogs/headlines/2014/03/teen-porn-star-belle-knox-will-return-to-college-despite-threats/, accessed August 24, 2015.

[15] Many ex-porn stars have shared what goes on behind the scenes in the industry, from the high rate of STDs and drug abuse, to the long-term psychological toll it takes on the actors.

context of sexual sin, our children are being increasingly exposed to depraved views on sexuality, and this at an earlier age than ever before.[16] There is a concerted effort to inculcate worldly views on sexuality into our young people. Anyone who has watched television programming change over the past forty years can attest to this. The media have been a powerful means through which a counter-Christian morality has been disseminated. I am appalled by what the movie industry thinks is appropriate for a young teenager in a PG-13 film.

This has affected how young people regard pornography. Barna Group reports that while half of adults age 25 and over perceive pornography as wrong, only 32% of young people age 13–24 think similarly. Nearly twice as many young adults consider not recycling as worse than viewing pornography.[17]

If it isn't bad enough that the media and corporations are encouraging promiscuity in our society, consider the push by governments and the United Nations promoting "comprehensive sexuality education" (CSE). The thirty-five-minute video produced by Family Watch International is something every Christian parent should see.[18] CSE seeks to change sexual and gender norms of societies, undermines the parent-child relationship, and even encourages children to sexually experiment. In the United States, battles have erupted in several states over this curriculum, which one Christian group contends is "pornography under the guise of education."[19]

The accounts of Jesus healing leprosy have a spiritual analogy to the

---

[16] This sobering ABC News Nightline report, "Porn before Puberty," deals with the easy access to pornography young people have today via social media, and the damaging effects it is having on their psyche: YouTube, www.youtube.com/watch?v=MnE8LobXoJY, accessed October 17, 2015.

[17] "Porn in the Digital Age: New Research Reveals 10 Trends," https://www.barna.org/research/culture-media/research-release/porn-in-the-digital-age-new-research-reveals-10-trends?utm_source=Barna+Update+List&utm_campaign=20c22a58ed-Barna_Update_Porn_in_the_Digital_Age_New4_3_2016&utm_medium=email&utm_term=0_8560a0e52e-20c22a58ed-172166833&mc_cid=20c22a58ed&mc_eid=94d9ce5e76#.V2f0ro0VgkL, accessed May 2, 2016.

[18] "The War on Children: The Comprehensive Sexuality Education Agenda," www.comprehensivesexualityeducation.org/videos/the-war-on-children-the-comprehensive-sexuality-education-agenda/, accessed June 28, 2016.

[19] "Parents Rage over Sex-Ed Class That 'Rapes Children of Their Innocence,'" Yahoo! News, https://www.yahoo.com/news/parents-rage-over-sex-ed-class-that-rapes-151034433.html, accessed June 27, 2016.

seeping silica of sin. Much like healing the blind and deaf has a parallel to people who spiritually cannot see and hear, leprosy could be equated with sin's deadening effects, slowly killing all sensitivity and eventually destroying the person.

The last stage in the petrification of a person's soul is recklessness. These people have "given themselves over to sensuality so as to indulge in every kind of impurity" (Eph. 4:19), with a continual greed for more. Like Israel in Jeremiah's day, they have become "skilled in doing evil" (Jer. 4:22).[20]

Why did God have to give the Israelites a command to not have sex with animals? Because they were occupying a land where its inhabitants practiced this vulgarity. They sacrificed their children to the fire gods, cut and sliced their bodies in their religious rituals, and had whole cities like Sodom and Gomorrah that reveled in their depravity. God warned the Israelites: "Do not defile yourselves in any of these ways, because this is how the nations that I am going to drive out before you became defiled" (Lev. 18:24). God's people were moving into a land whose occupants had succumbed to sin's seeping silica and who were evidently beyond redemption. They had become completely desensitized to evil, with an inability to judge right from wrong.

This slide is usually gradual, even though it has appeared rapidly in American culture. I do not think a person wakes up one morning and decides out of the blue to have sex with an animal. Such a descent typically takes time. As C. S. Lewis wrote, "The safest road to hell is the gradual one—the gentle slope, soft underfoot, without sudden turning, without milestones, without signposts."[21] James likens it to the birthing process:

> But each person is tempted when they are dragged away by their own evil desire and enticed. Then, after desire has conceived, it gives birth to sin; and sin, when it is full-grown, gives birth to death. (1:14–15)

We can all attest to this. Things we never did in the past can eventually become habitual over time. Herein lies the ultimate deceptiveness of sin. When it is practiced long enough, it feels so natural and normal that we

---

[20] Akin to Paul's comment: "they invent ways of doing evil" (Rom. 1:30).
[21] *The Screwtape Letters*, 56.

cannot help but think it is good. Proverbs 14:12 (NKJV) says, "There is a way that seems right to a man, but its end is the way of death." It is similar to the homosexual who claims that God approves of his lifestyle (despite God's biblical commands to the contrary); or the adulterer who sees in his mistress the perfect woman who, if only he could have her, he would treat in the most godly way (while he cheats on his wife); or the people who clothe abortion in the language of "rights" (while violating the rights of the unborn).

This kind of reasoning was driven home for me when I taught at a seminary in Namibia. A student was having trouble with an alcoholic wife. Studying to become a pastor, he admitted that he was having an affair with a woman who he claimed would make an excellent pastor's wife. While we sympathized with his marital situation, we had to question how godly his mistress was. After all, she was having an affair with a married man. Undeterred, he left his wife for the other woman.

This should not surprise us. Upon eating the forbidden fruit, not only did Adam blame "the woman" for his sin, but he implicated God in his downfall as well. "The woman *you* put here with me—she gave me some fruit from the tree, and I ate it" (Gen. 3:12).

When Adam and Eve realized they were naked, they hid from God because of their shame. Today's sinner, though, openly stands in the nude for all to see, defying God to do anything about it. His nakedness is his glory, and if God were around, he ought to approve it, not try to cover it up as he did in Eden. Adam ate one piece of forbidden fruit and was ashamed, while today's sinner gorges his belly on the stuff, defiantly declaring its goodness while bemoaning the fact there isn't more of it to devour.

Many gay Christians have taken a brazen stance. They not only say that God approves of their sin, they claim God's creative act as its cause. This shameless position is brasher than Adam's, who recognized his rebellion and fled from God's presence. For the militant homosexual Christian, God's favor rests on his act of rebellion. He saunters into the throne room of heaven, confident that the Almighty will approve.

How long does it take a society to move from natural views about sexuality to more depraved ones, until like Canaan it is condoning pedophilia and sex with animals? Once you move the line of acceptability when it comes to sin, the temptation is to move it farther. Our culture's debate about sexuality is important because if we recognize anything about the nature of sin, it is never content to stop at point B or C, but will drive relentlessly onward until it has consumed us entirely.[22] The following examples attest to this.

All in the Family

The 2013 comedy *Delivery Man* tells the story of a middle-aged butcher who discovers that anonymous sperm donations he made to a fertility clinic twenty years before as a cash-strapped college student have shockingly produced 533 children. It is the kind of movie that could only be made in the past decade, but not because it is fiction. In 2011, *The New York Times* reported a case involving 150 children conceived from the same donor's sperm.[23]

With the rise of sperm banks, there is increasing probability that people raised in different families may be biologically related. For this reason a Danish professor argued in 2014 for abolishing laws against incest.[24] Around the same time, a German ethics panel suggested de-criminalizing incest, calling it a fundamental right.[25] The German case was brought to the forefront when it was discovered that a German brother and sister, who met later in life, have four children together.[26]

---

[22] Sexual misconduct among American doctors is perhaps another sign of the eroding of our moral foundation, with 3,100 doctors publicly disciplined for sexual harassment of patients and employees since 1999 ("License to Betray," *Atlantic Journal-Constitution*, http://doctors.ajc.com/doctors_sex_abuse/?ecmp=doctorssexabuse_microsite_na, accessed July 7, 2016). Yahoo! News reports that more than 2,400 doctors in the United States have been sanctioned for sexually abusing their patients, yet more than half of them were allowed to keep their licenses ("The New Sex Abuse Scandal," https://gma.yahoo.com/sex-abuse-scandal-2-400-doctors-implicated-patients-105806732--abc-news-topstories.html#, accessed July 7, 2016).

[23] Jacqueline Mroz, "One Sperm Donor, 150 Offspring," *The New York Times*, www.nytimes.com/2011/09/06/health/06donor.html?_r=4&pagewanted=1&hp&, accessed September 2, 2015.

[24] Thaddeus Baklinski, "'Sibling Incest Should Be Legal' Says Danish Professor of Criminal Justice Ethics," Life Site News, "www.lifesitenews.com/news/sibling-incest-should-be-legal-says-danish-professor-of-criminal-justice-et, accessed September 3, 2015.

[25] "German Ethics Council in Favour of Lifting Ban on Incest with Siblings," DW, www.dw.com/en/german-ethics-council-in-favor-of-lifting-ban-on-incest-with-siblings/a-17950246, accessed October 27, 2015.

[26] Jenny Kutner, "German Committee Says Incest Is a 'Fundamental Right,'" Alternet, www.alternet.org/world/german-committee-says-incest-fundamental-right, accessed October 27, 2015.

If incest were de-criminalized, not only could siblings be allowed to marry each other, but so could a father and his adult daughter, or even his son for that matter.[27] Once we open the floodgates of sexual freedom, ultimately all boundaries will be erased.

Christians have long argued that as the sexual freedom of a society increases, children bear the brunt of its detrimental effects. Child pornography and sex trafficking are consistent problems in parts of the world. A French scandal in April 2015 involving pedophilia and school teachers sent shockwaves through that country.[28] And in early 2015, a massive Internet child porn ring was busted, with estimates of 70,000 members in more than thirty countries.[29]

Would it surprise you that some people advocate for pedophilia in first-world nations?[30] Along with the gay rights movement there has been a steady presence of pro-pederasty (adult men having sex with boys) groups, labeled with euphemisms like "intergenerational relationships" and "minor-attracted adults."

For example, a Dutch pedophile advocacy group fought for its existence in the Netherlands but was eventually banned by the Dutch Supreme Court in mid-2014.[31] While this is positive news, it wasn't that long ago that other forms of sexual deviancy were illegal in many Western countries too.

What amazes me is that people publicly stand up and say, "I'm a pedophile and I demand my sexual freedom." They employ the same arguments

---

[27] The term "genetic sexual attraction" refers to biological family members who never knew each other in childhood but who meet for the first time as adults and have an immediate sexual attraction.

[28] "Scandal of Paedophile Teachers Shocks France," The Local, www.thelocal.fr/20150401/france-rocked-by-paedophile-teachers-scandal, accessed September 17, 2015.

[29] "Massive Online Pedophile Ring Busted by Cops," NBC News, www.nbcnews.com/id/42108748/ns/us_news-crime_and_courts/t/massive-online-pedophile-ring-busted-cops/#.VcEQvY0VgkI, accessed September 5, 2015.

[30] Taking child brides is not uncommon in some parts of the world, despite the West's current abhorrence of the practice.

[31] "Dutch Paedophile Club to Fight Their Ban at the European Court of Human Rights," Independent, www.independent.co.uk/news/world/europe/dutch-paedophile-club-to-fight-their-ban-at-the-european-court-of-human-rights-9622112.html, accessed September 5, 2015. A Wikipedia list of pedophile advocacy groups has more than a dozen countries represented: https://en.wikipedia.org/wiki/List_of_pedophile_and_pederast_advocacy_organizations (accessed August 31, 2015).

that the gay rights movement has been using for decades: "Sexual orientation is not a choice," "I was born this way," "I can't help myself."[32] In 2014,
an article in *The New York Times* argued that pedophilia is inborn and not
a choice.[33] The author labeled it a "mental disorder," but that was the same
diagnosis for homosexuality forty years ago in the United States.

These arguments are analogous to the seeds sown by the gay rights
movement in the 1960s and 1970s that laid the foundation for what has
become an American society open to gays adopting and marrying. Why
would we expect our culture to put the brakes on now?

Michael Brown, author of *A Queer Thing Happened to America*, wrote a must-
read article in August 2011 about the similarity between arguments from
the gay rights movement and those used for pedophile rights.[34] In "Why Are
We Surprised with the Push for 'Pedophile Rights'?" Brown begins:

> Many Americans have been shocked by reports about a recent
> pro-pedophilia conference in Baltimore in which psychiatrists
> and other mental health professionals, representing institutions
> like Harvard and Johns Hopkins, sought to present pedophilia in
> a sympathetic and even positive light.
>
> Academic articles in scholarly journals have been present-
> ing pedophilia in a sympathetic light for years, and, as Matthew
> Cullinan Hoffman noted, the American Psychiatric Association
> (APA) released a report in 1998 "claiming that the 'negative poten-
> tial' of adult sex with children was 'overstated' and that 'the vast
> majority of both men and women reported no negative sexual
> effects from their child sexual abuse experiences.' It even claimed
> that large numbers of the victims reported that their experiences
> were 'positive,' and suggested that the phrase 'child sex abuse' be
> replaced with 'adult-child sex.'"

---

[32] Michael Brown, "Pedophilia Inborn and Adult Incest OK?" WND, www.wnd.
com/2014/10/pedophilia-inborn-and-adult-incest-ok/, accessed September 16, 2015.

[33] Margo Kaplan, "Pedophilia: A Disorder, Not a Crime," *The New York Times*, www.
nytimes.com/2014/10/06/opinion/pedophilia-a-disorder-not-a-crime.html?_r=1,
accessed August 30, 2015.

[34] Michael Brown, "Why Are We Surprised with the Push for 'Pedophile Rights'?"
Townhall, http://townhall.com/columnists/michaelbrown/2011/08/26/why_are_we_
surprised_with_the_push_for_pedophile_rights/page/full, accessed August 30, 2015.

That's the same APA that changed the policy on homosexuality in 1973 and has been itching to do similarly with pedophilia since the 1990s. I cannot help but feel that the APA is waiting for the cultural tide to turn. In the estimation of these esteemed psychologists, pedophilia is "no more a matter of voluntary choice than are left-handedness or color blindness." Brown lists eight typical arguments used by the gay rights movement, showing how each one has been co-opted by pro-pedophilia groups. Is it a matter of time before this sexual perversion is given the imprimatur of the APA and our society?

Before someone cries foul, claiming that America would never do this, keep in mind that removal of age of consent laws was one of the primary platforms in the early days of the gay rights movement. We will see in the following chapter that this goal went underground for a while but has once again begun to rear its ugly head in recent years.[35]

Like Miley Cyrus, anything goes as long as it is between "consenting adults." However, that is a rather fluid notion since the idea of "adult" can change, as can the concept of "consent."[36] South Africa, for example, dropped its age of consent to twelve, albeit for a child having sex with another child under sixteen. Regardless, what kind of society drops the age of consent to preteen years? By the way, South Africa has had legalized gay marriage since 1996.

Arguments based on consent will inevitably lead to legalized prostitution and incest, and may eventually be used to approve pedophilia and pederasty. I will speak more about the consent issue in the following chapter.

What Should Be Our Christian Response to Sexual Immorality?

The following four principles apply to this chapter as well as the following

---

[35] Fr. John Zuhlsdorf, "The Next Homosexualist Goal: Elimination of 'Age of Consent,' License for Pedophiles," WDTPRS, http://wdtprs.com/blog/2013/10/the-next-homosexualist-goal-elimination-of-age-of-consent-license-for-pedophiles/, accessed June 3, 2016.

[36] Apparently consent isn't watertight either. Good2Go is a phone app where parties first record their consent before engaging in sexual activity, in case one later claims it was not consensual. It is amazing what we need to invent once biblical norms are abandoned. Amanda Hess, "Consensual Sex: There's an App for That," Slate, www.slate.com/blogs/xx_factor/2014/09/29/good2go_a_new_app_for_consenting_to_sex.html, accessed December 1, 2015.

one, even though in chapter 9 further guidelines addressing homosexuality will be given.

1. We must admit our own sin.

We all struggle with sin at one level or another. Christian men apparently have a problem with pornography, with 55% of them viewing it at least once a month. One in three commit adultery.[37] Sin is as much our problem as it is for non-believers. Is this not why we turned to Christ?

2. We must not judge hypocritically.

Christians cannot strike out against some sins while ignoring others, the latter usually being the ones they commit. Jesus recognized this kind of hypocrisy when he said, "Do not judge." Unfortunately, this quotation is ripped out of context and used to shut down any "judging" by believers. Here is the full passage:

> Do not judge, or you too will be judged. For in the same way you judge others, you will be judged, and with the measure you use, it will be measured to you. Why do you look at the speck of sawdust in your brother's eye and pay no attention to the plank in your own eye? How can you say to your brother, "Let me take the speck out of your eye," when all the time there is a plank in your own eye? You hypocrite, first take the plank out of your own eye, and then you will see clearly to remove the speck from your brother's eye. (Matt. 7:1–5)

Jesus is not saying we should never judge sin, but rather we should not do so hypocritically. One aspect of the insidious tendency toward self-deception is when we rationalize sin in our own lives while we condemn the same sin in others.

One high-profile case involved Rev. Ted Haggard, one-time president

---

[37] Michael Haverluck, "Study: Alarming Rate of Christian Men Look at Porn, Commit Adultery," One News Now, www.onenewsnow.com/culture/2014/10/09/survey-alarming-rate-of-christian-men-look-at-porn-commit-adultery, accessed September 3, 2015.

of the National Association of Evangelicals and pastor of a church with several thousand members. In 2005, *Time* listed Haggard as one of the twenty-five most influential evangelicals in America. Haggard openly preached against the ills of homosexuality, yet was secretly involved with male prostitutes. He resigned from his ministry in 2006 when the scandal broke out.

An apropos biblical example is David and his sin with Bathsheba. Let it be a reminder that in each person lies the seed of deception and wanton disregard for God's ways. David was a man after God's own heart, someone who from an early age had evinced God's special hand upon him. From slaying the mighty Goliath to penning the greatest hymns of praise, David was without equal. Yet one evening he fell into lust, and then adultery, and ultimately murder of an innocent, principled man. Yet, while these sins germinated and grew in his heart, David continued to sing the praises of Yahweh.

The prophet Nathan later came to David and told him about a rich man who had taken the lone ewe from his destitute neighbor, and David's rage was kindled. In righteous indignation David pronounced judgment on the man: "As surely as the LORD lives, the man who did this must die!" Not surprisingly, upon hearing Nathan's rebuke, "You are the man!" David pled for mercy (2 Sam. 12:5-7, 13, 16; Ps. 51). Why is it that we want judgment to fall upon those who commit sin, while we do the same things and expect grace?

Paul's rebuke of his fellow Jews strikes a comparable tone. "You, there-fore, have no excuse, you who pass judgment on someone else, for at what-ever point you judge another, you are condemning yourself, because you who pass judgment do the same things" (Rom. 2:1). While the Jews were reproving the Gentiles for their depravity, God's people were behaving sim-ilarly (Rom. 2:21-24).

Christians must regard hypocrisy as wicked a sin as any other we put at the top of the list, lest unbelievers blaspheme our God as the Gentiles did (Rom. 2:24).

3. We must not back down from biblical principles.

Evangelicals often suffer from the following ailments, making our witness in the world ineffective:

- We lack biblical discernment. We have adopted the world's definition of love, which has more to do with tolerance and lust than the genuine love embraced in Scripture.
- We lack courage and conviction. It is much easier to adopt a bunker mentality, remaining in our "holy huddle" and not engaging the world.
- We lack compassion, finding it difficult to delineate between the militantly sexual and those who love God yet are enslaved by their sexual lifestyle.

The world confuses infatuation for love, and unfortunately some Christians have imbibed from this same poisoned well. "Love" in our culture is frequently equated with a feeling and nothing else. It can be here today and gone tomorrow. This kind of love usually drives people in and out of marriages with regularity. Once the initial butterflies in the tummy wear off, there is no true loving foundation on which to build. Is it any wonder that many movies and television programs depict the characters first hopping into bed and then "falling in love"?

The world also confuses tolerance for love. Many unbelievers have a contradiction in their thinking. They fashion a false image of God that is tolerant and easy-going, a divine being who will put up with anything you say and do because of his love affair with human autonomy. However, if this same portrayal of God were incarnated in, say, their neighbor, these people would have no patience for it.

Imagine a scenario where the tolerance-loving individual has a neighbor who kills his dog. The neighbor is taken to court but the presiding judge has nothing but kind words to say to the dog killer. In fact, the judge can understand why the barking dog disturbed his neighbor's sleep, and since his neighbor was sincere in his beliefs, no judgment need be pronounced.

We would rightly call that judge to account. Why, then, are people who embrace a tolerance-loving god shocked when injustice is done in the world? We demand justice when sinned against, but our own sins are never subject to it.

Lastly, the world mistakes lust for love, and this has worked itself out in the warped views of sexuality we have seen in this chapter.

As Christians, we cannot shy away from calling sin what it is, or allow our culture to dictate what is or is not sinful. After all, some very advanced civilizations viewed pedophilia as quite acceptable, even commendable. Because those societies accepted pedophilia, should followers of the biblical God in those days have kept quiet about it?

John the Baptist spoke against the immorality of the king's wife (Mark 6:18) and he lost his head for it. He did not change his views on morality to suit the times, nor did he back down despite the threat to his life.

Our deepest aspiration cannot be the approval of our friends and family, or the "attaboy" from our culture, or the skirting of persecution and mockery from the world. Our overriding desire should be to please Jesus Christ and do what he declares to be good and right. As Jesus said to his disciples, "Whoever acknowledges me before others, I will also acknowledge before my Father in heaven. But whoever disowns me before others, I will disown before my Father in heaven" (Matt. 10:32–33).

We must keep this in mind as even our Christian associations may become soft on this matter. For example, the Society of Biblical Literature (SBL) in 2016 put a temporary ban on evangelical publisher InterVarsity Press (IVP) for its orthodox views on sexuality, stating that IVP would not be allowed to exhibit at the annual SBL conference in 2017. SBL stated, among other things, that its "core values" concerning tolerance, diversity, and inclusivity necessitated the ban.[38] I wonder how censorship can be equated with tolerance in the view of the Christian leadership of SBL?

Religious freedom is rapidly eroding in America. The September 2016 report from the U.S. Commission on Civil Rights, euphemistically titled "Peaceful Coexistence," is nothing more than an assault on Christian values in American society. As the chair of the Commission states, "The phrases 'religious liberty' and 'religious freedom' will stand for nothing except hypocrisy so long as they remain code words for discrimination, intolerance, racism, sexism, homophobia, Islamophobia, Christian supremacy or any form of intolerance."[39] Note that Christianity is singled out as the culprit. Should the recommendations of this report find support in the American legal system, churches and other Christian organizations

---

[38] Bonnie Pritchett, "InterVarsity Press faces book conference ban," WORLD, https://world.wng.org/2016/10/intervarsity_press_faces_book_conference_ban, accessed October 29, 2016.

[39] Quote from page 29 of the report, which can be found on the USCCR website: www.usccr.gov/pubs/Peaceful-Coexistence-09-07-16.PDF.

may quickly find themselves in the crosshairs of an increasingly aggressive immoral sector of our society.

In light of this, evangelicals need to recapture a prophetic voice and the boldness that goes with it. As various Christian organizations embrace the world's standards of morality, believers who trust God's Word as eternal truth must take a stand much like the Old Testament prophets did in their day. Any notion that we should remain silent because we are losing the culture war concerning sexuality is pure cowardice.

The longer we are vocal in our opposition to sexual depravity, the longer it will hopefully take before other, more deviant forms become the accepted norm in our society.

4. We must address sin compassionately yet firmly.

Christians who insensitively show up at the funerals of homosexuals with offensive signs like "God hates faggots" surely are not communicating the love of Christ. At what point do we overstep the line of decency and Christian charity when conveying the real danger of sin? I will speak more about this as I turn specifically to the topic of homosexuality.

CHAPTER NINE

God's Created Order
and Homosexuality

As more believers are coming to realize [affirming same-sex relations] is, in fact, a requirement of Christian faithfulness.
—MATTHEW VINES[1]

A FRIEND RECENTLY RECOUNTED a conversation she overheard among children playing in the school yard. One nine-year-old boy said that a man should not "love another man." A fifteen-year-old girl then defended homosexuality, appealing to the arguments typically used by the gay rights movement.

I believe the boy has an innate sense of what is natural and normal, while the girl is a product of our culture's media-driven, pro-gay indoctrination. I do not trust a single television drama coming out of the United States that targets teenagers. For a segment of America that represents less than 2% of the population, gay characters and homosexual situations crop up too often in these dramas, and they are always presented as natural.

We live in the midst of a cultural revolution centered on sexual freedom, where traditional Christian morality is in the crosshairs. Militant homosexuality is on the rise, and what was done quietly in the dark is now openly paraded in the daylight. The gay rights movement has legally won the day, but this does not mean that Christians should no longer object. There are powerful reasons to voice our displeasure with our culture's fixation on sexual freedom.

---

[1] *God and the Gay Christian*, 25.

Doesn't the Bible Forbid Homosexuality?

There are clear-cut prohibitions in the Bible against homosexual activity, so it might strike readers as odd that gay Christians claim that God does not oppose homosexuality. Consider Leviticus 18:22: "Do not have sexual relations with a man as one does with a woman; that is detestable." There is nothing ambiguous about this command, or is there?

In *God and the Gay Christian*, evangelical Matthew Vines argues that there is nothing wrong with homosexuality in the context of a loving, consensual relationship. Vines goes through six biblical passages that most stand in the way of homosexuality being accepted by the Christian community.[2] Because he professes the Bible as God's inerrant and authoritative Word, this is not your characteristic pro-gay source.

I have no intention of providing a verse-by-verse rebuttal of Vines's book.[3] However, the arguments made by Christians for homosexuality largely overlap with those used by non-Christians supporting this lifestyle.

Typical Arguments Made by Supporters of Homosexuality

Below I provide a brief rebuttal of thirteen arguments gay rights advocates employ against Judeo-Christian morality.

1. "Christiansarefear-mongerstryingtoscarepeopleintotheirreligion."

If a mother tells her daughter not to touch the stove because it will burn her hand, is this fear-mongering? Of course not. The danger is real; the damage can be extensive. It is the same with abusing God's gift of sex. The negative consequences are tangible in both this life and the afterlife. Christians are motivated by love when they warn others of God's impending judgment.

---

[2] Genesis 19:5; Leviticus 18:22 and 20:13; Romans 1:26–27; 1 Corinthians 6:9; and 1 Timothy 1:10.

[3] An excellent rebuttal of Vines is the free ebook, *God and the Gay Christian? A Response to Matthew Vines*, edited by R. Albert Mohler Jr.: www.albertmohler.com/2014/04/22/god-the-gospel-and-the-gay-challenge-a-response-to-matthew-vines/, accessed June 22, 2016.

2. "Sexual orientation is a right that cannot be violated."

As we saw in chapter 7, there is a suppleness with the term "sexual orientation," as it is basically left to individuals to define it for themselves. People can claim to be heterosexual at one point in their lives, then homosexual at another, then bisexual at another, perhaps undergo a sex change operation, and at each stage claim that this is their orientation. Yet, the term is used by gay advocates as if it is an immutable law that can never be violated or questioned.

"Orientation" is either inborn or it is not. The constant moving between "orientations" by the same individual violates the very definition of the word as used by sexual freedom advocates. This exposes the fallacy that sexual orientation is a rights issue on par with ethnicity or a person's skin color. Clearly those traits are immutable. Conversely, sexual orientation as expressed by the gay rights movement is a choice.

An article about gay teens and pregnancy states, "Lesbian and bisexual females were three to five times more likely to have been pregnant than straight females, while gay males and males who are questioning their sexuality were four times more likely than straight males to report getting someone pregnant."[4] The article hotlinks several studies and surveys that report similar findings. Gay men are getting women pregnant? "Sexual orientation" is far more elastic than the homosexual rights movement leads us to believe.

The orientation argument cuts both ways. If it is true that one's orientation confers an inviolable right, then anything, as long as it is deemed an "orientation," is fair game. Gays cannot argue for homosexuality while denying incest for consenting adults, which we saw in chapter 8 must fall under the same "right."

Lastly, if homosexuality were genetically driven we would find about the same percentage in all cultures, but we do not.[5] This confirms what Scripture assumes. Humans are heterosexually predisposed, and any other forms of sexual activity are the result of sin, not genetic inclination.

---

[4] Joe Carter, "Gay Teens Have Higher Rates of Pregnancy Than Straight Teens," The Gospel Coalition, www.thegospelcoalition.org/article/gay-teens-have-higher-rates-of-pregnancy-than-straight-teens, accessed November 1, 2015.

[5] An old but thorough study of 191 cultures bears this out: Clellan S. Ford and Frank A. Beach, *Patterns in Sexual Behavior* (New York: Harper & Brothers, 1951).

3. "Homosexualsarebornthatway;theyhavea'gaygene';theycannothelp but be homosexual."

Gays assert that homosexuality is inborn, not learned, but have little evidence to back up this claim. They argue that if homosexuality is inborn, then gays cannot help being gay any more than a white person can help being white.[6] However, if homosexuality is a learned behavior (assuming God's heterosexual design of humans), then homosexual behavior can be curbed, or treated, or even cured.

First, not everything that is inborn is good. Babies are born with genetic defects that we regularly look to correct. Second, an argument could be made that *everything* that comes out of a person has an "inborn" basis. A man inclined to fits of rage may be acting out an inborn inclination. This hardly means we ought to condone it. Third, from a biblical point of view, *all* sin is inborn but this does not legitimize it. If we argue "I'm born this way" to justify homosexuality, we might as well use it to validate every sin.

Much ink has been spilled over this nature-versus-nurture debate. In the past, conventional wisdom was that effeminate men had domineering mothers, or men with same-sex attraction were molded by sexual experiences (particularly abusive) during puberty or early adolescence. Also, people experiment sexually. To eliminate all influence from experience in molding a person's sexual preference is too heavy handed. Our life experiences shape everything else about us, including our intellect, emotions, tastes, preferences, and personality. Why in the area of sexuality is it different?

What the inborn argument boils down to is a Freudian notion that humans are slaves to their basest sexual urges. As Christians who know that we are made in the image of God, we reject this argument. An individual's identity cannot come from whom he chooses to have sex with. It comes from God who has made us in his image and for his glory. Boiling down our identity to sexual orientation is wholly inadequate.

---

[6] Gay rights advocates will often ask their opponents, "Did you choose to be heterosexual?" to emphasize that their gay "orientation" is equally inborn, not learned. However, this ignores the biblical perspective. Heterosexuals do not need to choose their orientation; heterosexuality is designed by God and natural for everyone. However, to go against this design is indeed a choice.

Related to the inborn argument, gay advocates mock the idea that homosexuals can change to heterosexuals, and the high-profile collapse in 2013 of the Christian organization Exodus International, which for four decades claimed to help gays do just that, only seems to add credence to arguments that homosexuality is immutably inborn. However, as Christians we must submit to what God's Word says on the matter. In warning Corinthian believers about wrongdoers who will not inherit the kingdom of God, Paul lists among many sins "men who have sex with men" (1 Cor. 6:9). Then Paul notes, "And that is what some of you were. But you were washed, you were sanctified, you were justified in the name of the Lord Jesus Christ and by the Spirit of our God" (v. 10). Clearly, homosexuals can turn away from their sin and follow Jesus.

Homosexuals claim that twin studies prove a strong genetic predisposition. One of the foundational studies was conducted in 1991 by John Bailey and Richard Pillard, reported by *The New York Times* as the "strongest evidence yet that homosexuality has a genetic basis."[7] This was twenty-five years ago, so you would expect a mass of similar evidence to back up this claim, but this has not been the case.

Bailey and Pillard tested about 150 sibling couples, finding that 52% of identical twin brothers, 22% of fraternal brothers, and 11% of adoptive brothers were gay. Of interest is that *The New York Times* does not mention the fourth category in the study, that of non-twin siblings, which sat at 9.2%. This is no small omission. The correlation between genetically related brothers (9.2%) is actually *lower* than brothers not genetically related (11%), which runs contrary to the assumption that homosexuality is genetically driven.

Other twin studies in Australia, Scandinavia, and the United States have found a lower concordance rate, with one study of nearly five thousand twins having a 30% correlation in identical twins.[8] What we'd expect if homosexuality is an immutable genetic "orientation" is that identical twins would have a correlation rate approaching 100%. These studies prove that genes don't predispose people toward homosexuality.

---

[7] "Gay Men in Twin Study," *The New York Times*, www.nytimes.com/1991/12/17/science/gay-men-in-twin-study.html, accessed November 2, 2015.

[8] See Feinberg and Feinberg, *Ethics for a Brave New World* (374–81), who report that in some studies a concordance rate in twin boys is as low as 6.7%.

Environmental factors play a prominent role in the development of a person's sexuality. These factors include a culture that promotes homosexuality, being raised by gay parents, experiencing sexual abuse at an early age, poor parental role models for gender distinctions, and lack of inhibitions toward sexual experimentation. This is just common sense.

Nevertheless, while I think the current evidence strongly leans toward nurture, I am not willing to say we will never discover a genetic predisposition for homosexuality. Still, I am skeptical because of what I know about the self-deceptive nature of sin. Regardless, the way things are going now, it will not matter if a genetic predisposition is proved; the gay lobby has already won the rights battle.

4. "God made me this way."

While akin to the previous statement, this one warrants its own comments because it is so pernicious. If God has declared something to be sinful, how dare we declare it good? Consider the audacity that avers unholy behavior as approved by God and part of his design. The prophet Isaiah wrote about a similar attitude in his day:

> Woe to those who call evil good
> and good evil,
> who put darkness for light
> and light for darkness,
> who put bitter for sweet
> and sweet for bitter. (5:20)

Whenever we excuse our own sinfulness by blaming God for it, we invite his judgment.[9]

---

[9] Forty years ago homosexuality was categorized as a mental illness. Now opposing homosexuality is considered a "cultural-induced disease" in the words of the head researcher of a study involving Italian university students. Stephanie Pappas, "Homophobic People Often Have Psychological Issues," Yahoo! News, http://news.yahoo.com/homophobic-people-often-psychological-issues-121032115.html, accessed November 3, 2015.

5. "Homosexuality is natural, being seen in the animal kingdom."

Male lions eat their cubs. Certain spiders and insects kill their mates after copulating. Should humans behave similarly? Is it reasonable for human beings to consult seagulls and clownfish for cues on proper sexual behavior? The questions answer themselves.

6. "Jesus never condemned homosexuality; why do you?"

While Jesus never used the word "homosexuality," it is wrong to conclude he did not or would not condemn it. Here is what we know about Jesus:

a. Jesus was a Torah-following Jew who kept the Law perfectly. He said the Law was from God and not "one jot or one tittle" would pass from it, expressing its supreme authority (Matt. 5:18 KJV). This includes Levitical laws expressly condemning homosexuality (Lev. 18 and 20).[10] Whenever Jesus spoke about sexual immorality (Matt. 5:32; 15:19; 19:9), the Mosaic Law formed the background for understanding him.

b. In using the destruction of Sodom and Gomorrah as an example of the coming judgment of God (Matt. 10:15), Jesus gave implicit approval of his Father's condemnation of those cities, which participated in sexual immorality and particularly "men on men" sex (Gen. 19:5; Jude 7).[11]

c. Jesus never specifically denounced incest, bestiality, pedophilia, prostitution, pornography, rape, child abuse, and a hoard of other immoral activities. Are we to assume he approved of these too? Can you imagine someone saying, "Jesus never condemned pedophilia, so why do you?" An argument from silence—if Jesus did not explicitly condemn something, then he tacitly approved it—is a very dangerous way to read Jesus.

d. Jesus affirmed marriage as between a man and a woman. He spoke

---

[10] At times Jesus appears to disregard the Law, but he refused to accept manmade laws built around God's Law.

[11] Gay activists argue that God condemned homosexual rape with Sodom and Gomorrah, not consensual homosexual relationships. In the context of the whole Old Testament this is clearly false.

of ways in which this marriage covenant, when violated, leads to adultery (Matt. 19:4–6, 9).

e. It is clear in the way Jesus dealt with sinners that if he were here today he would show compassion and kindness to those trapped in homosexual sin. However, he would hardly endorse it as many Christians do.

To say that Jesus approved homosexuality is a deceptive argument that ignores the biblical facts about his life and his teaching.

Another tactic of the gay camp is to rewrite history in a pro-gay manner. One modern commentator has written that "the historical Jesus was a libertine Jewish magician who engaged in homosexual acts with his initiates."[12] Such comments are obviously slanderous. People who love homosexuality will see it everywhere.

7. "The Bible as an ancient source is not to be trusted when it comes to modern issues like homosexuality."

I have been told by gays that Jesus spoke about loving others, so I should accept homosexuals as they are. However, when I point out that Jesus said salvation is only found in his person and nowhere else, I am curtly asked how I can trust the biblical authors.

Yet, gay advocates claim Jesus never said anything about homosexuality and he taught that we should love others. Clearly they trust the veracity of the Gospels. When they then argue that the Gospels are not to be trusted when Jesus is declared the sole way, they reveal a contradiction in their reasoning.

It also reveals their ultimate authority: their own personal preference. When the Gospels record Jesus saying something they already believe, they are all for Jesus. But when the Gospels record something Jesus says that is contrary to their personal preference, then they are untrustworthy. A wise man builds his house on the foundation of *all* of Jesus' teaching, not just the parts he prefers (Matt. 7:24). Either the Gospels are reliable or they are not.

---

[12] Reported in *Biblical Archaeological Review* (December 2009): 50.

8. "Christiansarenotconsistentintheiruseofthe Bible, condemning homosexualitywithpassagesfromLeviticus, whileignoringotherthingsthe same book prohibits, like eating shell fish or pork."

Leviticus is not the only biblical book that condemns homosexuality, but this accusation does have a level of truth to it. Christians appear to accept parts of Leviticus while ignoring other parts.

One of the early struggles in the Christian faith was what to do with the Hebrew Scriptures (our Old Testament) and especially the Law of Moses. Some church leaders advocated ignoring these books, while others argued that because they pointed to the coming Messiah, Christians should adopt them. Ultimately the latter argument won the day.

Nevertheless, it was recognized that not every portion of the Old Testament had equal relevance for Christians. This sentiment was driven by the Christian writings (our New Testament) that came from the teaching of Jesus and the apostles. It became popular to categorize the Old Testament laws into three kinds: civil, ceremonial, and moral. Civil laws concerned the governing of the Israelite nation (e.g., punishment by stoning), and ceremonial laws dealt with religious rituals and obligations (e.g., laws pertaining to sacrifices and special days). Both kinds no longer apply to Christians as they are not repeated in the New Testament.[13]

However, moral laws apply equally to all people in all places at all times.[14] It is wrong to lie and steal and murder, whether you are a Jew or a Gentile. We find moral laws consistently repeated in the New Testament, including prohibitions against homosexual behavior. Therefore, the distinction between types of Old Testament laws is justified by the way the New Testament handles the matter.

Lastly, Leviticus not only censures homosexual sin, it similarly condemns adultery, bestiality, and incest. Christians consistently view all sexual relations outside marriage as sinful, which is the unswerving teaching of both the Old and New Testaments.

---

[13] Sometimes these laws are abrogated, such as with food laws (Mark 7:19; 1 Tim. 4:3–4), animal sacrifices (Heb. 9:10–14), and observance of special days (Gal. 4:8–11; Col. 2:16–17). This makes sense as Jesus came to fulfill the Law (Matt. 5:17; Heb. 8:6–13).

[14] The Canaanites were judged specifically for the sexual sins God prohibited the Israelites from committing (e.g., Lev. 18:24–25).

9. "TheNewTestamentauthorsdidnotunderstandthepsychologyof homosexuality,nordidtheyhaveanycategoriesforfaithful,committed homosexual relationships."

The biblical authors were not naïve. They were well aware of human ratio-nalizations for sin. They were well-traveled men who understood that the Greeks put high value on pedophilia and that temple prostitution was com-mon in the mystery religions. There were gay men in the first century who reveled in their homosexuality as much as twenty-first-century gays do.

Gay advocates argue that the biblical authors did not understand that homosexuality is inborn and natural. This argument is coupled with the idea that New Testament objections to homosexuality are driven by conser-vative Jewish roots, but today with our open-minded society we no longer adhere to these limitations.

At its heart, this tactic must eventually question all supernaturalism in the Bible. If the Bible is solely the product of a writer limited by time and circumstance, then the first century has no relevance for the twenty-first century. Conversely, if the Bible is the very words of God, who inspired its authors to record what he wanted them to record, then we can no lon-ger claim cultural irrelevance. God's perspective is not limited to looking through the keyhole of time.

It is one thing to claim limited knowledge for the human authors of Scripture, but quite another to accuse God of it. While an atheist could not care less about this point, evangelicals who support homosexuality should. Declaring a limited Bible is nothing less than declaring a limited God who inspired it.

10. "TheapostlePaulmerelyopposesmaleprostitution(e.g.,1Tim.1:10)or sexualimmoralityinthecontextofidolatry(e.g.,Rom.1),notloving,consen-sual, homosexual relationships."

Paul does indeed condemn idolatry, but only after noting that idolaters have rejected God's self-revelation in his creation. Paul argues in Romans 1:18–32 that humans suppress the truth about God because they prefer their own wickedness. As such, they are without excuse. Having rejected God's revelation, they instead turn to idols, which results in futile thinking and darkened hearts.

Therefore, God gives these people over to "sinful desires" (v. 24), "shameful lusts" (v. 26), and a "depraved mind" (v. 28). These idolaters are so immersed in their own depravity that they approve of those who act similarly (v. 32). Paul then catalogues the various sins that come as a result.

In the midst of this "giving over," Paul makes his clearest statements against homosexual immorality:

> Even their women exchanged natural sexual relations for unnatural ones. In the same way the men also abandoned natural relations with women and were inflamed with lust for one another. Men committed shameful acts with other men, and received in themselves the due penalty for their error. (vv. 26b–27)

Homosexual sin is not wrong only when attached to idolatry; Paul condemns them both. Such an argument is akin to saying that Paul, in speaking against Corinthian believers frequenting prostitutes, was not judging prostitution but merely its use in pagan temple worship.

Scripture says that humans have an awareness of God's existence but can suppress this truth (Rom. 1:18–20). Similarly, they have a sense of what is normal when it comes to sexuality but can, over time, also suppress it. Homosexual activity in Paul's thinking is a consequence of rejecting God's revelation. Christians who embrace homosexuality, then, are snubbing God's created design.

Pro-gay Christians attempt to remove Old Testament prohibitions against homosexuality, argue from the supposed silence of Jesus, and redefine Paul's terms, and then tell us the Bible supports their sexual preference. They excuse the Bible for what it clearly states: homosexuality is a sin in the eyes of God.

11. "Christians should never judge others, just like Jesus said."

I dealt with this in the previous chapter. Jesus is not speaking against making any judgments. Rather, he opposes hypocritical judging, similar to Paul's chastisement of the Jews in Romans 2. That is why Jesus says, "Before you remove the sawdust from your brother's eye, first remove the plank from your own. Then you will be able to assist your brother" (Matt. 7:5). In other words, help your brother from a position of moral authority, not hypocrisy. Christians are consistently called throughout the New Testament to make moral judgments.[15]

12. "Does God really care whom you have sex with?"

This question assumes sexual activity is harmless fun. "Why does God care about your sex life? Doesn't he have more important things to be bothered with?" Suppose that you gave your son a very generous gift of $100,000, but he squandered it on cocaine, burned his brains out, and now suffers from diminished mental capacity. Would it bother you that he misused your wonderful gift?

In the previous chapter we saw that sex has a spiritual dimension to it, affecting our very souls. Jesus is not pleased when we destroy ourselves; can his followers sit quietly by while others do it?

Ironically, those supporting sexual freedom are the ones who stammer and spit when Christians suggest that people with same-sex attraction remain celibate. On the one hand, they downplay sex as unimportant ("Why should God care?"), while on the other, it is made to be essential for any kind of contented life, and is used to define one's identity and self-worth.

13. "Anything consenting adults do in the privacy of their own bedroom is none of your business."

The notion that their homosexual behavior is "private" is rather disingenuous of gays since they have made it very public.[16] However, privacy is no guarantor of rights. Consenting adults who use heroin in the privacy of their own home are breaking the law based on the harm drug usage causes the greater community.

If consent is the main factor, then adult siblings or a parent-child couple should be permitted to marry, but the majority of Western countries do not allow these marriages on the grounds that they are genetically unsafe. Even marriages between first cousins are prohibited for the same reason.

---

[15] I deal with this command in greater detail in chapter 9 of *Ten Things I Wish Jesus Never Said* (Wheaton, IL: Crossway, 2006).

[16] As I heard from a speaker: "Oscar Wilde's 'love that dare not speak its name' has turned into a lifestyle that won't shut up."

Perhaps the more consistent argument by gay proponents is to say that it is not our business because it harms no one. However, this is not correct either, as the following health statistics prove. It is incongruous to prohibit certain lifestyles based on health hazards (e.g., first-cousin marriages), and yet approve the homosexual lifestyle with its heightened risks.

Homosexual Sex Is Dangerous Sex

The National Health Statistics Report from the U.S. Centers for Disease Control and Prevention (CDC) provides recent sexual orientation demographics for the United States.[17] It reports that almost 98% of Americans identify themselves as heterosexual, with 1.6% homosexual and 0.7% bisexual. We will use the round figure of 2% for gays in America.[18]

Some claim that Christian morality is needlessly repressive and the ideal of lifelong monogamy is outdated. Promiscuity, on the other hand, can be liberating and fun. But here is wisdom from the CDC for lowering your risk of contracting a sexually transmitted disease (STD). "Limit your number of partners. You can lower your risk for STDs if you only have sex with one person who only has sex with you."[19]

Even a governmental institution recognizes biblical wisdom. Taking this reasoning to its logical conclusion, if a man and a woman avoid premarital sex and remain together in lifelong monogamy, their risk of acquiring an STD is virtually zero. This is God's design, and moving away from it puts people in jeopardy.

Some studies indicate that more than one-quarter of gay men have had more than 1,000 sexual partners in their lifetimes, with nearly 80% engaging in sex with strangers. While various reports place heterosexual fidelity

---

[17] No. 77, July 15, 2014.

[18] This is in stark contrast to the figure I heard growing up, based on the discredited Kinsey Report from the late 1940s, that 10% of Americans were gay. Unfortunately, this false figure made homosexuality appear more common than it was. The media consistently play a role in this. A Pew Foundation study found that there is 500% more positive coverage of same-sex marriage than negative in the American media ("News Coverage Conveys Strong Momentum for Same-Sex Marriage," www.journalism.org/2013/06/17/news-coverage-conveys-strong-momentum/, accessed November 4, 2015).

[19] "CDC Fact Sheet: What Gay, Bisexual and Other Men Who Have Sex with Men Need to Know about Sexually Transmitted Diseases," www.cdc.gov/std/life-stages-populations/STDFact-MSM.htm, accessed November 7, 2015.

between 60% and 80%, homosexual fidelity is at an astonishingly low 4.5%.[20] We expect this to have a detrimental effect on the gay community.

In the United States, 110 million people have an STD, with the majority from the heterosexual population, but this merely looks at the raw figures. When we consider the proportions, those participating in gay sex have incredibly higher rates.

Syphilis was virtually wiped out in the United States, with just 6,000 cases documented nationwide in 2000. However, by 2013, more than 16,000 cases were reported, and 9 out of every 10 were found in gay men. When less than 2% of the population accounts for 90% of cases of a particular STD, alarm bells should ring. One director of the CDC referred to the problem as the "rising epidemic of syphilis among gay and bisexual men."[21]

The report lists the "individual risk factors" associated with the higher prevalence of syphilis among gays, from politically correct reasons like homophobia and stigma in our society to economically disadvantaged gays who have no access to adequate healthcare. Left out of this medical report is an actual medical possibility: that gay sex is inherently dangerous. Besides, how does homophobia or inadequate access to healthcare give a person an STD?

If we cast the net wider and include chlamydia, herpes, hepatitis A (mainly spread by ingesting infected fecal matter), and hepatitis B (spread through contact with infected bodily fluids such as semen and blood—not uncommon during anal sex), the picture for gays is even bleaker. The CDC reports that "about 10% of new hepatitis A and 20% of all new hepatitis B infections in the United States are among gay and bisexual men."[22]

At first blush, this might not sound bad. However, the incidence of hepatitis B among gays is more than 12 times higher than among heterosexuals,

---

[20] This webpage provides several reports on gays and their number of sex partners: "What Is the Average Number of Sex Partners a Gay Man Has in His Lifetime?" Answers, www.answers.com/Q/What_is_the_average_number_of_sex_partners_a_gay_man_has_in_a_lifetime, accessed June 23, 2016.

[21] Steven Reinberg, "Syphilis Cases Climbing among Gay Men: CDC," WebMD, www.webmd.com/sexual-conditions/news/20140509/syphilis-cases-climbing-among-gay-men-cdc, accessed June 25, 2016.

[22] "Viral Hepatitis," www.cdc.gov/msmhealth/viral-hepatitis.htm, accessed June 25, 2016. However, when I accessed this webpage in 2015, the report said "men who have sex with men." It has now been changed to "gay and bisexual men."

meaning gays have a more than 1,200% more likelihood of contracting the disease than straight men. This is shocking.

The human papillomavirus (HPV) comes in about 40 varieties and usually results in genital warts. Estimates are as high as 50% of gay men with an HPV, while 25% have rectal gonorrhea, which often leads to gonorrhea of the throat and penis. Australian research has shown that out of 100 gay and bisexual men, statistically there are 57 new anal HPV infections every year.[23] If one of every two gays has an HPV, in time it will become extremely difficult to find a gay man who does not have genital or anal warts.

Suggestions have been made in the United Kingdom, the United States, and Australia to give vaccinations across the board to males age eleven and twelve, to guard against the spread of HPV.[24] The whole time we are encouraging young boys that gay is okay, we are telling them to get a shot because the gay lifestyle is destructive to the male body.

The Foundation for AIDS Research calls unprotected anal intercourse "high risk behavior," and this from an organization that encourages homosexuality.[25] Gay men are twenty times more likely to get anal cancer than heterosexual men, and gay men with AIDS are forty times more likely.[26] Yet we continue to encourage homosexuality in our society.

Sexual immorality is big business in the United States, with twenty million new STD cases annually costing "nearly $16 billion a year in direct medical costs, according to the CDC."[27] That is money that could be better spent on cancer research, dialysis, and the like. If a particular community habitually practices unsafe sex, this eventually affects us all. It is counterproductive that our culture both bemoans increasing healthcare costs while

---

[23] "HPV Infections Common among Gay, Bisexual Teen Males," Fox News, www.foxnews.com/health/2014/12/04/hpv-infections-common-among-gay-bisexual-teen-males/, accessed June 25, 2016.

[24] "UK's Gay Men Should Receive HPV Vaccination, Says Expert Panel," POZ, www.aidsmeds.com/articles/HPV_vax_gays_1667_26563.shtml, accessed June 25, 2016.

[25] "High Infection Rates Continue among Gay Men," amfAR, www.amfar.org/content.aspx?id=140, accessed June 28, 2016.

[26] Liz Margolies and Bill Goeren, "Anal Cancer, HIV, and Gay/Bisexual Men," The Body, www.thebody.com/content/art54524.html, accessed June 28, 2016.

[27] "CDC: 110 Million Americans Have STDs at Any Given Time," CBS Atlanta, http://atlanta.cbslocal.com/2014/10/06/cdc-110-million-americans-have-stds-at-any-given-time/, accessed June 25, 2016. See also "CDC Fact Sheet: Incidence, Prevalence and Cost of Sexually Transmitted Infections in the United States," www.cdc.gov/std/stats/STI-Estimates-Fact-Sheet-Feb-2013.pdf, accessed June 25, 2016.

encouraging homosexual activity, which by its very nature is unhealthy. Smokers have been castigated over the past decade for the health risks they cause others (e.g., second-hand smoke) and the public costs incurred. Yet similar arguments are never used with gays.

Instead of taking these risks seriously, gay activists attack those who report the statistics. In the past, diseases common among the gay community were labeled "gay bowel syndrome," which refers to sexual activity involving contact with fecal material. Gay activist Michael Scarce criticized the concept of "gay bowel syndrome" in his book *Smearing the Queer*, saying that "gay bowel syndrome has been, and remains today, a powerful tool for the specific surveillance, regulation, definition, medicalization, identification, and fragmentation of gay men's bodies"[28] This is most unfortunate. While the gay lifestyle is ravaging the gay community, activists like Scarce are more concerned with politicizing the issue.[29]

God prohibits sodomy—not just between two men, but involving a man and a woman too—because it is unhealthy. It is clear that problems ensue when the human body is used contrary to its basic design. Putting the male sex organ in an orifice designed to expel bodily waste products is a case in point. God is not a sourpuss who does not want his creatures to have fun. He hates sodomy because it destroys the human body; it is harmful to his very precious creatures. God made humans and he knows what is best for them.[30]

This opinion usually gets derided with slurs like "homophobe" and "bigot," but if you objected to someone who wanted to take a pencil and drive it into his eye, would this make you a bigot? Of course not. Yet people who deface the design of God destroy themselves, which is what sin does.

This is particularly the case with sexual sin. Paul writes that sexual immorality is a sin against your own body (1 Cor. 6:18), and he warns that men who seek after unnatural relationships with other men bear the

---

[28] Michael Scarce, *Smearing the Queer: Medical Bias in the Health Care of Gay Men* (New York: Routledge, 1999), 13.

[29] A typical rebuttal to the health risks associated with homosexuality is that the same risks do not apply to lesbianism. However, the American College of Pediatricians states otherwise: http://factsaboutyouth.com/posts/female-homosexual-behavior.

[30] Anal sex increases the risk of "rectal prolapse, perforation that can go septic, chlamydia, cryptosporidosis, giardiasis, genital herpes, genital warts, isosporiasis, microsporidiosis, gonorrhea, viral hepatitis B and C, and syphilis" (Robert Reilly, *Making Gay Okay* [San Francisco: Ignatius Press, 2014], 55).

consequences in their own bodies (Rom 1:27). The statistics we have noted attest to this.

Christians also argue that the gay lifestyle decreases the life expectancy of homosexuals. For example, a comprehensive study in Denmark (the first country to allow gay marriage, in 1989) tracked mortality rates of married homosexuals and heterosexuals. The report concluded in 2009, "Despite dramatic reductions in AIDS-associated mortality over the past decade, our study shows that same-sex–marrying Danish men and women have overall mortality rates that are 33% to 34% higher than those of the general population."[31]

There is something also to be said for quality of life. Factor in living with the constant threat of STDs and the medical treatment they necessitate, as well as the pain, discomfort, and inconvenience created.

If we encourage activity that goes against God's design for sex, we should not be shocked if more detrimental diseases appear. Homosexuals have chosen a lifestyle that is self-destructive. The irony is that a monogamous, heterosexual couple who enjoys a lifelong relationship is hardly affected, at least directly, by the prevalence of STDs in the gay community. The people destroyed are the gays themselves. Yet, the healthcare risks and costs borne by the greater society must be considered. It is not a private matter when the whole community bears the financial burden for this lifestyle.

So what do I say to the very lucky gay man who never gets a venereal disease; who remains in a monogamous, loving, gay relationship his entire adulthood where he and his partner never cheat on each other; whose life expectancy is hardly affected by his gay lifestyle; who never gets anal cancer or genital warts unlike the vast majority of his gay friends; and who experiences life like a typical heterosexual man?

First, such a person is virtually non-existent given the statistics we have already discussed. The above description is an anomaly bordering on the fictional. Nonetheless, I might word a question about a heterosexual man in the same way. What do I say to the very lucky heterosexual man who has had dozens of sexual partners, many of them involving one-night stands, and who never contracts an STD or any health problems as a result of his promiscuous lifestyle?

---

[31] Morten Frisch, "Mortality among Men and Women in Same-Sex Marriage: A National Cohort Study of 8333 Danes," National Center for Biotechnology Information, www.ncbi.nlm.nih.gov/pmc/articles/PMC2636618/, accessed June 27, 2016.

He too would be a statistical anomaly (although not to the extent of the gay man), but my answer to both men is the same: your lifestyle is displeasing to God, who has graciously allowed you to continually rebel against his intention for his special gift of sex, without the typical deleterious effects endemic to your lifestyle. Yet, do not confuse God's temporal grace with his eternal pleasure. God has promised to judge the sexually immoral. Now is your time to repent, not flaunt your sexual open-mindedness and test God's patience (1 Cor. 6:9–10; 1 Peter 3:9).

Responding to Homosexuality

In the previous chapter we covered general principles for a Christian response to sexual sin in our society. However, something further needs to be said about homosexuality because it serves as a watershed issue in our culture.

I believe there are genuine, born again believers who struggle with same-sex attraction and are nonetheless saved, just as there are believers who struggle with addiction to pornography or alcohol, or losing their temper and using foul language. Christians struggle with sin. If Jesus can only save us once we cease being confused, rebellious sinners, then none of us has any hope. Therefore, we must show compassion, but lying to people and telling them that God approves of their sin is not compassionate, it is sinister.

There are self-professed Christians who revel in their homosexuality. It is similar to the adulterous believer who claims God gave him these natural desires so having an extramarital affair is in line with how God designed him. Such rationalization of sin is equally sinister.

Should our response to a teen struggling with same-sex attraction be any different than with a militant homosexual on the march for depravity? Jude's short epistle in the New Testament provides some clues. The first is that we must contend for the faith (v. 3).

The Greek word for "contend" is *epagonizesthai*. Maybe you can see that our English "agonize" comes from this word. It is not a simple thing to contend for the faith, especially among people who are contending against it. But if in the name of Christian love we approve of sin, we cannot say we have obeyed Jesus. Christian love devoid of truth is appeasement mixed with hypocrisy.

Jude 22–23 shows how Christians should respond to godlessness:

> Be merciful to those who doubt; save others by snatching them
> from the fire; to others show mercy, mixed with fear—hating even
> the clothing stained by corrupted flesh.

Some in our churches doubt that the traditional Christian mores are valid
today. They claim homosexuality is acceptable because they do not know
the Bible well, or they have succumbed to the world's standards. With these
people we can deal gently and patiently.

Jude speaks of a second group who need to be snatched from the fire.
Perhaps these are believers who are same-sex attracted or who have participated in homosexual activity. They are confused, though, about whether to
accept homosexuality or condemn it, and they experience significant angst
over the issue. These are honest Christians who are struggling with sin and
have to be compassionately yet firmly kept from the fire.

However, there is a third group of Christians who are decidedly vocal
that God approves homosexuality. With these Christians we require considerably less patience. Jude speaks of hating anything to do with their
depravity. Yes, even for Christians, hatred is a proper response. We hate
what God hates.

Speaking the truth about sexual sin makes the most sense, not simply
because it is biblically mandated, but for pragmatic reasons too. If we tell
gays that homosexuality is a sin, they may repent and turn to God for his
grace.

Unfortunately, it does not matter how lovingly we state the truth; many
will hate us as long as we do not approve their lifestyle. There is no "loving"
way to tell a sinner to stop sinning when he is looking for affirmation of
his immorality.

Sensing this pressure, some evangelicals have adopted a moderating
position, one where they affirm that homosexuality is an "orientation,"
while calling for the gay person to abstain from sex. In other words, the
biblical prohibitions concerning homosexuality only apply to the gay act,
not the gay desires. However, this hollow distinction yields to the subtle
arguments of the gay rights movement, which has worked hard to establish
an understanding of "orientation" that basically defines the terms of the
debate.

Part of the problem with evangelical disputation in the public square is that we yield too easily to emotional arguments used by those opposed to Christian morality. Here is how non-Christian propaganda often works. When dealing with the rape of a twelve-year-old girl who falls pregnant by her uncle, non-Christians say, "Are you really that cold-hearted to force this pre-teen girl into motherhood? How can you not allow her to have an abortion?" Statistically, this scenario accounts for less than one percent of all abortions. However, once the emotional appeal is won on this level, the other 99% of the cases are smuggled in.

The same rhetoric applies in the gay rights debate. "Are you really going to deny a healthy, happy, monogamous marriage to homosexual couples? How dare you?" Statistically speaking, though, fidelity in the homosexual community is virtually non-existent. However, once the emotional appeal is won on this level, all the other cases are smuggled in.

In essence, the tactic is to make a fringe instance the central focus, and in so doing, to then quietly slip in all the other cases. This was a key tactic used to defend gay marriage, which is at best a façade, when statistics clearly prove that the vast majority of homosexuals are not interested in monogamy at all.

This approach can be used with virtually any issue. For example, a sister and brother meet for the first time as adults, fall in love, and are married, only later to find they are genetically related. In order to avoid such scenarios, it is argued that we need to make all forms of incest legal. A fringe case is used to "backdoor" all the other scenarios. The beauty with this tactic is that once you allow the fringe case, you will eventually allow all of them. Evangelicals must be ready to expose this sort of fallacious argumentation.

Compromising on biblical principles is never a good idea, especially when we appease immorality.[32] If we know anything about sin, we recognize that it is insatiable. The gay lobby is not interested in privacy. It is not even interested in tolerance. What it is interested in is approval. Unless we stand up and cheer their homosexual lifestyle, they will not be satisfied.

---

[32] In a recent Pew poll 54% of American Christians said homosexuality should be accepted: Tom McKay, "This Poll Shows How Christians in America Really Feel about Homosexuality," Yahoo! News, www.yahoo.com/news/poll-shows-christians-america-really-203719289.html, accessed June 1, 2016.

Attacks on Religious Freedom

One of the key emotional arguments in the gay rights movement has been the problem with homosexuals who are bullied at school because of their sexual orientation. While this is a legitimate concern, the irony is that the militant homosexuals have become the real bullies. They shout you down. They do not argue the facts. They make slanderous comments and slurs against anyone who deigns to question their lifestyle. Their chief tactic against "bullies" is to become bullies.

Some bullies cause trouble when you happen upon their path on the playground, but there is another kind who cannot wait for the recess bell to ring. They go out of their way to find you. Today's militant homosexuals are that kind of bully. They harass Christians who have a moral objection to baking a cake for a gay wedding or renting their farm out for a same-sex marriage. They purposefully target a Christian business and then sue when it is unwilling to condone their lifestyle, when all the while they could walk down the street a few blocks and easily get the same services elsewhere.[33]

Lest American Christians think they are alone, consider the June 2015 case of Zizipho Pae, acting president of the Student Representative Council (SRC) at the University of Cape Town (UCT). South Africa recognizes sexual orientation as a basic right in its constitution and has allowed same-sex marriage since 1996. Pae expressed her personal opinion on her Facebook page about the U.S. Supreme Court decision to legalize gay marriage: "We are institutionalising and normalising sin! Sin. May God have mercy on us."

The UCT administration quickly removed Pae from her SRC post and sent out an email from the Vice Chancellor's Office to its constituents. It stated that UCT recognizes "the rights of members of the lesbian, gay, bisexual, transgender, queer, intersex and asexual (LGBTQIA+) community." It then ironically noted the problem with individuals in South African society who "still experience prejudice, harassment and abuse, whether because of sexual orientation, gender, race, nationality, economic status, etc." Conspicuously absent from that list is religious persecution, with Pae being the latest victim.

A main avenue for this bullying is through the courts. More than a

---

[33] Several of these examples are noted in chapter 10.

decade ago, Swedish pastor Åke Green was arrested for preaching against homosexuality. He received a thirty-day prison sentence that was later overturned.[34] In Europe, Canada, and the United States, legislation is annually brought before government bodies to widen hate speech laws to include sexual orientation, with Christian morality particularly targeted.[35] Now that gay marriage is legal in America, I expect similar legislation against Christianity in an increasingly aggressive manner.

The Canadian and Swedish courts eventually sided with the arrested Christians due to freedom of speech laws. Forgive me if I am less than encouraged, simply because it was less than a decade ago that the traditional view of marriage won sweeping victories in state constitutional referendums. I put little trust in human courts to uphold Christian values. I will not be surprised if we get to a point where someone can say "homosexuality is a sin" in the meekest tone, and still be thrown into prison.

Author J. Alan Branch notes that the word "homophobia" is meant to intimidate and coerce people who disagree with the homosexual agenda, much like the words "bigot" and "racist" are used in other contexts. "Calling someone a 'homophobe' is intended to express contempt for anyone expressing moral objection to homosexual behavior while simultaneously participating in socially acceptable abuse of the opponent."[36]

"Phobia" is a misplaced word. I do not fear homosexuals, but I do find sexual activity that regularly involves ingesting microscopic amounts of fecal matter repulsive. It is dangerous, and the data on STDs in the gay community bears this out. I am troubled by people who redefine the institution of marriage, created by God "in the beginning," and what that will do to the fabric of our society. And I am deeply concerned for the spiritual well-being of people who declare good what God has determined to be against his will. If the above earns me the label "homophobic," so be it, but

---

[34] Lee Duigon, "Swedish Pastor Faces Jail for Preaching against Homosexuality," Chalcedon, http://chalcedon.edu/Research/Articles/Swedish-Pastor-Faces-Jail-For-Preaching-Against-Homosexuality/, accessed November 1, 2015.

[35] Melissa Stefan, "Major Hate Speech Ruling in Canada Affirms Biblical Principle," *Christianity Today*, www.christianitytoday.com/gleanings/2013/february/major-hate-speech-ruling-in-canada-affirms-biblical.html, accessed October 29, 2015.

[36] *Born This Way?* 9. This book exposes the underlying ideologies of the gay rights movement and the "science" used to support it.

the people who should genuinely fear are those who wantonly flaunt God's created order.

Recapturing a Prophetic Voice

What is our proper response to this aggression? Do we "lie down like dogs," or do we fight? Some Christians argue that the former response most resembles Jesus, but this misses the instances where Christ took a hard stand against immorality and religious hypocrisy, such as when he overturned the moneychangers' tables in the temple. It certainly ignores the rather aggressive stance we see in the New Testament, where, for instance, Paul opposes a false gospel or Peter and Jude declare judgment on the "godless men" of their day (John 2:15; Gal. 1:8–9; 5:12; 2 Peter 2:3b, 12b; Jude 7). If we are concerned with being popular, or not rocking the boat, or not wanting to say something that will hurt another's feelings, then we may be tempted to back down from the biblical truth. For a while we may be popular with the gay rights camp, as some evangelicals are when they say the Bible approves of homosexuality. In time, though, our lies will be exposed and neither we nor the people we misled will benefit. Christians must show a little backbone and stand up for biblical truth, not waffle with the whims of the day.

We need to recapture a prophetic voice. Declaring God's truth is not contrary to Christ's teaching. Jesus knew that the men whose tables he overturned in the temple would be the ones shortly thereafter yelling, "Crucify him! Crucify him!" We cannot flinch from our duty to stand for God's righteousness because we fear persecution. When we communicate the truth of God in a firm yet gentle way, as Jesus did, we are doing what God expects us to do.

The Old Testament prophets lived in a land turning away from the one, true God to follow the false gods of the Canaanites, but the prophets did not cease to speak about Yahweh and his ways. We must continue this prophetic voice in our time, especially in the face of a rising ethic that is hostile to Christianity.

CHAPTER TEN

God's Created Order
and Marriage

Life is short; have an affair.

—ASHLEY MADISON

IN 2015, ASHLEY MADISON, "the most recognized and reputable married dating company," had the email addresses of their 37-million-member clientele compromised. Their website facilitates adulterous flings for married people. The promise of anonymity and the ability to browse thousands of willing adulterers was apparently too tempting for many. At the time of the hack, only three zip codes in the entire United States did not have an Ashley Madison account.[1]

Marriage as we know it is fast disappearing and with it the traditional family. The fundamental building block of healthy societies is yielding to an array of configurations. Marriage forms the capstone for topics we have already touched on. In chapter 7 we noted how the poor modeling of gender roles—best done in a heterosexual marriage—has encouraged gender confusion in our society. Chapter 8 spoke about limiting God's gift of sex to the marital relationship, and in chapter 9 we saw how homosexuality is a perversion of that gift. It stands to reason that gay marriage is a similar distortion. Even chapter 5 and our discussion about the sanctity of life impinges on the present topic, as it is in the confines of a heterosexual marriage that life is meant to be created and nurtured.[2]

---

[1] Nathan McAlone, "There Were Only 3 ZIP Codes in America without Any Ashley Madison Accounts—Here They Are," Yahoo! Finance, http://finance.yahoo.com/news/were-only-3-zip-codes-175956661.html, accessed June 17, 2016.

[2] Some argue that divorce is bad for the environment: Olivia Zaleski, "Is Divorce Bad for the Environment?" *The Huffington Post*, www.huffingtonpost.com/olivia-zaleski/is-divorce-bad-for-the-en_b_88065.html, accessed June 16, 2016.

After everything previously said, it would be easy to pick on gay marriage as the main issue for this chapter. While I will speak about it, the real problem facing the American church is not the handful of homosexuals who want ecclesiastical sanction of their nuptials. There are far more troubling issues, ones where heterosexuals are largely at fault. In this chapter we are going to look at the importance of marriage and the family, and how a spiritual battle is taking place that intends to destroy these cornerstones of a healthy society.

Biblical Marriage

If I were Satan and wanted to destroy humanity, I would attack male headship and through it the family. I would also pervert the very special gift of sex that God has given to his creatures. This combination of assaults would powerfully rip apart the basic family structure that is designed to protect individuals and societies.

Liberal Christian scholars argue that the Bible never sets down a clear formula for marriage, thus maintaining the acceptability of same-sex marriage. They attempt to distance the biblical material from us chronologically ("it was written long ago and is thus irrelevant") or qualitatively ("Genesis isn't really meant to be literal history"). Both of these arguments, though, are eliminated when we realize how Jesus viewed the biblical material. Christians can hardly say that what Christ said is irrelevant for a Christian view of marriage.

When questioned by the Pharisees about divorce, Jesus affirmed the created order of Genesis 2:24:

> "Haven't you read," he replied, "that at the beginning the Creator 'made them male and female,' and said, 'For this reason a man will leave his father and mother and be united to his wife, and the two will become one flesh'? So they are no longer two, but one flesh. Therefore what God has joined together, let no one separate." (Matt. 19:4–6)

This is what Jesus upholds about marriage.

·   It is between a man and a woman, which excludes same-sex marriage.
·   It involves only two people, which excludes multiple-partner marriages.

- Because the two become one flesh, adultery and divorce are unacceptable.
- Marriage is an institution created by God.

The last point is worth dwelling on because we often forget that marriage is God's intention for humanity. It is not simply a civil or ceremonial exercise; the state and the church did not create marriage, the Creator did. In this light, I paraphrase Franklin Graham, who had perhaps the best response to the U.S. Supreme Court's decision to legalize gay marriage: "The Supreme Court did not create marriage, so it has no right to redefine it." Jesus affirms marriage as God's institution from the beginning.

While the two "become one flesh," this is not merely referring to sex. There is a spiritual aspect to marriage that Paul elaborates on in Ephesians 5:31–32. Like Jesus, he refers back to the created order in Genesis:

> "For this reason a man will leave his father and mother and be united to his wife, and the two will become one flesh." This is a profound mystery—but I am talking about Christ and the church.

Paul sees in the marriage of a man and a woman a spiritual reflection of the relationship between Jesus and his bride, the church. As we noted in chapter 8, sexual activity has a spiritual component. It is designed to bring a husband and a wife into deep physical, emotional, and spiritual communion.

The imagery of marriage was frequently used by God to portray his relationship with his wayward wife Israel (e.g., Isa. 54:5–8; Ezek. 16:32). It can be seen in the second commandment, where God refers to himself as a "jealous God" (Exod. 20:5) who is incensed when his covenant people commit spiritual adultery.

Christians who argue for alternative forms of marriage are ignoring the roots of an institution that was founded in Eden, codified in the Law, and affirmed by Jesus and the apostles.

Non-Traditional Marriage

"You can choose your friends but you can't choose your family" is no longer true. The legalization of gay marriage opened the proverbial floodgates, such that one day we may find marriage not so much redefined as undefined.

Humor has been an effective tool in the gay rights movement, as light-hearted scenes frequently appear on television and in cinema depicting gay relationships. We laugh with the characters and soon our guard is down; what is unnatural eventually becomes acceptable. *Modern Family*, a comedy series that follows three families involving a mixture of step-children, remarried divorcees, and a gay couple with an adopted daughter, has won twenty-one Primetime Emmy Awards, including five straight seasons for Outstanding Comedy Series. Mixed-up families are seen as the norm.

In our first term as missionaries in Namibia in the mid-1990s, we served on the field with a couple who had four children: one child from their present marriage, one each from their previous marriages, and an adopted child. This was certainly an oddity for a missionary family.

Today, though, it would not be so strange. The wordy article "All in the (Nonnuclear, Totally Unorthodox) Family" looks to debunk the "traditional family" notion.[3] The article recounts the story of Lake, a two-year-old boy who lives with four people: his birth parents and an infertile woman who after two failed marriages is now in a relationship with a transgender male. This unmarried couple has legally adopted Lake.

Another story involves a gay man who wanted to be a father and had a relationship with a lesbian couple in the hopes of getting one pregnant. When that did not materialize, he entered a relationship with another man. They subsequently met a single, infertile woman who wanted children. Using an egg donated by another woman and the sperm of one of the men, she gave birth to twins. The three share parenting responsibilities and believe their arrangement is better for children than a traditional one-mother, one-father family.

In the United Kingdom, the DNA from three people can be legally used to produce one child in a process called "mitochondrial replacement."[4] Today, you can have sperm donated by one person, an egg by another, the womb from yet another, and the product of this creation can be adopted by a heterosexual or homosexual couple who have no biological connection with the child.

---

[3] Lisa Belkin, "All in the (Nonnuclear, Totally Unorthodox) Family," Yahoo! News, http://news.yahoo.com/all-in-the--non-nuclear--totally-unorthodox--family-214743763.html, accessed June 17, 2016.

[4] "MPs Vote in Favour of 'Three-person' Embryo Law," *The Guardian*, https://www.theguardian.com/science/2015/feb/03/mps-vote-favour-three-person-embryo-law, accessed June 19, 2016.

The 1972 gay rights platform, created by the National Coalition of Gay Organizations convention held in Chicago, set some heady goals nearly a half century ago.[5] Repealing all laws prohibiting transvestism, removing adoption prohibitions for homosexuals, repealing age of consent laws, and demanding federal support for sex education that portrays homosexuality as "a valid, healthy preference and lifestyle as a viable alternative to heterosexuality" were just a few of the objectives. Most of the aims have already been met.

The last one on the list remains: "Repeal of all legislative provisions that restrict the sex or number of persons entering into a marriage unit; and the extension of legal benefits to all persons who cohabit regardless of sex or numbers." Yes, you read that correctly. If twenty people want to enter into "marriage," the gay rights movement is all for it. It has never been about "loving monogamy" in the gay camp.

Polygamy will be the next front of the marital culture wars. Pressure is mounting for both religious reasons (e.g., Mormons and Muslims want it) and political motives (liberals in the "free sex" movement have always argued that marriage should not be limited to only two people). Already we are beginning to see cases where polygamists are using the U.S. Supreme Court decision legalizing gay marriage as a springboard for marriage with multiple partners.[6]

While there is no outright condemnation of polygamy in the Old Testament, it is portrayed as a source of marital conflict and interpersonal grief. Jealousy is a constant problem throughout polygamous Old Testament marriages. Solomon's multiple partners were an impediment for him to rightly worship God, and the Lord commanded the king to not take too many wives, lest his heart be led astray (Deut. 17:17). God tolerated polygamy, but he never mandated it or approved it.

Is polygamy acceptable for Christians today? From our look at what Jesus and Paul say about marriage, we must answer in the negative. The two become one flesh. It is difficult to see how polygamy could be justified when marriage is a reflection of Christ and the church, unless you argue that Jesus has many brides, a ridiculous notion.

---

[5] All Things Queer, "The 1972 Gay Rights Platform," www.rslevinson.com/gaylesissues/features/collect/onetime/bl_platform1972.htm, accessed June 21, 2016.

[6] John Witte Jr., "The Case Against Polygamy," First Things, www.firstthings.com/article/2016/04/the-case-against-polygamy, accessed June 21, 2016.

Militant Marriage

Now that gay marriage has received the imprimatur of the highest court in the land, I expect an increasing number of homosexuals to purposefully try to trap Christians in their "illegal" biblical position. The media typically portray homosexuals as people who simply want to be left alone in their loving relationships. However, the truth is much starker, as this sampling of cases from the past few years shows:[7]

- Barronelle Stutzman is a Christian florist who was sued by a gay couple when she refused to provide flowers for their wedding. In early 2015, the state of Washington found that Stutzman violated anti-discrimination laws. She was fined and ordered to pay court costs.[8]
- Blaine Adamson founded Hands on Originals, Inc., a promotional printing company. The Gay and Lesbian Services Organization sued Adamson when he declined to print gay pride shirts with words that violated his conscience. A lower court ruled against Adamson, citing anti-discrimination laws. Thankfully, a higher court overturned the conviction.[9]
- Sweet Cakes by Melissa was fined $135,000 by the state of Oregon for refusing to bake a cake for a lesbian couple's wedding, when the couple could have easily gone to a dozen other places. The owners paid the fine in late 2015 but have appealed the ruling.[10]
- Cynthia and Robert Gifford were fined $13,000 by the state of New York for refusing to hold a lesbian marriage on their private property that had regularly been used for weddings and receptions. The couple

---

[7] Many more can be found at AllianceDefendingFreedom.org.

[8] Samuel Smith, "Christian Grandma-florist Fined," *The Christian Post*, www.christianpost.com/news/christian-grandma-florist-fined-1001-ordered-to-work-gay-weddings-but-refuses-says-she-wont-betray-jesus-state-threatens-to-take-her-home-business-away-136613/, accessed June 17, 2016.

[9] Jamie Dean, "Christian Print Shop Wins Discrimination Case," World, https://world.wng.org/2015/04/christian_print_shop_wins_discrimination_case, accessed June 1, 2016.

[10] Curtis Wong, "Bakers Who Discriminated against Same-Sex Couple Just Won't Admit Defeat," *The Huffington Post*, www.huffingtonpost.com/entry/sweet-cakes-by-melissa-appeal_us_5723aecae4b0f309baf0d510, accessed June 19, 2016.

was also ordered to attend anti-discrimination training classes.[11] The lesbian couple taped the initial phone call requesting the venue, clearly looking to trap the Christian couple.

There are similar cases around the country involving Christian bakers and florists and photographers and wedding hosts and planners. In some instances, Christians have had to close their businesses because they would otherwise be forced to violate their consciences.

We are moving to a situation not unlike the early centuries of the Christian faith, where believers could not hold certain jobs because they contradicted Christian principles. Third-century apologist Tertullian argued that believers could not become teachers as it involved lecturing on the gods. Today, a number of doctors and nurses who have strongly held principles against abortion are being pressured to provide assistance.[12] The high-profile cases of Kentucky county clerk Kim Davis, who initially refused to sign marriage licenses for gay couples, and Oregon judge Vance Day, who declined to perform same-sex marriages, have made it clear that Christians will find it increasingly difficult to occupy certain positions in government.

One way the gay rights movement was able to win the argument was to redefine the conditions of the debate. As a 2014 article from *US News* notes, about a decade ago, "Gay leaders stopped talking about 'rights' and started talking about 'love and commitment.'" A former Justice Department lawyer under President George W. Bush explained it this way: 'If you are a conservative, how could you be against a relationship in which people who love one another want to publicly state their vows . . . and engage in a household in which they are committed to one another?'"[13]

If marriage truly has a stabilizing effect on societies, then why not

---

[11] Rick Moran, "New York Couple Fined $13,000 for Refusing to Host Gay Marriage," American Thinker, accessed www.americanthinker.com/blog/2016/01/new_york_couple_fined_13000_for_refusing_to_host_gay_marriage_.html, accessed June 17, 2016.

[12] Hans von Spakovsky, "Illinois Abortion Bill Would Force Doctors to Violate Their Religious Convictions," CNSNews, http://cnsnews.com/commentary/hans-von-spakovsky/latest-assault-religious-freedom-ill-abortion-bill-restricts-doctors, accessed June 25, 2016.

[13] Carrie Wofford, "Why Equality Is Winning," US News, www.usnews.com/opinion/blogs/carrie-wofford/2014/03/26/how-did-public-opinion-on-gay-marriage-shift-so-quickly, accessed June 7, 2016.

allow gays to marry? The problem with this argument is manifold. First, we cannot condone what God condemns; homosexuality is a sin. Second, one benefit of marriage is that it teaches children proper gender roles, and homosexual marriages can never do that.

Third, gay relationships are dominated by consistent infidelity as we saw in chapter 9. Slapping the "marriage" label on one is not going to change that. An advocate of gay marriage recognizes this when he writes, "Male-male marriages that survive are likelier to have some kind of informal level of permission."[14] In other words, they agree that every so often, it is quite okay to cheat on your partner. According to one study conducted by two homosexual authors, only 7 of the 156 homosexual couples surveyed had maintained sexual fidelity, and of the 100 that had been together for more than 5 years, none had remained faithful.[15]

Fourth, raising children in a gay environment will give them a warped sense of right and wrong, natural and unnatural, and will further our culture's descent into sexual immorality and gender confusion.

Broken Marriage

Imagine a world where monogamous, heterosexual marriages dominate. Where divorce and unwanted pregnancies are unheard of, and where parents are solid male and female role models for their children. A world where premarital sex is frowned on, adultery a fiction, and sexually transmitted diseases non-existent; where promiscuity is seen as unwise, pornography eliminated, and sexual perversions absent. How healthy would a society be when built on these ideals?

Of course, such a world can never exist as long as sin is present. Our corrupt hearts have produced broken families, unwanted children, and a view of sex that is egocentric and selfish. Of my youngest son's core group of friends, only one lives with his biological parents. This was similar with my daughters and their friends.

Part of the problem is not how marriages end, but how they often

---

[14] "The Unique Quality of 'Lifelong Heterosexual Monogamy' Ctd," *The Atlantic*, www.theatlantic.com/daily-dish/archive/2010/08/the-unique-quality-of-lifelong-heterosexual-monogamy-ctd/183637/, accessed June 1, 2016.

[15] Quoted in Jeffrey Satinover, *Homosexuality and the Politics of Truth* (Grand Rapids: Baker, 1996), 55.

begin. More than half of all marriages in America start with cohabitation.[16] "Why not kick the tires and take her for a test drive?" is the
approach many take to marriage. However, out of eight couples who
cohabit, four will never get married, and of the ones that do, three will
end in divorce.[17] "Couples who cohabit before marriage (and especially
before an engagement or an otherwise clear commitment) tend to be less
satisfied with their marriages—and more likely to divorce—than couples
who do not."[18]

Many people treat marriage like purchasing a new pair of pants. Try
them on and if they don't fit, put them back on the rack and pick another
pair. The reality television show *Married at First Sight* sensationalizes what
our culture has already approved. Four experts pair three couples who first
see each other on the wedding day. After a honeymoon they live together for
six months, after which time they have the option of divorcing or staying
together. Not surprisingly, in the three seasons of the show, the majority of
the couples separated or divorced.[19]

The church has spent far too little time teaching children about the
importance of abstinence before marriage. Premarital sex is seen as harmless fun in our culture, and our children regularly imbibe the media's cavalier portrayal of sex before marriage. We protect our children, not limit
their enjoyment, when we teach them that sex should be practiced solely
within marriage. As one ethicist notes, "where all the benefits of marriage
are available without any of its responsibilities, society, and particularly
children, will suffer."[20]

---

[16] According to Barna Group, 65% of American adults believe cohabitation is acceptable (https://barna.org/research/family-kids/research-release/majority-of-americans-now-believe-in-cohabitation?utm_source=Barna+Update+List&utm_campaign=573151e2e6-Cohabitation_2016&utm_medium=email&utm_term=0_8560a0e52e-573151e2e6-172166833&mc_cid=573151e2e6&mc_eid=94d9ce5e76#.V27t040VgkJ), accessed June 27, 2016).

[17] Walt Larimore, "Poll Shows Sex within Marriage Is More Fulfilling," imom.com, www.imom.com/poll-shows-sex-within-marriage-is-more-fulfilling/#.V2BtToOVgkI, accessed June 21, 2016. For more statistics, see David Gudgel, *Before You Live Together* (Ventura, CA: Regal Books, 2003).

[18] Meg Jay, "The Downside of Cohabiting before Marriage," *The New York Times*, www.nytimes.com/2012/04/15/opinion/sunday/the-downside-of-cohabiting-before-marriage.html?_r=0, accessed June 22, 2016.

[19] Internet Movie Data Base, www.imdb.com/title/tt3868860/, accessed June 1, 2016.

[20] Feinberg, *Brave New World*, 281.

The CDC reports that 40% of births are to unwed mothers.[21] This is all the more shocking when you consider that since the 1970s, the use of birth control has skyrocketed, and one in four pregnancies ends in legal abortions. Yet, the Guttmacher Institute reports that the rate of unintended pregnancy in the United States is at a thirty-year low.[22] This means that marriage is falling out of favor.

The year I was born, the illegitimacy rate was less than 3%.[23] I am included in that statistic, brought into this world by an unwed, eighteen-year-old mother for whom I am most grateful. Virtually everybody she knew encouraged my mother to give me up for adoption, with arguments I might have used as well. "You are too young to raise a child." "You don't have the financial means to afford a baby." "Find a childless couple who can give your baby a good home." I am glad she ignored the well-intentioned advice.

My mother gave me a caring home, but she could not model maleness for me no matter how much she loved me. Thankfully she married.

I do not think we realize yet how devastating to children these anti-marriage trends are. There is a clear link between out-of-wedlock birth rate and poverty on a state-by-state basis.[24] Also, is it a coincidence that as the nuclear family has disintegrated, gender dysphoria has increased? While I have the deepest respect for single parents, they are at a disadvantage compared to a two-parent home.

Evangelicals rightly bemoan our country's embrace of gay marriage, saying it is the end of marriage as we know it, but let's not fool ourselves.

---

[21] CDC, "Unmarried Childbearing," www.cdc.gov/nchs/fastats/unmarried-childbearing.htm, accessed June 8, 2016. *The Telegraph* estimated three years ago that by 2016, more children will be born outside marriage in the United Kingdom than in it. In 1979, it was 11% (Steven Swinford, "Most Children Will Be Born Out of Wedlock by 2016," www.telegraph.co.uk/news/politics/10172627/Most-children-will-be-born-out-of-wedlock-by-2016.html, accessed May 17, 2016).

[22] "U.S. Unintended Pregnancy Rate Falls to 30-Year Low," https://www.guttmacher.org/news-release/2016/us-unintended-pregnancy-rate-falls-30-year-low-declines-seen-almost-all-groups, accessed June 1, 2016.

[23] Stephanie Ventura, "Changing Patterns of Nonmarital Childbearing in the United States," CDC, 2016, www.cdc.gov/nchs/data/databriefs/db18.pdf, accessed May 29, 2016. The CDC notes that children born to single mothers "typically have more limited social and financial resources." Foreign trends are similar.

[24] Steven Nelson, "Census Bureau Links Poverty with Out-of-Wedlock Births," *US News*, www.usnews.com/news/newsgram/articles/2013/05/06/census-bureau-links-poverty-with-out-of-wedlock-births, accessed June 21, 2016.

Heterosexual Christians have been ruining marriage for some time now. Even if all the gays and lesbians of the world married today and divorced tomorrow, that still would not constitute as much of a statistical impact on the institution of marriage as the generally cavalier way heterosexuals have approached it.

According to Barna Group, the divorce rate in America among evangelicals and born again believers is roughly the same as that for atheists and agnostics, around 30%.[25] The Christian community must take some of the blame for the deterioration of marriage in our country.

There is considerable debate about the effect divorce has on children. Not surprisingly, on the secular side are those who argue that it isn't all that bad, like those at Live Science[26] and *The Huffington Post*.[27]

On the other side are those who take a more sober view, like the Yahoo! article, "'Kids Are Resilient' and 7 Other Lies Divorcing Parents Should Stop Believing."[28] The gist of the article is that couples habitually put the welfare of their children behind their own selfish wants. Let's not fool ourselves: divorce damages children, which is one of the reasons why God hates it (Mal. 2:16). As a Harvard University report stated more than twenty years ago, "Through divorce and remarriage, individuals are related to more and more people, to each of whom they owe less and less."[29]

Christians who vehemently oppose homosexual marriage yet take a lax position on divorce are being hypocritical, especially since Jesus connects divorce and adultery: "But I tell you that anyone who divorces his wife, except for sexual immorality, makes her the victim of adultery, and anyone who marries a divorced woman commits adultery" (Matt. 5:32).

---

[25] "New Marriage and Divorce Statistics Released," https://www.barna.org/barna-update/family-kids/42-new-marriage-and-divorce-statistics-released#.V2L-l40VgkI, accessed June 11, 2016.

[26] Rachael Rettner, "Divorce Not Always Bad for Kids," www.livescience.com/6648-divorce-bad-kids.html, accessed June 12, 2016.

[27] Brette Sember, "Why a Good Divorce Is Better Than a Bad Marriage for Kids," www.huffingtonpost.com/brette-sember/why-a-good-divorce-is-better-than-a-bad-marriage-for-kids_b_6925236.html, accessed June 12, 2016.

[28] Debra Macleod, "'Kids Are Resilient' and 7 Other Lies Divorcing Parents Should Stop Believing," Yahoo! News, https://www.yahoo.com/news/kids-are-resilient-and-7-other-lies-divorcing-107330654983.html, accessed December 11, 2015.

[29] Quoted in David Clyde Jones, *Biblical Christian Ethics* (Grand Rapids: Baker, 1994), 179.

Most evangelicals argue that divorce is allowed when one partner commits adultery, as the passage above implies, or deserts her or his spouse (1 Cor. 7:15). Even if this is true (and some evangelicals argue that divorce is *never* an option for a believer, regardless of the circumstances), it is clear that many Christians have divorced on less than biblical grounds. This cavalier approach to marriage negatively impacts our culture's attitude toward it.

Still, the Law allowed for divorce if a husband found something "indecent" about his wife (Deut. 24:1–2).[30] By Jesus' time, the Pharisees approached divorce almost the way "no fault" divorces are conducted today, "for any and every reason" (Matt. 19:3). However, Jesus points out that the Law was an allowance because the hearts of the people were hard, "but it was not this way from the beginning" (19:8b). In other words, the disciples of Jesus should practice marriage the way God intended it to be engaged.

By connecting divorce and adultery, Jesus lays the foundation for a righteousness his disciples must possess, one that "surpasses that of the Pharisees and the teachers of the law" (Matt. 5:20). It is the adverse condition of a person's heart that yields divorce and adultery (Matt. 15:17-20).

Under the Mosaic Law, adultery was punishable by death (Lev. 20:10; Deut. 22:22), so what Jesus says about divorce is shocking. In fact, Jesus' answer to the Pharisees is so stark that his disciples exclaim: "If this is the situation between a husband and wife, it is better not to marry" (Matt. 19:10). Because Jesus sees marriage as a vow before God, it is unthinkable to break such a covenant.

Infidelity has become something of a spectator sport with our culture, with programs like *Cheaters* crassly doing what soap operas have been doing for decades: tempting viewers to sit on the edge of their seat, wondering if Joe will get caught in bed with Sue. Do Christians give a bump in the ratings to these programs? How much money have evangelicals spent supporting television and movie industries that propagate this promiscuity?

The book of Proverbs has more to say about adultery than any other book in the Bible, and its focus is not eschatological (i.e., "God will punish you in hell for it"), but practical. Adultery involves a monumental breach of trust and a supreme act of foolishness.

---

[30] Most Old Testament scholars see Moses' certificate of divorce as a law protecting women from wanton abandonment by their husbands.

While God "sees" the adulterer (Prov. 5:21), the emphasis in Proverbs is on the here-and-now. The adulteress is likened to bitter gall, a double-edged sword, and death (5:4–5), and a deep pit and a bandit (23:27–28). The adulterer is compared to an ox led to the slaughter, a deer caught in a noose, and a bird trapped in a snare (7:22–23). Adulterers subject themselves to loss of honor and dignity (5:9), and public shame and humiliation (5:14–16; 6:33). Proverbs 6:32 sums it up best: "But a man who commits adultery has no sense; whoever does so destroys himself."

Jesus intensifies the prohibitions when in the Sermon on the Mount he likens lust harbored in the heart to adultery (Matt. 5:28). His corrective is drastic: cut off the offending hand or pluck out the wandering eye (vv. 29–30). Notice the progression: from the heart to the eyes to the hands. Again, it is the condition of the heart that leads to marital destruction. As one pastor notes, "There can be no healthy spiritual life where there is no absolute faithfulness in marriage."[31]

Marriage must be safeguarded. "Marriage should be honored by all, and the marriage bed kept pure, for God will judge the adulterer and all the sexually immoral" (Heb. 13:4).

Healthy Marriage

We've come a long way from *Father Knows Best*, the 1950s television sitcom starring Robert Young as the sage title character who offered sound advice each episode when one of his children had a problem. As the show's name attests, the father is the head of the household to whom all others look for guidance.

Modern television shows that have a family as their centerpiece are regularly less flattering to the parents. The father figure in particular is frequently portrayed as a bumbling idiot who needs to be corrected by his much-wiser teenagers or primary school kids, prompting one writer to ask, "Why Do So Many Father-Daughter Movies = Feisty Kid + Bumbling Dad?"[32]

---

[31] Brian Edwards, *The Ten Commandments for Today* (Leominster, England: Day One, 2009), 204.

[32] Hugo Swyzer, "Why Do So Many Father-Daughter Movies = Feisty Kid + Bumbling Dad?" *The Atlantic*, www.theatlantic.com/sexes/archive/2013/06/why-do-so-many-father-daughter-movies-feisty-kid-bumbling-dad/276773/, accessed June 24, 2016.

An article from *The Atlantic*, "The Distinct Positive Impact of a Good Dad," highlights the importance of fathers.[33] There is a "statistically significant" impact on lowering depression, unwanted pregnancies, and teen delinquency in boys in homes where fathers play an active role. Biblically speaking, this is just common sense, but it is good to see a secular source acknowledging it, especially when the other side is quite vocal.[34]

The Ten Commandments provide a clue for how important marriage and the family are in God's reckoning. The first tablet contains the four commandments that regulate our relationship with God. The second tablet lists the six commandments that order our relationship with our neighbor. Of these six laws, the first defines our relationship with our parents, the next covers the sanctity of life, and the following commandment the institution of marriage. The second tablet is front loaded with the importance of the family.

It begins with the parent-child relationship, the fundamental level of authority in human associations. A person who does not honor his father and mother will ultimately not honor anybody. From this family disobedience will flow all other forms of insubordination. Once the family breaks down—the principal building block of any community—all else will begin to fail as well. Scripture envisions strong communities flowing from strong families. No doubt this is the reason underlying God's command in the Old Testament to stone to death a rebellious son if he will no longer honor his parents (Deut. 21:18–21).

When respect for parents is lost, all forms of anarchy and corruption will follow. In the list of sins in Romans 1:29–31, Paul includes "they disobey their parents" along with evils like murder, slander, and greed. Such a person will find it much easier to justify disobedience with employers, the church, and the state. We are told in the pastoral epistles that a man should not be a pastor or elder unless he properly orders his own household (1 Tim. 3:4–5; Titus 1:6).

---

[33] W. Bradford Wilcox, "The Distinct Positive Impact of a Good Dad," *The Atlantic*, www.theatlantic.com/sexes/archive/2013/06/the-distinct-positive-impact-of-a-good-dad/276874/, accessed October 11, 2015.

[34] See the article by Jane Mattes, founder of Single Mothers By Choice, "Fathers Can Be Valuable, But Not Indispensable," *The New York Times*, www.nytimes.com/roomfordebate/2013/06/03/what-are-fathers-for/fathers-can-be-valuable-but-not-indispensable, accessed June 22, 2016.

Unfortunately, some parents sacrifice their children for their careers. Sticking a child in day care while both spouses work is a necessity for certain couples, but for others, it is just an excuse to drive a Mercedes instead of a Hyundai. Our children can make godly decisions, as they sift through the garbage our society sends their way, the more time we spend with them. Parents have awesome power to shape the lives of their children, but when we off-load that responsibility onto others, we allow for greater negative influences to capture them.

While it is not wrong for women to be in the workplace, the disintegration of the family has produced some troubling trends in America. Nearly half the workforce is composed of women, and 40% of working moms are either the primary or sole earners in their families. In 62% of families with children, all adults are working.[35] This often leaves the raising of children to someone other than the parents, and the distinct contribution of mothers is muted or lost.

Absentee fathers are no better. Men encourage their children to take risks, and they mete out discipline in ways far different from mothers. As the two genders are complementary one to the other, so are they complementary in the way they raise children.

Turning to the husband-wife relationship, as we noted in chapter 7, the order of creation establishes male headship in both the family and the church. It is the erosion of this headship that has precipitated the decay of the family. While husbands are instructed to love their wives, wives are called to submit to their husbands (Eph. 5:22–28). Neither command has opt-out clauses attached. Husbands are not told to love their wives "as long as she remains beautiful in your eyes," nor are wives told to submit to their husbands "as long as he treats you well."

Marriage also serves to sanctify the spouses and helps guard them from sin. Nonetheless, it is the distinct responsibility of the husband to protect the purity of his wife, as Christ does the church (Eph. 5:25–27).

Lastly, marriage has sexual benefits missed by our secular society. The prevailing ethos of our culture and the one promoted through the media is that sex is more fulfilling the more partners you have. Conversely, sex

---

[35] Lindsay Power, "White House: Why All Families Need Paid Leave," Yahoo! News, https://www.yahoo.com/parenting/white-house-why-all-families-need-paid-leave-128515895932.html, accessed June 22, 2016.

within a monogamous, heterosexual marriage is deemed boring and pedestrian. However, there is a fair amount of research that proves that thesis wrong.

According to Walt and Barbara Larimore, authors of *His Brain, Her Brain: How Divinely Designed Differences Can Strengthen Your Marriage*, numerous surveys show that sex is most satisfying in a monogamous relationship between very religious people. Walt Larimore writes, "Forty-two percent of wives said that they found sex emotionally and physically satisfying, compared to just 31% of single women who had a sex partner. Forty-eight percent of husbands said sex was satisfying emotionally, compared to just 37% of cohabiting men. The higher level of commitment in marriage is probably the reason for the high level of reported sexual satisfaction."[36]

Marriage Matters

When compared to animals, humans have inordinately longer childhoods where they are under the care of their parents. God designed childhood development to make it necessary for children to stay with their parents much longer and thus learn more. Masculinity and femininity are modeled by the father and the mother. Girls learn what it means to be women, and they experience what secure love from a man involves. Likewise, boys see what it means to be men, and how to relate to women in a healthy way. Single-parent households miss this vital aspect, as do gay and lesbian couples.

Strong marriages make strong families that in turn produce strong societies. While Christians will probably not be able to stem the tide as our society slips further from God's design, we can honor marriage by conducting *ourselves* the way God expects us to. Perhaps the seeds of our obedience will be the eventual return of our culture to Christian principles.

---

[36] David Popenoe, "Ten Important Research Findings on Marriage," For Your Marriage, www.foryourmarriage.org/ten-important-research-findings-on-marriage/, accessed June 17, 2016.

A Word about Godly Wisdom

IN MY EARLY TWENTIES, I took two pieces of paper and read through the book of Proverbs. On one piece I put everything Proverbs declares about a fool, and on the other I recorded what the book says about a wise man. I compared the lists to my own life, noting that while a number of items were true about me on the wise page, there were quite a few on the foolish paper. I then determined to inculcate more of the wise ideals while attempting to correct the foolish inclinations. It was a profitable exercise.

Proverbs contains godly wisdom for prudent living. These wisdom sayings deal with how we handle our money, the way we view sexuality, and how a healthy work ethic brings prosperity. This type of biblical wisdom is "worldly" because it deals with how to productively live on this earth.

In the early chapters of Proverbs, Solomon weaves a picturesque personification of wisdom. Chapter 8 begins with the call of Wisdom out to the world. This material is juxtaposed with the call of the adulteress in the previous chapter. While the fool listens to the adulteress, the wise man heeds Wisdom, also personified as a woman.

> Does not wisdom call out?
> Does not understanding raise her voice?
> On the heights along the way,
> where the paths meet, she takes her stand;
> beside the gates leading into the city, at the entrances,
>   she cries aloud:
> "To you, O men, I call out;
> I raise my voice to all mankind.
> You who are simple, gain prudence;
> you who are foolish, gain understanding."

(vv. 1–5)

Wisdom then declares that her words are more valuable than silver and gold, that they are faultless, that kings and rulers value their just fruit, and that they are worked out in prudent and godly living.

All of Wisdom's words are rooted in the "fear of the LORD" (v. 13), a common theme throughout Hebrew wisdom literature. It is this godly fear that results in contentment (19:23), prosperity (22:4), prolonged life (10:27), walking uprightly (14:2), and hating evil (8:13). In light of the ills discussed throughout this book, perhaps the best summation of the positive effect of fearing God and respecting his ways is found in Proverbs 14:27: "The fear of the LORD is a fountain of life."

Conversely, people who do not fear the Lord reconfigure the world to conform to their ungodly desires. This works out in numerous ways:

- Because they don't fear God's judgment, they redefine his love.
- Because they don't fear God's omniscience, they create false knowledge.
- Because they don't fear God's omnipresence, they secretly practice depravity.
- Because they don't fear God's immutability, they change the gospel.
- Because they don't fear God's omnipotence, they cling to human autonomy.
- Because they don't fear God's holiness, they openly flaunt their wickedness.

This is why in Romans 3:18 Paul summarizes the root cause of sin this way: "There is no fear of God before their eyes."

In light of the world's absence of godly fear, Christians can be tempted to fear the world. When you don't fear God, you will fear men, especially as they become more and more depraved. It is increasingly problematic to be a believer, even in countries with long exposure to Christianity. We live in a day when a Christian in the United Kingdom can be suspended from her job for "harassing and bullying" a work colleague, simply for giving her a Christian book to read and inviting her to a church service.[1]

This is nothing new. Abel, the first righteous man, was murdered by his

---

[1] BBC News, "NHS Christian Worker Loses Appeal after 'Giving Book to Muslim Colleague,'" www.bbc.com/news/uk-england-london-35988115, accessed June 1, 2016.

unrighteous brother. The persecution of the godly has happened since the beginning. The chronicle of Hebrews 11 recounts many instances of righteous individuals persecuted for their faith. In the face of similar opposition, some Christians cower.

However, believers must act as "salt" and "light" in the world (Matt. 5:13–16): as salt by preserving humanity from slipping more quickly into corruption, and as light by illumining the way of life and exposing evil. Now is not the time to shrink back and be destroyed (Heb. 10:39). Now is the time to persevere.

Much of what we have seen in this book has come from a denunciation of what God did "in the beginning" (Gen. 1:1), so it should not surprise us that Christ—who was also "in the beginning" (John 1:1)—was likewise rejected. The apostle John records the snubbing of Jesus: "He came to that which was his own, but his own did not receive him" (1:11).

Jesus viewed the Hebrew Scriptures as the very words of God, and he linked belief in himself directly with trust in God's Word when he told the Jewish leaders, "If you believed Moses, you would believe me, for he wrote about me" (John 5:46). Unfortunately, some Christians have lost their faith in God's Word.

In his personification of Wisdom, Solomon goes back to the beginning.

> The LORD brought me forth as the first of his works,
> before his deeds of old;
> I was appointed from eternity,
> from the beginning, before the world began.
>
> (Prov. 8:23–24)

Those who reject God's created order are acting like fools because Wisdom was there observing, applauding, and participating in the creation. There is great insight in concurring with God's design, and incredible folly in going against it. Whether it be the gender roles that God laid out in Eden, or the supremacy of humankind in God's created hierarchy, the wise person applauds God's design. Only the fool kicks against the goads.

As sinners, we are adept at taking things God has made—innocent, pure, and decent things—and perverting them to suit our immoral inclinations. Until we admit this despicable tendency in fallen humans, we cannot expect the world to improve.

In the previous chapters we saw countless examples of people who believe they are free as they reject God's design. This attitude is expressed whether it concerns sexuality or gender roles or the scientific enterprise. Unfortunately, this is a wrongheaded view of freedom. Godly wisdom recognizes that when we act against God's design, we destroy ourselves. This self-destruction is a form of slavery, not liberty.

James refers to God's Word as "the perfect law that gives freedom" (1:25). The world sees God's Word and liberty at odds with each other, but believers understand that in obeying the Law of God, there is complete freedom. We live in agreement with his will, which brings liberation, because we live in the way we were intended to live, to his glory, according to his design.

Those who pursue righteousness will be persecuted by a world that snubs God and embraces evil. The world has rejected the Prince of Peace and runs after a worldly "peace" that is hollow. Genuine peacemakers will experience opposition from a world that revels in depravity. As long as contentment with God and his design is neglected, peace in the world will be a fleeting hope.

> Now all has been heard;
> here is the conclusion of the matter:
> Fear God and keep his commandments,
> for this is the duty of all mankind.
> For God will bring every deed into judgment,
> including every hidden thing,
> whether it is good or evil.
>
> (Eccl. 12:13–14)

PUBLICATIONS ARE LISTED BELOW if they were substantially used in this book, or can provide readers with further research. Sources that were only used for a quotation or for illustrative purposes can be found in the footnotes, as well as all periodicals and Internet sources.

Ager, Derek. *The New Catastrophism: The Importance of the Rare Event in Geological History*. Cambridge: Cambridge University Press, 1995.

Alexander, Denis. *Creation or Evolution: Do We Have to Choose?* Oxford: Monarch Books, 2008.

Andreades, Sam. *enGendered: God's Gift of Gender Difference in Relationship*. Bellingham, WA: Lexham Press, 2018.

Ashton, John F., ed. *In Six Days: Why 50 Scientists Choose to Believe in Creation*. Green Forest, AR: Master Books, 2005.

Barbour, Ian. *When Science Meets Religion*. New York: HarperCollins, 2000.

Barrick, W. D., D. Lamoureux, J. H. Walton, and C. J. Collins. *Four Views on the Historical Adam*. Grand Rapids: Zondervan, 2013.

Branch, J. Alan. *Born This Way? Homosexuality, Science, and the Scriptures*. Bellingham, WA: Lexham Press, 2018.

Collins, Francis. *The Language of God: A Scientist Presents Evidence for Belief*. New York: Free Press, 2006.

Dawkins, Richard. *The Blind Watchmaker: Why the Evidence of Evolution Reveals a Universe without Design*. New York: W. W. Norton & Company, 1986.

_____. *The Greatest Show on Earth: The Evidence for Evolution*. London: Transworld Publishers, 2009.

DeFranza, Megan. *Sex Difference in Christian Theology: Male, Female, and Intersex in the Image of God*. Grand Rapids: Eerdmans, 2015.

Dembski, William A., and James M. Kushiner, eds. *Signs of Intelligence: Understanding Intelligent Design*. Grand Rapids: Brazos Press, 2001.

DeYoung, Kevin. *Taking God at His Word*. Wheaton, IL: Crossway, 2014.

Driscoll, Mark, and Gerry Breshears. *Doctrine: What Christians Should Believe*. Wheaton, IL: Crossway, 2010.

Erickson-Schroth, Laura. *Trans Bodies, Trans Selves: A Resource for the Transgendered Community*. Oxford: Oxford University Press, 2014.

Feinberg, John, and Paul Feinberg. *Ethics for a Brave New World*. 2nd ed. Wheaton, IL: Crossway, 2010.

Ferngren, Gary, ed. *Science & Religion: A Historical Introduction*. Baltimore: Johns Hopkins University Press, 2002.

Field, Weston. *Unformed and Unfilled: A Critique of the Gap Theory*. Green Forest, AR: Master Books, 2005.

Gentry, Kenneth, Jr. *As It Is Written: The Genesis Account, Literal or Literary?* Green Forest, AR, Master Books, 2016.

Giberson, Karl, and Francis S. Collins. *The Language of Science and Faith*. Downers Grove, IL: InterVarsity Press, 2011.

Glover, Gordon. *Beyond the Firmament: Understanding Science and the Theology of Creation*. Chesapeake, VA: Watertree Press, 2007.

Grudem, Wayne. *Systematic Theology: An Introduction to Biblical Doctrine*. Grand Rapids: Zondervan, 2000.

Hawking, Stephen. *A Brief History of Time*. New York: Bantam, 1988.

Larimore, Walt, and Barbara Larimore. *His Brain, Her Brain: How Divinely Designed Differences Can Strengthen Your Marriage*. Grand Rapids: Zondervan, 2008.

Lewis, C. S. *The Screwtape Letters*. New York: Macmillan, 1964.

Lubenow, Marvin L. *Bones of Contention: A Creationist Assessment of Human Fossils*. Grand Rapids: Baker, 2007.

McGrath, Alister. *A Fine-Tuned Universe: The Quest for God in Science and Theology*. Louisville, KY: Westminster John Knox Press, 2009.

Mock, Janet. *Redefining Realness: My Path to Womanhood, Identity, Love & So Much More*. New York: Atria Books, 2014.

Mohler, R. Albert, Jr., ed. *God and the Gay Christian? A Response to Matthew Vines*. Lexington, KY: SBTS Press, 2014.

National Academy of Sciences. *Science, Evolution, and Creationism*. Washington, DC: National Academies Press, 2008.

Roberts, Alice. *The Incredible Human Journey: The Story of How We Colonized the Planet*. London: Bloomsbury, 2010.

Sailhamer, John. *Genesis Unbound*. Sisters, OR: Multnomah, 1996.

Sanford, John. *Genetic Entropy*. Waterloo, NY: FMS Publications, 2014.

Sarfati, Jonathan D. *The Genesis Account: A Theological, Historical, and Scientific Commentary on Genesis 1–11*. Powder Springs, GA: Creation Book Publishers, 2015.

Sunderland, Luther. *Darwin's Enigma: Ebbing the Tide of Naturalism*. Green Forest, AR: Master Books, 2002.

Tamas, Richard. *The Passion of the Western Mind: Understanding the Ideas That Have Shaped Our World View*. New York: Random House, 1991.

Vines, Matthew. *God and the Gay Christian*. New York: Convergent Books, 2014.

Wells, Jonathan. *Icons of Evolution: Science of Myth? Why Much of What We Teach about Evolution Is Wrong*. Washington, DC: Regnery, 2002.

White, Andrew Dickson. *History of the Warfare of Science with Theology in Christendom*. 2 vols. Amherst, NY: Prometheus, 1993.

Wiker, Benjamin, and Jonathan Witt. *A Meaningful World: How the Arts and Sciences Reveal the Genius of Nature*. Downer's Grove, IL: InterVarsity Press, 2006.